NIET

THE BIRT

Continuum *Reader's Guides*

Continuum's *Reader's Guides* are clear, concise and accessible introductions to classic works of philosophy. Each book explores the major themes, historical and philosophical context and key passages of a major philosophical text, guiding the reader towards a thorough understanding of often demanding material. Ideal for undergraduate students, the guides provide an essential resource for anyone who needs to get to grips with a philosophical text.

Reader's Guides available from Continuum

Aristotle's Nicomachean Ethics – Christopher Warne
Aristotle's Politics – Judith A. Swanson and C. David Corbin
Berkeley's Principles of Human Knowledge – Alasdair Richmond
Berkeley's Three Dialogues – Aaron Garrett
Deleuze and Guattari's Capitalism and Schizophrenia – Ian Buchanan
Deleuze's Difference and Repetition – Joe Hughes
Derrida's Writing and Difference – Sarah Wood
Descartes' Meditations – Richard Francks
Hegel's Philosophy of Right – David Rose
Heidegger's Being and Time – William Blattner
Heidegger's Later Writings – Lee Braver
Hobbes's Leviathan – Laurie M. Johnson Bagby
Hume's Dialogues Concerning Natural Religion – Andrew Pyle
Hume's Enquiry Concerning Human Understanding – Alan Bailey and
    Dan O'Brien
Kant's Critique of Aesthetic Judgement – Fiona Hughes
Kant's Critique of Pure Reason – James Luchte
Kant's Groundwork for the Metaphysics of Morals – Paul Guyer
Kuhn's The Structure of Scientific Revolutions – John Preston
Locke's Essay Concerning Human Understanding – William Uzgalis
Locke's Second Treatise of Government – Paul Kelly
Mill's On Liberty – Geoffrey Scarre
Mill's Utilitarianism – Henry West
Nietzsche's On the Genealogy of Morals – Daniel Conway
Plato's Republic – Luke Purshouse
Rousseau's The Social Contract – Christopher Wraight
Sartre's Being and Nothingness – Sebastian Gardner
Spinoza's Ethics – Thomas J. Cook
Wittgenstein's Tractatus Logico Philosophicus – Roger M. White

NIETZSCHE'S
THE BIRTH OF TRAGEDY

A Reader's Guide

**DOUGLAS BURNHAM AND
MARTIN JESINGHAUSEN**

continuum

Continuum International Publishing Group

The Tower Building	80 Maiden Lane
11 York Road	Suite 704
London SE1 7NX	New York, NY 10038

www.continuumbooks.com

British Library Cataloguing-in-Publication Data
A catalogue record for this book is available from the British Library.

ISBN: HB: 978-1-8470-6584-1
PB: 978-1-8470-6585-8

Library of Congress Cataloging-in-Publication Data
Burnham, Douglas.
Nietzsche's *The birth of tragedy*: a reader's guide / Douglas Burnham
and Martin Jesinghausen.
p. cm.
Includes index.
ISBN-13: 978-1-84706-584-1 (HB)
ISBN-10: 1-84706-584-8 (HB)
ISBN-13: 978-1-84706-585-8 (pbk.)
ISBN-10: 1-84706-585-6 (pbk.)
1. Nietzsche, Friedrich Wilhelm, 1844–1900. Geburt der Tragödie.
2. Aesthetics. 3. Music – Philosophy and aesthetics. 4. Tragedy. 5. Greek drama
(Tragedy) – History and criticism. 6. Tragic, The. 7. Wagner, Richard,
1813-1883.
I. Jesinghausen, Martin. II. Title.
B3313.G43B87 2010
111'.85--dc22   2009035023

Typeset by Newgen Imaging Systems Pvt Ltd, Chennai, India
Printed and bound in Great Britain by CPI Antony Rowe Ltd,
Chippenham, Wiltshire

CONTENTS

CONTENTS

INTRODUCTION

This commentary does not aim to summarize or replace *The Birth of Tragedy,*[1] but to help it to be read in depth. We imagine readers with both books open, side by side. The reader can follow the line of Nietzsche's labyrinthine argument by resorting to the commentary as an accompaniment. We have aimed at covering each of the sections and most of the book's individual paragraphs. Wherever possible we have cross-referenced between the different sections. Apart from illustrating the argument and formal aspects of the text, we also provide contextual information. It is hoped that the commentary manages not to obliterate the text, which still needs to work its magic on the reader as the best way for it to be understood.

Repetition and variation are two of the most obvious stylistic features of Nietzsche's book, and we have tried to understand the underlying intentions of these overlapping waves of argument. Another key feature of the text is its use of metaphor, employed by Nietzsche with a critical, anti-academic intention. This critique is directed against the lifeless and 'hardened' language of concepts used in the long established academic 'disciplines', philology, for instance, Nietzsche's original home subject. The book also has an axe to grind in particular with the conceptual language of modern philosophy, the second major thrust of Nietzsche's critique. The assumption is that metaphors are the closest linguistic form of human correspondence with the outside 'true nature of things' (Schopenhauer's phrase, much used by Nietzsche, as we will see; cf. particularly **Section 16**). Concepts to Nietzsche are nothing but dried-up metaphors, emaciated to such an extent that they have lost all of their originally intuitive meaning: concepts have forgotten that they are metaphors; they have stopped corresponding with that which they are aiming to capture. In opposition to the dead language of 'learning', Nietzsche proposes to inaugurate a language more

1

perceptive, elemental, dynamic and occasionally poetic, – in short: more *attuned* to and *in tune* with the forces of life which this book is tackling in its themes and form (see our discussion in **Section 8, Note: Philosophy and Language in Nietzsche**). Taking Nietzsche seriously as regards linguistic experimentation, as we will be doing, seems to create a methodological dilemma for a commentary such as the present one, because the task of furthering an understanding of *The Birth of Tragedy* for the contemporary reader is to a large extent dependent on a reversal of Nietzsche's philosophical stylistics: namely on a conceptualization and discursive translation of *The Birth of Tragedy*'s language of metaphors. Thus, commentary could be regarded as going against Nietzsche's intentions of stylistic reform and invalidating his project for an aesthetic overhaul of philosophical standards of conceptual writing. This methodological objection to explaining Nietzsche in the language of conceptual discourse has been addressed (and resolved, we think) in Sarah Kofmann's excellent book on *Nietzsche and Metaphor*, who holds that writing about Nietzsche in a style emulating or even simulating Nietzsche amounts to an 'impossible task'. What is more, it also does Nietzsche a disservice. We are going along with Kofmann when she argues that it is 'more Nietzschean to write conceptually in the knowledge that a concept has no greater value than a metaphor and is itself a condensate of metaphors'; it is more productive therefore 'to write while opening up one's writing to a genealogical decipherment, than to write metaphorically while denigrating the concept and proposing metaphor as the norm'.[2] Here, we will follow this path: we will seek to explain in more conventional academic prose Nietzsche's intentions while also drawing attention to those points where such prose does and must fall short.

Let us ask in what way readers, both those with a general and with a more specialized interest in Nietzsche, will benefit from reading this first of Nietzsche's published books. The shortest possible answer is this: this is a riveting book that reflects and responds in condensed form to vast areas of nineteenth-century thought; and, being Nietzsche's first book, it both anticipates his others and foreshadows many cultural and intellectual movements in the century that followed. So, in Chapters 1 and 2 we will look backward to some of the things that influenced Nietzsche, leaving others to be covered in the main text of the commentary, and in Chapter 4, devoted to the book's reception history, we will be looking forward to the immediate and longer-term reception or influence of *The Birth of Tragedy*.

AUTHORS' NOTE

Much of the preparation and research for this book was undertaken in Nietzsche collections and libraries in Germany and Switzerland. Accordingly, we would like to thank Mr. Erdman von Wilamowitz-Moellendorff, cicerone through the Nietzsche holdings in the Herzogin Anna-Amalia Bibliothek, Weimar; also the Klassik Stiftung, Nietzsche Kolleg and Nietzsche Haus, Weimar; particularly the Stiftung Nietzsche Haus, Sils Maria, Upper Engadine, Switzerland, and particularly the kind guardians of Nietzsche's Swiss bequest, Prof. Peter André Bloch and Dr. Peter Villwock. The picture of 'the Swiss Nietzsche' took on further, firmer contours thanks to Dr. Alfred Heinimann and Ms. Kathrin Engels, both Basel, and Dr. Jürg Amann, Zürich. We would also like to thank the Research Fund of Staffordshire University, which generously funded the archive visits. Thanks also to the British Society of Phenomenology, at whose annual conference in 2009 some of the ideas animating this commentary were given a first public airing. Finally, we would like to thank our colleagues and families for support, guidance and patience.

CHAPTER 1

CONTEXT

NIETZSCHE'S VIEW OF *THE BIRTH OF TRAGEDY*

Nietzsche himself was among the harshest of this book's serious critics. In 'An Attempt at Self-Criticism', written more than a decade after *The Birth of Tragedy* was published, Nietzsche asks himself whether he has delivered successfully a new form of philosophical writing equal to a new type of metaphysics. With hindsight, Nietzsche thinks that his first book has thrown open more questions than it answered. There are also a considerable number of things that are wrong with it, he thinks: it is wordy in all the wrong ways, coy about its anti-moral and anti-Christian tendencies, and far too enthralled with Schopenhauer and Wagner. We will turn to all these issues in detail in our commentary. Nevertheless, it is clear that the book remains in some ways dear to him because it contains his mature philosophy in the making – it at least asks the right questions, if not necessarily in the right way – and is valuable as the first step on a writing career that culminates in *Zarathustra*, in Nietzsche's view the most 'successful' and consistently 'artistic' of his works (with the exception of his poetry).

Nietzsche's later assessment of the early work is certainly evidence for the maturing of his position. However, we should keep two points in mind. First, Nietzsche's self-criticism is strategic: he deliberately under-emphasizes the continuity of his philosophical career in order to avoid contamination from that small handful of early ideas he has indeed come to regret. Moreover, it may still be the case that some of those areas which Nietzsche later considers failures might be of interest and relevance for future generations.[1] This introduction, and the commentary as a whole, will be defending both of these positions.

4

ORIGINS AND DIRECTIONS OF *THE BIRTH*
OF TRAGEDY: SOME LINKS

In spite of all its youthful ingenuity and recklessness, *The Birth of Tragedy* has not dropped from the skies. Nietzsche absorbs a vast amount of cultural baggage, some of it by way of osmosis, as an intellectually active, ambitious young academic, another large amount through consciously adopting attractive positions without naming them (for various complex reasons), and a third area of influences which the text clearly acknowledges, such as those emanating from Kant, Schopenhauer and Wagner and from the circle of writers of Weimar Classicism, particularly Schiller and Goethe.

   In the first group of influences, the German Romantics loom large in the background, particularly perhaps Friedrich Schlegel (1772–1829), although his brother August Wilhelm (1767–1845) gets a critical mention in **Sections 7** and **8**.[2] (The English Romantics fare better: Shelley's [1792–1822] re-creation of Aeschylus' lost sequel *Prometheus Unbound* [1820] is singled out in the **Foreword**. The title vignette of the first edition,[3] an etching depicting Prometheus freed from his shackles, was executed on Nietzsche's own orders. Consequently, Nietzsche in the 'Attempt' accuses his earlier self of the crimes of Romanticism.) Another area of such osmosis-like influence is German Transcendental Idealism. Nietzsche probably knew Fichte's work (1762–1814), the most famous alumnus of his boarding school.[4] It is also unlikely that Nietzsche did not know Schelling (1775–1854), who also is not mentioned. Nietzsche's critical sense of history, manifest here and everywhere else in his work, makes it likely that he engaged at some stage with Leopold von Ranke (1795–1886), founder of the German Historical School and another famous pupil of his elite school, *Schulpforta*, near Naumburg.

   Unmentioned, but one of the most significant influences (apart from Schopenhauer, Wagner and Schiller, who are cited) is Friedrich Creuzer (1771–1858) who wrote the pioneering *Symbolik und Mythologie der alten Völker, besonders der Griechen* (*Symbolism and Mythology of Ancient Peoples, Particularly the Greeks*) in 1812. Creuzer clearly had an influence on Nietzsche's central theory of symbolization in *The Birth of Tragedy*. For example, not unlike Nietzsche (cf. **Section 2**), Creuzer establishes a typology of symbolization and distinguishes between mystic and plastic symbolization.[5] In this context of influences also belongs Johann Jacob Bachofen (1815–87), Nietzsche's colleague at Basel, whom he revered and with whom he socialized. Bachofen, never so much as mentioned in *The Birth of Tragedy* (as is also not Jacob Burckhardt [1818–97], idolized as historian of the Renaissance and cherished as a colleague and 'friend'), contributed with a pioneering study of *Mother Right, An Investigation of the Religious and Juridical Character of Matriarchy in the Ancient World* (1861)[6] to the foundation of Cultural Anthropology as a new academic discipline. Nietzsche's interest in archaic, 'pre-historical' phases of history, and the particular importance allocated to anthropological aspects of gender clearly show the influence of Bachofen's work.[7] The quasi-independent Swiss line of approach to early culture as pioneered by Bachofen, with the *The Birth of Tragedy* as transmitter, is picked up in C.G. Jung's theory (breaking away from the Freudian mother lode of psychoanalysis) of the 'Collective Unconscious'.

The second group of unacknowledged influences is easier to deal with because there are more concrete hints. For example, the figure of Prometheus is present both as the tragic hero of Aeschylus' tragedy, Goethe's '*Sturm and Drang*' poem (both **Section 9**), and Shelley's play (**Foreword**); furthermore, Nietzsche embraces Prometheus as a sublime criminal and a Dionysian mask worn by the tragic hero. Thus, *The Birth of Tragedy* shows an implicit affinity with the intentions and literary ambitions of German *Sturm und Drang* (Storm and Stress), the groundbreaking literary and philosophical movement of angry young hotspurs (the early work of Goethe, Schiller and Herder belongs here), who inaugurated modern German literature and culture after 1770, and for whom Prometheus features as a symbol for the movement's aesthetic and political rebellion. *Sturm und Drang* is one of the key influences clearly discernable beneath the surface of the text. Its often-exuberant style, the fact that at strategic moments it resorts to a rhetoric of direct address, passages of exulted hyperbole and epiphany-like excitement: all these are features also of *Sturm und Drang*-writing. There are other unacknowledged major sources: the proximity of Nietzsche's view of the Greeks with Hölderlin's (1770–1843) is remarkable, as is the central importance of Hölderlin as a 'dithyrambic' poet with a philosophical mission (see our **Note** in **Section 3, Nietzsche, German 'Hellenism' and Hölderlin**). Also of significance is the underlying presence of one of Nietzsche's favourite writers, the American 'transcendentalist' Ralph Waldo Emerson (1803–82).[8] Mention needs to be made also of Heinrich von Kleist (1777–1811), one of the most important unacknowledged sources, we think, for Nietzsche. Kleist's philosophy of history (if this is not too grand a name for the slender sketch outlined in the essay relevant here, *The Puppet Theatre,* 1810[9]), Nietzsche replicates in several key ideas, one of them being that 'we have to eat again of the Tree of Knowledge to fall back into the state of innocence' (p. 416). Kleist is also the author of some of the most striking tragedies ever written in German, particularly *Penthesilea* (1808). These are the best non-musical modern illustrations for Nietzsche's theory of tragedy as a balancing act of two competing fundamental drives. Hegel (1770–1831) belongs also in this group of hidden references, although as a less than benevolent presence. Hegel seems to be the unacknowledged bête noire of *The Birth of Tragedy.* His towering influence is manifest in the text struggling for an alternative to Hegelian logic and historical teleology. And finally, Nietzsche's favourite poet (apart from Hölderlin, mentioned above) needs mentioning: Heinrich Heine (1797–1856), who is present in Nietzsche's more satirical, parodistic moments, and also in the central thematic focus of the text on dreams. Heine's first major collection *Buch der Lieder* (Book of Songs, 1827) deals with the contrasting worlds of dream and waking: the poetic exaltation of dreams is contrasted with a drab reality of post-Romantic disillusionment. Much of what *The Birth of Tragedy* has to say about dreams and their mediating role is prefigured poetically in Heine.

We cannot go into detail here concerning any further of these indirect reference points. The commentary will give more detail. Still one observation may be useful following from the listing of the above: the reader needs to be aware that the text processes a great deal of unreferenced influences, both those present in the background by default, and a second type, not identified by the author for various reasons. Darwin (1809–82) occupies a special position in between the two categories of non-acknowledgement. Is Nietzsche consciously blanking the *Origin of the Species* (1859), as he does Hegel or Jesus, or is he so steeped in Darwin's evolutionary theory that its presence as a fixed component of his thought must be taken for granted? (We will go into this in more detail in our **Note: Nietzsche and Darwin** in **Section 1**.) It is evident, however, that the named sources of influence in the text as we have it before us are only the tip of the iceberg of a vast underground mass of material that has contributed to the making of this text. It is perhaps another sign of its youthfulness that the author is not yet fully empowered to discuss openly what moved him or provoked his ire.

How does *The Birth of Tragedy* fit into European debates on history, aesthetics and politics in Nietzsche's time? The book defends the realm of the aesthetic against that of the political and social. Thus, it fits in well with a growing tendency in the European cultural and literary debates of the time to set up the aesthetic as a bulwark against emerging mass culture based on industrialization, mechanization and democratization, as well as the intrusion of cheap commodity standards into all areas of cultural production. In other words, *The Birth of Tragedy* can be read as a German contribution to the European movements of Symbolism and Aestheticism. These movements react against a then prevalent doctrine in the arts and literature, that of Naturalism, an extreme form of earlier-nineteenth-century Realism. Thus, in its attempt at creating a metaphysics of aesthetics, *The Birth of Tragedy* is surely a true product of German philosophical culture, but also corresponds well with French and English attempts, for instance as outlined in Charles Baudelaire's (1821–67) *The Painter of Modern Life* (1863), and applied in the poetic cycle of the *Fleurs du mal* (1857),[10] or in the conclusion to Walter Pater's (1839–94) *Renaissance* (1873),[11] to overcome the crisis of modernity by capturing and transcending it aesthetically. When Nietzsche polemicizes against Euripides (**Sections 11 to 13**), his critique implies Émile Zola (1840–1902), who had outlined the basic principles of Naturalism in a Preface to his novel *Thérèse Raquin* (1862). Another place of Nietzsche's attack on Naturalism is in **Sections 7** and **8** where a naturalist view of the Greek chorus is refuted.

CHAPTER 2

OVERVIEW OF THEMES

THE BIRTH OF TRAGEDY AS UNTIMELY MEDITATION: DANGEROUS LIAISONS

Aligning himself with Wagner against the 'mediocre' culture of the establishment and academic parochialism of his time turns the whole enterprise of this book into one of great risk-taking. This is because the Nietzsche/Wagner union provides solace and support (much more to Nietzsche than to Wagner[1]) only for as long as it lasts. It encourages Nietzsche to be reckless, and his later isolation will be all the more shattering and absolute. From around the middle of the 1870s, there comes a lonely point for Nietzsche when he realizes that Wagner cannot help him any further in his fight against the status quo of contemporary 'philistinism'. Wagner had never been the harbinger of cultural renewal, Nietzsche now thinks; he had been simply wrong to see in him the 'dithyrambic dramatist' on a par with Aeschylus, as he is idolized in *The Birth of Tragedy*. Nietzsche now realized that Wagner was not a modern composer at all, but one steeped in the Romantic tradition. 'All Romantics end up Christians' as Nietzsche reports his disillusioning findings in section 7 of 'An Attempt at Self-Criticism'. Nietzsche manages to hide his changing attitude quite well publicly for a while; only Wagner notices that Nietzsche is condemning him with faint praise in the essay *Wagner in Bayreuth* of 1876, the last of the *Untimely Meditations*.

The radicalism of his ideas and the innovative, experimental nature of his style have the effect of catapulting Nietzsche out of his own time. *Untimely Meditations*, as already mentioned, is the title of his second series of publications of 1873–76, which contains four essays devoted to appraising or critiquing misunderstood contemporary role models (Schopenhauer, Leo Strauss and Wagner) and investigating the flaws of thought in the paradigm of contemporary Historicism. In a way, *The Birth of Tragedy* could be called Nietzsche's first untimely meditation because it alienates so many of his friends as Nietzsche takes on established orthodoxies in classical studies, history, philosophy, aesthetics and even the sciences. This book wants to shake things up. Though Nietzsche still had a contemporary public in mind when he wrote it, within all of Nietzsche's published work he had that public in mind only to the extent he could change it and help deliver a different future.

INTENTIONS, FORM AND STRUCTURE OF *THE BIRTH OF TRAGEDY*

One of this book's priorities is the wholly unusual way in which it is written. In fact, what makes it special is that it is the trial run for Nietzsche's lifelong experiment of exploring new ways in composing philosophical ideas. *The Birth of Tragedy* springs this experiment on the reader whose participation in it is essential for its success. Nietzsche's text deliberately breaks with the 'established' conventions of explication in philosophy and classical philology, the first major transgression being that it disregards the boundaries traditionally dividing these two academic disciplines. The text is a hybrid of the two (plus at least psychology and anthropology), largely unconcerned with rules of subject-specific methodological purity. And it goes further: rather than aiming at clarity and logical development, Nietzsche (perhaps following F.W. Schlegel's advocacy of incomprehensibility[2]) employs irony and rhetorical tricks, plays with the reader, and approaches and then backs away from key subjects like an accomplished seducer. There is a planned educational or 'heuristic' dimension to Nietzsche. 'Making sense' for the reader means to struggle free from obscurities, laid out for us to be overcome. In this way, there is a labyrinthine quality to the experience. This unusual type of reader activity accounts for part of the excitement in the reading. It is also one of the justifications for this commentary which, even though it cannot release the reader from the task Nietzsche demands, wants to provide at least some assistance.

'The medium is the message': Marshall McLuhan's infamous adage[3] emphasizing the predominance of form over content in modern mass media might help to illustrate Nietzsche's intentions of a century earlier. More than any other major writer in the history of philosophy (perhaps with the exception of Plato who chose to present his ideas in the unusual form of dialogue; Nietzsche talks about this in **Section 14**), Nietzsche is concerned with embedding the form of his writing in his 'message', so that the writing itself, in its structures, metaphors, allusions, repetitions, etc., takes on a leading role in steering the reader in the desired direction. The form of the book is intended to be symbolic of what Nietzsche wants to say: it is a theory of symbolic forms in – symbolic form.

The Birth of Tragedy aims at squaring a theory of fundamental human anthropology with one of the development of European cultural history. Nietzsche posits a perennial ensemble of forces of human cultural production. These forces or drives are understood from a broadly Schopenhauerian metaphysical point of view as specific modes of objectification or expression of the underlying Will. The drives have metaphysical meaning and, in their realizations in cultural forms, are symbolic of that meaning. Culture, broadly speaking, is metaphysics made actual. The struggles and combinations of these forces are behind historical change. More specifically, the twin basis of human cultural expression are the two artistic drives of the Dionysian and Apollonian, engaged in an alternately benign and violent (but always productive) struggle (this is the subject of the book up to **Section 12**). This activity, already visible in very early stages of cultural history, is interfered with by a historically later malignant third force, the 'Socratic tendency' of consciousness-led reflectivity (from **Section 13**). Nietzsche defines this change as the difference between the Greek pre- or subconscious epoch of culture, driven by natural instinctual forces of artistic production, and the modern one premised on the controlling agency of consciousness and abstract logic removed from instinctual drives.

The Birth of Tragedy is subdivided into two main parts, like a diptych of two panels.[4] The first studies the interplay in Greece between the art-drives of the Apolline and Dionysiac. This is the age of myth (*mythos*) describing the Apolline drive in *agon*-like interplay with the Dionysiac, and culminating in their unique combination in tragedy and going into decline with Euripides. The second part sets up the epochal antagonism between the age of tragedy and the modern age, dominated by ascending consciousness and theoretical reason, which leads to the death of tragedy and the *Weltanschauung* or the world view it represents.

This is the age of reason and logic (*logos*), and Nietzsche investigates the disease that is caused when the 'to-ing and fro-ing' (cf. **Section 4, p. 28**) between the two mythical drives is suppressed by the hegemonic expansion of *logos* as a powerful new cultural agent: with Euripides and Socrates consciousness that knows its name, and theoretical man, arrive on the scene. The agon of the mythological sparring partners, the Apollonian and Dionysian, is interrupted; they are driven underground by an out-of-control logical drive which Nietzsche regards as 'pathological' (cf. **Sections 1 and 13**). Part one charts the rise and fall of tragedy as a literary form symbolic of a metaphysically tenable world view. Part two ascribes the decline and death of this symbolic form to a fundamental anthropology whose metaphysical meaning is deluded; it then also tries to establish conditions for its revival.

This revival, though, cannot be a form of simple return to preconscious conditions of Greek life. A re-establishment is envisaged instead, a 're-birth' of the preconscious world view of tragedy *under modern conditions*. Since the clock of history cannot be turned back it has got to be pushed forward. A radically modern, highly synthetic form of art is propagated, Wagner's music drama, as vehicle to achieve the tragic depth of existence, but born from within consciousness. In modernity, the highest forms of consciousness, abstract scientific logic and 'systematic' philosophy, have been achieved and already begun to implode, creating fertile conditions for this rebirth. This idea of an historical event 'squared', as it were, is prefigured in the aforementioned essay by Heinrich von Kleist of 1810, which poses the problem of how to regain the innocence of artistic transfiguration in an age where human instinct is choked with abstractions and overruled by reason.

Each of the two parts is relatively self-contained. Some critics have argued that only the first one is worthy of critical attention, because it is here that Nietzsche develops his theory of tragedy.[5] In our view, nothing could be further from understanding the book's intentions. It could even be argued that it was written entirely from a modern perspective: the Greeks are only an example, or case study, underpinning a theory of art and culture based on modern models of thought. (Nietzsche more or less says as much in Section 6 of 'An Attempt at Self-Criticism' [cf. p. 10].) Both of these polar arguments fail to do the book justice, because it is only in its symmetry of construction in two main parts that its statement achieves full validity. Only together do they encompass Nietzsche's grand historical theory of cultural anthropology. Nietzsche's 'theory of tragedy' derived from Greek models is incomplete and therefore does not make sense without its modern equivalent in the theory of musical aesthetics derived from Wagner. Besides, the way that culture moves, from Asia Minor and via Athens and Rome to Bayreuth, is at the very centre of Nietzsche's interest. This 'genealogical' perspective on culture also makes it necessary to consider the book as a whole, in both its parts.

The second set of twelve chapters, from 14 to 25, constitutes the right-hand panel of the diptych. It is a back-to-front mirror image of the historical development traversed in panel one, leading from the incubation of diseased culture in and since Socrates, to its full blown crisis unfolding over more than two millennia, down to the point where the prospect of the demise of diseased culture is raised through the reawakening of tragedy in Wagner's operas. The problem posed for us moderns is the opposite one to that encountered by the Greeks. Whilst they had to tame the Dionysian – to make it productive in the domain of culture – we have to find a way to break open the ever tightening straightjacket of modern culture by letting ourselves get back in touch again with the primeval life forces of Dionysian sensuality. We have inherited from the Greeks a desire to control nature, but thereby have lost absolutely what we set out to control – a very topical message still for the twenty-first century.

CHAPTER 3

READING THE TEXT

'AN ATTEMPT AT SELF-CRITICISM'

'An Attempt at Self-Criticism' was written long after the original text, for the 1886 second edition of *The Birth of Tragedy*. It is nearly as close to the end of Nietzsche's career as *The Birth of Tragedy* is to the beginning. For best effect, we strongly recommend readers to first read the main text, and to leave this retrospective re-evaluation for later.

Nietzsche is here confessing from a position of mature sovereignty of the assured theorist and stylist to *The Birth of Tragedy's* faults, informing us what it really wanted to achieve, and where and why it partially failed to do so. He apologizes for its youthful blemishes, the insufficiencies of form, logic, organization, style and argument, and for the fact that it has its basis in 'precocious, wet-behind-the-ears personal experiences' (p. 5). This admission serves as a strategic move to enable the author to salvage some of the underlying truths of the book. It is after all the embryonic cell from which all his future works are spawned, both thematically and stylistically. Nietzsche embraces the earlier work's tentative rejection of Schopenhauer's cultural pessimism and its groping steps towards a cultural and psychological theory of Dionysian life-affirmation. However, he rejects the metaphysics of art as *solace* (the philosophical core of the early text), as a misguided late Romanticism under the besotting influence of Wagnerian toxins.

We must not forget that Nietzsche looks back to the earlier text from a vantage point where all his mature theoretical positions are fully developed. That creates a certain bias of his view. He also to an extent wants to compensate for the embarrassment inflicted on him by the early critics of the book (cf. **Chapter 4, Reception and Influence**), and for his own self-inflicted humiliation caused by dissociating himself from Wagner, the book's hero. It is remarkable that Nietzsche here deploys his later methodology of genealogy autobiographically, as he also does in his last (self-) critical work *Ecce Homo*. Nietzsche asks: what made this book possible and necessary? What were the wider cultural and specific personal conditions and motivations that led to just this formulation of *The Birth of Tragedy*'s theoretical positions and formulations? Nietzsche crystallizes the book's rambling argument in a series of seven short interrelated key questions or statements, together with self-critical concerns, one for each section of the 'Attempt'. The compressed brevity is an indication of the gulf that separates Nietzsche's early and late styles.[1] Although there remain the rhetorical shadow-boxing and hyperbolic tomfooleries of the text's surface, there is a highly distinct voice here. As in all his more critically, that is, less poetically ambitious work of the 1880s, this voice is more sober, determined, considered and 'realistic' (if this term is permissible).

'Is There Pessimism of *Strength*?'

Section 1 illustrates the incongruity between the stormy political conditions in which the book was conceived and written, and its seemingly esoteric academic concern and the idyllic personal conditions of the author. The German nation is at war and the author is for most of the time tucked away in Switzerland, 'sitting in some corner of the Alps' (p. 3). He briefly joins the war effort, gets ill, and by way of recovery settles down to a considered view of the arcane intellectual project. The use of the third person is striking: Nietzsche's earlier self is held at a distance, awaiting the revelation of the 'question' that 'underlies' the book, and thus awaiting the evidence that this young author deserves to share a first person pronoun with the philosopher of 1886. A similar distancing strategy is employed in the last section of the 'Attempt'. As the **Foreword** to the main text informs us, Nietzsche sees his book as contributing to the conflict between academic enquiry and political engagement. Nietzsche's falling out with 'philistine' warmongering and nationalist German politics is therefore already prepared in *The Birth of Tragedy*, and, as we will see here in Section 6, fully realized in the 'Attempt'.

Section 1 goes on to list the original concerns of *The Birth of Tragedy* in a series of clipped questions and conjectures, culminating in the re-evaluating question quoted above. Pessimism and optimism, like truth and lying, good and evil, are no longer opposed as negative/positive binary opposites. The conceptual oppositions are not original, but derivative; they are not neutral descriptions of values but already intrinsically valued. A more fundamental contrast, Nietzsche hints, is between a weak or sickly pessimism (also to be called 'nihilism'), and a 'pessimism of strength'. Nietzsche emphasizes with particular urgency in this retrospective the role of pain and suffering as basis for cultural responses that have widely different metaphysical meanings. The pessimism of strength is an antidote to Schopenhauer's pessimism of resignation; it does not seek to annul pain and suffering. This new stress on the concept of pessimism accords with the new subtitle Nietzsche gave the book for its second edition: it is now entitled *The Birth of Tragedy, Or: Hellenism and Pessimism*. The original book certainly distinguishes between two modes of optimism or, more generally, cheerfulness. The first being the shallow serenity of the later Greeks under the influence of the scientific optimism of Socrates; the other (more aesthetically and metaphysically interesting) is characteristic of the pre-Socratic Apolline (see **Section 3**). Already pointed to in that same section, though, are the two modes of pessimism. For Nietzsche cleverly introduces the triumphant confidence of the Apolline by way of the incomprehension of an observer of 'another religion' (Christianity, of course) in whose 'asceticism, spirituality and duty' we should hear something of what the later Nietzsche is calling a pessimism of weakness (see the 'desire for nothingness' in **'Attempt'**, **Section 5**). Likewise, again in Section 3 of the main text, the Apolline 'magic mountain' is shown to be resting upon 'the terrors and horrors of existence', something equally incomprehensible no doubt to the Christian view. Here, though, is where Nietzsche disagrees with himself: for where the later Nietzsche calls for a pessimism of strength as the only healthy and metaphysically appropriate response to these terrors, his earlier book turns to the solace of art. This is the substance of Section 7 of the 'Attempt'.[2]

With this opening discussion of the 'Attempt', and with the new subtitle, Nietzsche is claiming that his first book was always about the nature of pessimism. Read in this way, Nietzsche thus confirms the validity of the categories introduced in the earlier book, and that they have become cornerstones of his mature methodology of revalidating cultural values. He can accept many of *The Birth of Tragedy*'s philosophical views, and many of the methodological innovations that led to them – but he cannot accept the Romantic, Christian, nihilist conclusions at which his younger self arrived.

'It Is Necessary to Look at Science "through the Prism of the Artist" and "at Art through the Prism of Life"'

What cultural form propagates this 'weak' pessimism? Section 2 identifies the real problem Nietzsche had set himself in *The Birth of Tragedy*: not the Greeks, not even ancient and modern tragedy as such are the prime objects of investigation, we are astonished to learn, but the 'problem of science'. He calls it an 'impossible' book because it treats an 'old man's problem' with youthful reckless-ness. It is too long (though shorter than most of Nietzsche's out-put), full of 'storm and stress' (the name of the proto-Romantic artistic movement in Germany at the end of the eighteenth century, see **Chapter 1, Origins and Directions**). However, it is an independent book ('standing defiantly') and it enjoyed some success, not least with Wagner, its addressee.

Nietzsche explains that he approached the problematic of science through an artistic lens,[3] and had to do so, because this problem cannot be raised 'within the territory of science'. In the main text of the book, Socratic science is described as 'optimis-tic'. One thing this means is that it is self-universalizing, unable to comprehend that something might not be part of its proper territory. The problem of science – the genealogical claim that science at its foundation is not scientific – is not a scientific prob-lem. The artist then doubles up as philosopher who goes on to inspect art through the lens of life. 'Through the lens of life' is repeated in the question that ends section 4 of this 'Attempt'. The nature of life – its health, production of manifold cultural forms and so forth – are indeed an absolutely fundamental concept for both the earlier (see **Section 7** of the main text, for example) and later Nietzsche. Nevertheless, the counterfactual return to phi-lology proposed in the next section, and the large number of texts on the physical and biological sciences in his library, sug-gest that Nietzsche *could* have continued: 'one must in turn inspect life, if not through' then at least *using* the lens of science.[4] Nietzsche thinks of his project – then as now – as a layering of perspectives, artistic and philosophical, building upon and reciprocally informing one another. And even though he rejects here, in Section 7, the early mystification of art as a vehicle for metaphysical solace – Benjamin and other critics have rejected this aspect of the book as Nietzsche's 'aestheticism'[5] – he still maintains the need for a fusion of artistic and philosophical (not to mention historical, scientific and so forth) perspectives as an epistemological and methodological necessity of the ongoing project. The use of optical metaphor is interesting here; it draws attention to the innovative method of perspective shifts as a central element of Nietzsche's mature critique.

'I Ought to Have *Sung* This "New Soul", and Not Talked!'

This section posits that *The Birth of Tragedy* is badly written, 'lacking the will to logical cleanliness, very convinced and therefore too arrogant to prove its assertions'. It preaches to the converted, and makes no attempt to communicate with those not admitted into the inner sanctum of musical delirium. There are two related points here. First, Nietzsche accuses his earlier self of a lack of philosophical or even 'logical' rigour.[6] Secondly, the first point was either caused or exacerbated by the fact that the book was for the initiated. Nietzsche mixes these points together with others that are recognizably about style. This section of the 'Attempt' contains a curious tension: Nietzsche seems to be simultaneously accusing himself of being too little a scholar (insufficient rigour, and if only he had written as a philologist) but also too much (something 'concealed' under the 'cowl of a scholar', talking not singing).

The question of adequacy of *The Birth of Tragedy*'s style is particularly relevant in relation to what Nietzsche with hindsight identifies as the real but as yet partially hidden agenda of the book, at the time not yet fully understood by himself: *The Birth of Tragedy*, so Nietzsche wants us to believe, is a covert hymn devoted to Dionysus; there is a wild, disembodied, dithyrambic voice audible in the background singing the god's praise. Underneath the monk's hood of scholarship, hides 'the voice of a mystical and almost maenadic[7] soul which stammers in a strange tongue'. Occasionally, the reader can clearly see what Nietzsche means, as for example, in the last paragraph of **Section 20**. Nietzsche holds that on the whole the book does not sufficiently accommodate 'this "new soul"'. Nietzsche asks himself whether he would not have been better able to say what he had to say 'at that time as a poet'. Alternatively, he might have stuck to his more modest guns as a trained philologist, excavating textual evidence. Thus, Nietzsche strategically agrees with his early critics (see **Chapter 4, Reception and Influence**) conceding one of the points of Wilamowitz-Mollendorff. He accused the book of falling between the chairs of philology and something new and, not understood by anyone (Nietzsche here calls it poetry), performing unsatisfactorily in both areas.

One way of understanding this double failure is in terms of the notion of 'wrong semblance' that we employ in discussing **Section 1** of the main text. In its symbolic form, the writing does not manage to match the depth of the underlying chthonic existential experience which it more hides than reveals. The Apollonian symbolization of Dionysian experience is found wanting.[8] Another way is employing the idea of layers of perspective that was discussed just above. The in-between style of *the Birth of Tragedy* fails to take seriously the domains of its constituent perspectives of the overall genealogical movement: it is half-hearted poetry together with half-hearted scholarship. One of the results of the early book, however, is precisely a call for a truly hybrid art: one that brings the Apolline and Dionysiac together, without compromising either, by forcing them into a higher dialectical unity (see the comment about 'dialectically disinclined[9] [*Unlustigkeit*] Germans'). It could be argued that Nietzsche later failed to follow the stylistic imperative found in the discoveries of his own first book.

'Is Madness Perhaps Not Necessarily a Symptom of Degeneration?'

One of the intentions of this self-critical retrospective is to reframe the earlier work in terms of the question: 'Yes, what is Dionysiac?' *The Birth of Tragedy* already set out to find an answer, Nietzsche maintains, but using a flawed method and style. As a drive that belongs to human beings (and whole cultures), the Dionysiac is linked with a psychological question. There follows a series of questions that repeat in miniature the peeling back of layers within the main text, as we move from the 'demand for beauty' to the 'demand for ugliness' and from there to its source in strength, desire and health.

At stake is mental health, both on personal and historical cultural levels. Continuing on the note struck in the previous section where the 'maenadic' Dionysian was mentioned as the author's 'new soul', in this section the phenomenon is broadened out and projected into the sphere of cultural identity. The question of the Dionysiac is now more clearly seen as one of *madness*, individual but especially collective: is madness 'perhaps not necessarily a symptom of degeneration, of decline, of culture that has gone on too long'? Is it perhaps possible, Nietzsche asks – he passes the question to 'psychiatrists' – 'to speak of neuroses of *health*, of national youth and youthfulness?'[10] This is the core of the debate *The Birth of Tragedy* has thrown open. The book seeks to re-evaluate the relationship between madness and civilization by proposing the unsettling and futuristic insight that what appears as madness from a point of view of highly developed standards of civilization – collective Dionysian ravings of primeval man – can also be regarded as a sign of healthy connectivity between humanity and nature, provided we in turn equally evaluate that same highly developed civilization as atrophied, diseased and solipsistically turned in on itself. This is clearly a highly destabilizing insight, unpalatable to Nietzsche's contemporaries. We can also see the importance of this untimely realization in the wake of the twentieth-century crises of culture and civilization which invite the diagnosis that destructive madness is not opposed to civilization but is its natural consequence. Thus, *The Birth of Tragedy* anticipates twentieth-century formulations of theories critical of Western civilization as varied as Freud's *Civilisation and its Discontents* and *Totem and Taboo*, Deleuze and Guattari's *Anti-Oedipus*, Horkheimer/Adorno's *Dialectic of Enlightenment*, Foucault's *Madness and Civilisation*.

'"What, When Seen through the Prism of Life, Is the Meaning of Morality?" For Want of a Better Word, "the True Name of the Antichrist" Is Dionysus'

The question we quote ends the previous section. Here, Nietzsche clarifies another central element of the critique he pursued with *The Birth of Tragedy*. As an advocacy of life the book is directed first and foremost against morality and here especially against the life-denying crimes of Christian morality. Nietzsche's premise then and now is that morality does not belong to 'life' as its immediate expression. Life is *per definitionem* amoral, and morality is a human protection mechanism, like science, from life's cruel, inhuman depths. In this way, morality tries to get the better of life; it is in essence a rejection of life, and 'before the court of morality . . . life *must* constantly and inevitably be proved wrong' and 'unworthy'. The fact that any explicit discussion of Christianity is virtually absent from *The Birth of Tragedy* Nietzsche now (perhaps disingenuously) claims as 'the best indication of the depth of the *anti-moral* tendency in the book'. Our commentary partially confirms this belated insight by pointing to a number of passages (cf. for instance **Section 13**) where the critique of Christianity is implicit.

The implicit anti-moral thrust of the book, however, is directly linked to the weight given in it to the metaphysics of art. Morality versus art is indeed one good way of expressing the struggle that followed the advent of Socratic and Christian morality. Now, after providing a fine and energetic description of this metaphysics of art, Nietzsche very carefully and playfully writes '*one may say* [emphasis added] that this whole artiste's metaphysics is capricious, otiose, fantastical'. Is he, or is he not, disowning it? The situation is more complicated than it might appear. The book's aestheticism is its instinctively constructed bulwark against Christian morality and a lever for unhinging it; he 'baptized it' (ironically) with the name of Dionysiac. In this respect, *The Birth of Tragedy* proves absolutely true to its author's mature intentions as a critic of Christian morality. Moreover, this metaphysics is the 'invention' of a healthy instinct responding to such morality; and as such, Nietzsche lauds the instincts of his earlier self. 'The only thing of interest in a refuted system is the personal element', Nietzsche writes in a second preface to his never completed book, *Philosophy in the Tragic Age of the Greeks*, which was written around the same time as *The Birth of Tragedy*. In other words, this 'artiste's metaphysics' discloses as possible a mode of human existence that is forever irrefutable and valuable (as an educational tool for cultural renewal in the present) even if the particular philosophical claims made – and especially the *general* or *intrinsic* value ascribed to existence on their basis – are 'one great mistake'.[11] Nevertheless, this metaphysics has a weakness that condemns it to falling back into the arms of the anti-life drives against which it battles. This weakness is the subject of the next two sections.

'What Would Music Be like If It Were No Longer Romantic in Its Origins, as German Music Is, but *Dionysiac*?'

Sections 6 and 7 contain Nietzsche's admission of the key failures of *The Birth of Tragedy*. These are areas in which he has since moved on to clearer and more sustainably radical positions. To us as readers with one and a half centuries distance, Nietzsche's self-criticism may seem justified but perhaps harsh and also in the end illegitimate; a case could be made for letting the early work stand as it is, 'warts and all'. The need may arise to protect the text to an extent from the critique of its own author. Particularly appealing to us now may seem for example the text's special complexity forced upon it by Nietzsche's original notion of duplicity (cf. commentary **Section 1** of main text) of the two forces in agonistic interplay. Nietzsche's essentially non-teleological, Darwin-influenced thinking represents – as we argue throughout the commentary – Nietzsche's early attempt to take a stance against Hegelian dialectics, which for Nietzsche exemplified the derelict end of Socratic culture.[12] In the 'Attempt', the Apolline is sacrificed on the altar of Dionysus. For Nietzsche in 1886, his earlier thesis of the Apolline as a basic art-drive plays into the hands (as we shall see) of Romanticism and nihilism, and also closes down the range of metaphysically justified possibilities open to cultural forms. The Apolline does not disappear in later Nietzsche, but is both reduced and expanded. The role is reduced in that its full status as a 'brother' to the Dionysiac is taken away; but it is expanded in that it comes to cover that aspect of the Dionysiac that is form *creating*.[13]

One key point of difference between early and 'mature' Nietzsche is that the former lacked 'a language of my own'. 'Language' here, as we have seen, not only refers to stylistic considerations, but also more particularly to the philosophical language Nietzsche has adopted from others. Thus the early book is forced to 'express strange and new evaluations in Schopenhauerian and Kantian formulations'. This is indeed a major youthful dilemma of *The Birth of Tragedy* which follows Schopenhauer by borrowing his formulations but expresses positions that entail fundamental criticisms of Schopenhauer. Nietzsche is saying the same about Wagner, and he could have made the same argument with regard to Schiller, whose aesthetics *The Birth of Tragedy* substantially replicates, though it disagrees with most of the substance of

Schiller's classicist and idealist notions of aesthetics and history. Nietzsche mentions resignation as a main element of Schopenhauer's pessimism, particularly as regards tragedy. 'How differently Dionysus spoke to me!', Nietzsche exclaims, but that difference of language *The Birth of Tragedy* could not fully transmit. This is the same as to say that *The Birth of Tragedy* squandered the opportunities it had of realizing the new Dionysian language. In the end, therefore, *The Birth of Tragedy* does not do justice to either Schopenhauer or to Dionysus.

The second error, and one Nietzsche regrets still more, is to have mixed up 'the grandiose Greek problem' 'with the most modern things'. This was a bold methodological move at the time from which stems – as we argue in the commentary – the explosive radicalism of the original text: the Greek solution is embedded as an inner motivational drive in history itself. Therefore, the Greeks are incorporated in modern culture, not in the detail of the past, or as a superimposed transcendental idea of teleological fulfilment, but in the structure of the psychological components involved that may be replicated in the contemporary period and under conditions of modernity. Moreover, it is difficult to see how this greatly differs from the attempt to return to the beginning of religious and moral systems by fictionalizing the figure of Zarathustra, in order to provide the present with an alternative.

The issue, of course, is not with the problem of modernity in general (Nietzsche's concern with this never goes away), but with the particular 'modern things' with which Nietzsche was mixed up. Above all, he is referring to Wagner. In Nietzsche's self-criticism this entails the rejection as 'Romantic' – by now a term of abuse for Nietzsche – of the Wagnerian aesthetic upon which the aesthetic theory of *The Birth of Tragedy* is built. The distancing from Wagnerian Romanticism includes the repudiation of German nationalistic sentiments in which – as part of the Wagnerite package – *The Birth of Tragedy* occasionally, but generally half-heartedly, indulges (see particularly our commentary to **Section 23**). The German spirit has 'finally and definitively' 'abdicated'; the nation drowns in 'mediocrity'; German culture has lost its legitimacy to lead in Europe.[14] An interesting open-endedness ensues: *The Birth of Tragedy* projects the vision of a culture of the future inspired by Greek tragedy which is in the process of being revived under modern conditions in Wagner's music drama. Now Nietzsche restates the vision but excludes Wagner's operas from it as its erstwhile artistic paradigm. The search is on again for a Dionysiac music 'no longer Romantic in its origins'. Mahler's Sixth, Schönberg's tone poem *Verklärte Nacht*, Webern's musical miniatures[15], and Berg's opera *Lulu* might have answered Nietzsche's question.

'Would It Not Be Necessary' to Desire a New Form of Art, the Art of Metaphysical Solace, in Fact, to Desire Tragedy?

Nietzsche's self-criticism culminates in the negative answer to this, his own rhetorical question. He quotes from section 18 of *The Birth of Tragedy* where he advocates 'metaphysical solace' through tragedy, quoting Goethe's *Faust II*. Both the metaphysical solace, even in the guise of the early book's aestheticism, and tragedy, even in the form of Wagner's operas advocated there, are now surplus to requirements. With reference to Zarathustra, 'that Dionysiac monster', Nietzsche laughs off the aspiration of the earlier book to heal the world's woes through the magical reconciliation of artistic forces in tragedy. The pessimist of strength – if determined to remain a pessimist – should learn to laugh and dance, responding in a healthy, thoroughly anti-metaphysical[16] manner to the burdens of existence. 'Metaphysical solace' means Romanticism, and Romanticism for Nietzsche always ends up as Christianity. This is a reference to the ending of Wagner's last opera, *Parsifal* (1882),[17] which Nietzsche believes propagates, true to the Christian spirit of abnegating life, the scholastic solution of 'redemption of the redeemer'. Singing and dancing, the irreverent figure of Zarathustra, the divine human and wise anti-metaphysical fool, cuts through all of these complications, which are in the end the ones that have made *The Birth of Tragedy* the influential book it turned out to become. The question remains of the validity of the earlier text in the light of Nietzsche's later work. The fact that it is riddled with complications might greatly speak in its favour.

FOREWORD: ART, WAGNER AND WAR

The Foreword serves as an introduction (as Nietzsche says in the first sentence) and as a dedication (in the last). We have already briefly discussed in **Chapter 2** Nietzsche's relationship with Richard Wagner. Not surprisingly, then, the dedication is to Wagner, and the Foreword is clearly written in a spirit of admiration bordering on sycophancy. As an *introduction*, though brief, it has some interesting things to say.

First, Nietzsche imagines himself on the same side of a battle as Wagner; not a military battle, but rather a much more important cultural one. Although often hidden from sight, this battle is the central focus of the book. The battle is for a cultural revolution within Germany (or within European culture more generally). What is meant by 'culture'? In both German and English, its broad meaning refers to any regional, national or ethnic group and to the features that give that group identity (e.g. political or educational institutions, traditions, a shared language or religion). So, Nietzsche's book addresses the question of what does, and what should, it mean to be German. Since Germany is a brand new country (the minor German states merged with Prussia for the first time as Nietzsche was writing), this is highly topical. Nietzsche is clearly trying to enter into the debate about what this new country should be, culturally, and especially he is trying to steer it away from what he sees as its crass militarism and nationalism, represented in Bismarck.

A narrower meaning of culture refers to the 'highest' or 'clearest' products of a particular group and its identity. These might include philosophy and science, but are especially identified as music, literature and the other arts. Nietzsche concerns himself with tragic drama and (later in the book) with Wagnerian musical drama. For Nietzsche, Wagner represents an important new struggle for achievement in culture. Nietzsche intends to battle for a revolution in German culture (in the broader sense of the word) by way of a new understanding and direction for culture in the narrower sense. The foes in this battle are the current 'aesthetic public' – that is to say, those people who are typical consumers of art, literature and music – and also those incapable of taking art, literature and music as a 'serious' issue. (These two groups may overlap, of course.) The battle is thus primarily *within* Germany and is not *against* a European enemy.

Secondly and accordingly, although the book would appear to be merely a history of events that happened 2,000 years previously in ancient Greece, Nietzsche claims this historical dimension is actually a device for addressing a contemporary issue. A few years later, in the second volume of *Human, All Too Human*, Nietzsche writes:

> The Greeks as Interpreters – When we speak of the Greeks we involuntarily speak of today and yesterday: their familiar history is a polished mirror that always radiates something that is not in the mirror itself. [. . .] Thus the Greeks make it easier for modern man to communicate much that is delicate and hard to communicate.[18]

The central topic is the contemporary cultural (in both broad and narrow senses) environment within Germany (or Europe); and the historical study of Greek culture and tragedy is a way of understanding this environment and bringing about the cultural revolution that will change it. As we shall see, for at least the previous hundred years, European and especially German intellectuals had been struggling with how to understand the ancient Greeks and their relation to the contemporary world. So, in one sense, this idea of the Greeks as a mirror is not new. However, what is much more original is the notion that the Greeks might represent a vital interpretative *detour*, permitting one to understand and express something about the 'modern' that would otherwise be impossible. At stake in this idea, and something posed very clearly in the Foreword here, is a whole philosophy of history. We will return to this notion in more detail later.

Thirdly, we encounter, here in the Foreword, a contrast between being caught up in everyday concerns, and a clearsighted contemplation of those concerns. In the summer of 1872 Nietzsche wrote:

> The philosopher is a self-revelation of nature's workshop – philosopher and artist tell nature's trade secrets. The sphere of the philosopher and the artist exists above the tumult of contemporary history, beyond need. The philosopher as the *brake shoe on the wheel of time*. Philosophers appear during those times of great danger – when the wheel keeps turning faster – they and art take the place of disappearing myth. But they are thrown far ahead of their time, because they only gain the attention of their contemporaries very slowly.[19]

This 'above' and 'beyond', though, is not simple indifference, nor a kind of purity with respect to the 'tumult' (see the very end of **Section 15**). On the contrary, the trade secrets that are revealed are in fact the inner meaning or structure of this 'tumult'. It is merely that the functions of the philosopher or artist do not exhaust themselves in the present. The clear-sighted contemplation is thus a means by which the philosopher or artist engages with the serious problems of his or her day. Accordingly, Nietzsche can argue that we must not see patriotism and 'aesthetic self-indulgence', or seriousness and play, as opposites. In each case, the latter is an indirect but ultimately more successful mode of the former. Similarly, the historical study of ancient Greek tragedy turns out to be the best way of understanding contemporary cultural needs.

Finally and fourthly, Nietzsche directs attention here to the central concern of this book, 'the conviction that art is the highest task and true metaphysical activity of this life'. Such a conviction explains why culture in the narrower, higher sense realizes itself most fully in the arts. This conviction here points forward to one of the key statements of *The Birth of Tragedy* in **Section 5**, repeated in modulated form in **Section 24**, that 'only as an aesthetic phenomenon is existence and the world eternally justified'. Thus, by moving art from its marginal position as 'an amusing sideshow' into the centre-ground of anti-French contemporary debate on culture, Nietzsche hopes to contribute more substantially towards national renewal than joining in with the nationalist chorus of belligerent propaganda of the time.

These four notions are important for understanding Nietzsche's purposes and methods in this book.

SECTION 1

The Apolline and Dionysiac as Art-Drives and 'Living Concepts'; Envisaging a New Science of Aesthetics.
Note: Nietzsche and Darwin

This starting section lays out some key general ideas, which appear to be anthropological or psychological in character. These ideas form the foundation of Nietzsche's historical analysis, which commences in **Section 2**. In particular, **paragraph 1** introduces the central notions of the Apolline and the Dionysiac.

Also, with the **first sentence** Nietzsche's stylistic ambition is fully revealed, this being one of the most extraordinarily rich sentences that Nietzsche ever wrote. It becomes clear right from the start that Nietzsche invests much effort into 'composing' his language of ideas. How this works exactly will become clearer as we move through the text. Suffice it to say here that it is possible to detect an analogy in Nietzsche's style, and in the way his argument is structured, to certain compositional techniques of Wagner, who is not only his modern idol, but also, as we will see, his artistic role model.

Superficially, Nietzsche claims that the Apolline and Dionysiac are essential for understanding art. Immediately, we should be asking questions, such as: What kinds of things are these – a few lines later Nietzsche calls them 'drives' (*Triebe*), but what exactly does that mean? This will become clear gradually, but for the moment we will not go far astray if we think of the Apolline and Dionysiac as claims about the fundamental nature of human beings. These claims are offered up as explanations of the activities and forms of human life. Human beings, like any other animal, are driven towards activity by a set of drives or instincts. Insofar as these result in artistic activity or cultural productions, there are these two drives, which Nietzsche calls Apolline and Dionysiac.[20] There will be many opportunities to introduce refinements to this initial conception. In any case, it turns out that the implications of the pairing of these two 'drives', named after mythological gods[21], extend far beyond the remit of art, or rather, the significance of art is widened to such an extent that it encompasses the whole of human life. The two art drives can therefore also be regarded as the two most fundamental *life drives*.

There are no less than five additional subtleties in the first sentence we need to bring out.

1. Aesthetics as 'Science'
Nietzsche does not just write of 'aesthetics' (since the eighteenth century, the name for the branch of philosophy dealing with art or with, for example, natural beauty); he writes of the 'science' of aesthetics. To be sure, the word 'Wissenschaft' in German has a broader meaning than in English, where its primary meaning is 'hard' or 'laboratory' science. Nevertheless, even in granting

this broader meaning, there is a *frisson* in pairing aesthetics and science. In part, then, this combination reiterates the point made in the Foreword that we should not see seriousness (in this case, scientific enquiry) and play (anything concerning art) as opposites. It also emphasizes a point that might otherwise have escaped notice. The Apolline and Dionysiac drives have received their names, certainly, from Greek mythology. That is to say, they appear to be historically specific. However, whatever these drives turn out to be, they are not confined to ancient Greece. Rather, as befits the scientific approach, Nietzsche claims an extended 'generality' for these drives, as principles of a fundamental (or philosophical) anthropology. This generality of the Apolline and Dionysiac as basic human drives allows Nietzsche to employ them in such a way as to be able to analyse ancient Greek art, *and also* to use them later to diagnose the cultural world of modernity and of contemporary German and European culture.

Another aspect of linking aesthetics with science is Nietzsche's groundbreaking assumption, on which the whole enterprise of *The Birth of Tragedy* rests, of the concrete, documentary evidence of the presence of the two anthropological drives in the material products of cultural history. We can actually see these forces in action both in the backdrop of history gone by and in the latest cultural and artistic products. Even the most spiritual of cultural forms – tragic drama, for example – are a manifestation of the basic anthropological forces. As basic human instincts, the two drives interact, and their specific interaction at any one moment in history allows us to distinguish distinct cultural forms and periods. Thus, for example, the Dionysiac is active in the realm of music and particularly associated with harmony and melody, whilst the Apollonian has its main domain in sculpture, architecture, tragedy and theatrical stagecraft. In terms of cultural periodization, for example, Nietzsche clearly sees the Apolline as active in the age of Homer and again (though in a highly modified way) in Roman and Baroque art and culture. In contrast, he regards pre-Socratic Greece and (again, in a modified fashion) medieval music and drama (see **Sections 16** and **19**) as under the spell of the Dionysiac.

However, there is a complication to this apparent positivism. To look out for these art-drives in texts (as we would say today) is what Nietzsche claims should be the new task of the age-old 'wissenschaftliche' discipline of philology. Philology is an academic discipline that combines linguistics (the study of language) with the study of literature, particularly as these have a comparative or historical dimension. Nietzsche at this time was a young professor of philology at the University of Basel. His way here of combining philology with aesthetics on the one hand, and with something like anthropology or psychology on the other, was already controversial. Still more groundbreaking is Nietzsche's claim that *criticism*, and indeed philology generally, are also themselves such a manifestation of drives: all cultural productions provide clear evidence for the action of the basic art-drives, but only for those not rendered incapable of seeing by still *other* intervening drives (see **Section 5**). Not surprisingly, such claims raised the ire of Nietzsche's philologist colleagues, who accused him of going off on unscholarly tangents (see **Chapter 4, Reception and Influence**). Nietzsche will return to the subject of the nature of science later in the book, on lines akin to our comments on criticism above. As we will see, aesthetics as Nietzsche envisages it here, with an existentially widened portfolio intersecting with metaphysics and cultural history, is conceived of as an alternative project to the single-minded pursuit of modern 'positive' science, and indeed perhaps even breathing new life into science, as the first sentence suggests.

2. Intuition ('Anschauung')
Our second observation concerning this first sentence is that conceptual insight is contrasted with direct apprehension or, better, 'intuition' [*Anschauung*]. 'Anschauung' is the term used by German philosophy since Kant to designate an immediate sensible relation with things, as opposed to one mediated through concepts. The significance of this distinction for Nietzsche is emphasized by the fact that, in the next sentence, he employs it again ('penetratingly vivid figures of their gods'). We have already discussed the notion that the effects of the drives are present to intuition in cultural objects, that even the highest forms of art are produced to satisfy basic instincts, and that criticism and philology (with their concept-driven analytical techniques) are often blinded to this direct evidence by other dominant drives. All this points to an underlying critique of the value of abstraction and

abstract thought, although this will not become explicit until much later (**Section 12**). Nietzsche is also pursuing a revaluation of the mind-body distinction: mind is spiritualized body, and thus the same drive can manifest itself in physiological, psychological or even conceptual effects. Thus we can also speak of the drives as 'principles' or 'concepts' in a conventional philosophical sense only derivatively, or perhaps metaphorically.

Nietzsche will have been conscious that writing about the history of culture, and about the dynamic mechanisms of the development of culture in terms of two antagonizing principles, will have reminded many of his readers of Hegel. Nietzsche refuses to tackle Hegel head-on in this text, but *The Birth of Tragedy* represents a deliberate break with abstract forms of conceptualization of German Idealism (that set of works that emerged around 1800, after and under the influence of Kant) – above all Hegel. Kant, and particularly Schiller, as we will see, are still treated with a high degree of reverence here, but otherwise Nietzsche evidently feels German thought went astray till Schopenhauer. The Apolline and Dionysiac are in conflict with one another, but they are not *opposites* or *negations* in the Hegelian sense of thesis and antithesis. Their occasional, cyclically recurring conciliations are, like historical occurrences in Hegel, real historical events, but they do not amount to logical *syntheses* that yield a new drive or principle. True, the emergence of Socratism, dealt with from **Section 13** onwards, represents such a new drive or principle bursting onto the scene of cultural history. But this new event is not the result of a synthesizing logical operation in the Hegelian sense, because, as we will see, in Socrates the Dionysian and the Apolline are not preserved according to Hegel's dialectical notion of *aufheben*. On the contrary, in Socratism the Apolline and Dionysiac are misunderstood, repressed, and only permitted as activities in truncated form. The emergence of the 'Socratic tendency' therefore represents the opposite to what Hegel conceives of as world spirit progressing to a higher conception of itself. (We will return to Nietzsche's relation to Hegel in the context of **Section 4**.)

3. Evolution ('Fortentwicklung')
This term could indicate just a general notion of change or development over time. The word held valuable currency in

German thought since the late eighteenth century, and it featured prominently as a key building block for historical theory of whole schools of literary and cultural criticism from *Sturm und Drang* to the German Historical School. It is from within this tradition that Nietzsche is using the term (**see below, this section, for our comment on** 'Triebe', from p. 35). However, the biological analogy of reproduction that follows suggests that Nietzsche is referring to more recent evolutionary theory, perhaps to Darwinism. This is interesting, because Nietzsche's relation to contemporary biology will add an extra dimension to his thought – we have suggested that Nietzsche appears to be speaking anthropologically and psychologically, perhaps we should also be thinking of drives in a still more basic biological sense. Moreover, and this is an idea we introduced above, we are by no means used to speaking of 'culture' and 'biology' in the same breath. We *tend* to think of culture as a dimension of deliberate, spiritual human activity and thought, above of and separate from biological processes. It is clear from this first sentence that Nietzsche will attack this tendency as a profound misunderstanding.

Note: Nietzsche and Darwin
The Birth of Tragedy is conceived in the wake of debates around Darwin's theory of evolution. It profiles the struggle for realization between forces located on the intersection between biology and culture. Thus, it makes a contribution to solving a problem left behind by Darwin's original theory outlined in 1859 with *The Origin of Species*, namely whether the laws of biological development are applicable also in the sphere of human history and culture. The existence of consciousness in the human species and the social and culture-building faculties of human beings necessitate a special investigation of this sphere which is both analogous to nature in the wider sense and also to an extent independent from it. Darwin himself addressed the problem of cultural evolution in 1871 in *The Descent of Man, and Selection in Relation to Sex*, which discusses – amongst a number of related issues – the applicability of evolution in the social realm. This leads to a whole new European movement of social theory in the 1880s and 1890s: 'Social Darwinism'.[22] Reading *The Birth of Tragedy* allows no other conclusion than to regard it as a contribution to the contemporary debate in this field. The more

unsavoury offshoot of these concerns is the prominence given later to race and eugenics as issues of 'serious' theoretical consideration.[23] It is not clear whether Nietzsche read Darwin's work (the first German translation appeared in 1860). The problem thus is similar as with Hegel or Fichte, for example, whose ideas are evident only as subcutaneous influences, though in Darwin's case we at least know that Nietzsche's source of transmission was Friedrich Albert Lange's *Geschichte des Materialismus und Kritik seiner Bedeutung in der Gegenwart* ('History of Materialism and Critique of its Significance for the Present'), published in 1866, where also the attempt is already being made to transpose Darwin's biological notion of struggle into the social realm. Nietzsche had a copy of the book in his library.

There is also present in the background here a peculiar German variety of evolutionary thinking which precedes Anglo-Saxon attempts by more than half a century. A German strand of evolutionary theory originates in the 1770s as part of the *Sturm und Drang* movement mentioned above (see **Chapter 1, Origins and Directions**). This German strand of *Entwicklungsdenken* encompassed aspects of art criticism, human and cultural anthropology as well as earth science and the physiological study of geographical environments, single-handedly breaking new ground in all these areas.[24] It is within this context that Nietzsche uses the notions of development and drive.[25] We will discuss these connections further shortly.

* * *

4. Duality ('Duplicität')
'Duality' suggests that the occurrence of both drives together in Greece was not a mere accident. The two drives are not separable, but originally tied together and belong to one another. This original tie becomes clear shortly; nevertheless, many readers have missed it and misinterpreted the nature of the Apolline especially. It is important, and Nietzsche makes this very clear right from the beginning here, that the drives cannot be reckoned with other than as a pair, even if they deny one another. A historically specific culture (and its dominant underlying drive) always needs to be struggling against what it conceives of as opposed to it. Thus the opposing drives are interdependent. Moreover, they complete

each other, bringing both to their highest realization (in tragedy). The Apolline and the Dionysiac are two halves that complete the whole, which needs to be thought of as no longer perfectly classically rounded, but more like an elongated, imperfect circle, like an ellipse, with two foci. Because of this 'bifocality', we can call *The Birth of Tragedy* an 'anti-classicist' book (see **Section 3, Note: Nietzsche, German 'Hellenism' and Hölderlin**). Or, again, the relationality of the drives is analogous to musical counterpoint: as we will see, Nietzsche actively encourages analogies with musical composition.

On Nietzsche's account, the drives are active both outside and inside of us, as individuals. Their relationship is part of the determination of our psychological make-up, our beliefs and values, and our well-being. However, Nietzsche also speaks of them as impersonal, as if they belonged to groups of human beings, perhaps the whole species (indeed, this is precisely what he does claim, as we will shortly see). Finally, these art-drives are materially manifest *outside of ourselves*, namely in the succession of products in human cultural history. This book is essentially devoted to the notion of historical development arising from the struggle of drives or instincts to realize themselves, an issue far removed from the historical projections of progress or a unifying teleology more typical of the Enlightenment or German idealist tradition. However, there is a vision of reconciliation of opposites also on Nietzsche's horizon. As we already know, in this first book he seeks support for the formulation of this vision in Wagner's new music drama. But reconciliation for Nietzsche does not mean synthesis or unification of opposites. Quite the opposite: for Nietzsche it means the acceptance of opposition as constitutive of the highest cultural achievements, and of the nature of the human. '[I]magine dissonance assuming human form – and what else is man?' he writes at the end of the book (**Section 25**). This is Nietzsche's revolutionary idea; this is what (at this stage of his career) he thinks Wagner teaches, and is later on developed as the notions of 'will to power' and the 'overman': the formation of a new mode of humanity through the recognition and positive celebration of difference and conflict. The central message of *The Birth of Tragedy* is that the denial of opposites entails the downfall of the human race. Nietzsche's primary example of this is the history of what he calls 'Socratism', right up to the present. This, as we will see, is a history of triumphs in a narrow sphere, surrounded by cultural failures and impending intellectual and moral crises. The first half of the book investigates the historical moment in ancient Greece where this recognition first bore fruit, albeit briefly, and where subsequently the history of European culture took a dramatically wrong turning. The rationale of this historical turn is to discover possibilities for a cultural renewal of the present.[26]

5. The Sexes and Reproduction
Implied in the analogy with sexual reproduction is the possible gendering of the two drives. We are tempted to speculate which of them represents the female and which the male principle in the reproductive act. There are playful references to sex, to the sexes, and to the 'battle' of the sexes, throughout this book. Later in his career, for example in *Thus Spoke Zarathustra*, Nietzsche thematizes these much more clearly, developing an elaborate symbolic vocabulary of sex and gender. There are numerous passages in Nietzsche's work where gender roles are allocated to make a philosophical point; that is not in doubt. It is equally clear that this domain is a fertile one for Nietzsche's peculiarly warped sense of humour.[27] The question is whether the roles are allocated in meaningful ways and what philosophical enquiry gains thereby. Many critics have detected unpalatable clichés of male domination and found this area of Nietzsche's metaphorical style contaminated with the clichés of late-nineteenth-century German sexual politics.[28] Others hold that the symbolic system he constructs is both more subtle, and less value-laden, than it first appears. In this passage, perhaps we can detect an undertone of 'tongue-in-cheek', or at least a stylized post-romantic disillusion (a lá August Strindberg) in the matter-of-fact way Nietzsche characterizes the relationship of the sexes here as mostly stormy with occasional periods of communicative, that is, reproductive relief. In any case, the main purpose of linking the relationship of the two drives with the relationship of biological partners is to demonstrate the essential nature of their dependency upon each other. Thus, this analogy reinforces the third and fourth observations above (the link to the theory of evolution and the original tie between the two drives).[29]

Obviously, we cannot spend this long on the ins and outs of every sentence in Nietzsche's book – although plenty will merit it. The above unfolding of a single sentence is merely an illustration of a general principle: despite the energetic and free style, Nietzsche is an extraordinarily careful writer who makes every phrase do double or triple duty. The first sentence thus already leaves the impression of an intense stylistic ambition. This writing deliberately scintillates as if it were through-composed.[30]

Apolline and Dionysiac are names for what Nietzsche calls 'drives' [*Triebe*; occasionally also translated as 'instincts']. The term is applied much in nineteenth-century biology, where it refers to overall, and generally strong, impulses within an organism to act in this or that way with respect to basic biological functions. In the human 'animal', a drive is to be located at a lower or more fundamental level than conscious decisions. In English, we are used to hearing about the 'reproductive drive' or a 'survival drive'. As we noted above, in Nietzsche's conceptualization of drives English and German scientific theories of evolution are implied. As Nicholas Martin[31] has demonstrated, the concept of drives in Nietzsche is also an application of the key principles of Schiller's anthropological aesthetics as outlined in the *Aesthetic Letters*. Schiller, in turn, builds on the pioneering forays into cultural anthropology of Johann Gottfried Herder (as laid down, for example, in the experimental essay *This Too a Philosophy of History for the Formation of Humanity*, 1774). All of Herder's early work emphasizes the predominance of archaizing instinctive drives over conscious rationality in the process of artistic creation. This theorem is one of the central items on the original manifesto of the new German art movement of *Sturm und Drang*, from which springs forth modern German literature after 1800. It is present as a key inspiration not only in the backdrop of Weimar Classicism – Goethe's and Schiller's ideas are built around it – but can also be detected as a central influence on international Romanticism, particularly the English variety. Coleridge and Shelley are familiar with it; it is the launching platform for Byronism.

Under the influence of Herder and Schiller, Nietzsche first posits that these are drives towards the production of types of art. He calls them 'Kunsttriebe'. (Schiller used the term 'Spieltrieb'.[32]) In the light of this, art is to be understood as a basic biological function. This is the essence of Schiller's reflections on art, which anchor the dimension of production and enjoyment of artistic beauty in the foundations of human anthropology: man as *homo ludens* (playful [in the sense of games, and also theatre] human) and *homo aestheticus* (artistic human). Human beings are naturally predisposed to express what is essentially human via art. We are reminded of our observation above, that Nietzsche will argue for dispensing with our tendency to think of culture and biology as quite distinct spheres; we are also reminded of the **Foreword** where Nietzsche wrote that art is the 'highest task' of this *life*. Secondly, and still more surprisingly, nothing here suggests that 'drives' have to be located in individual organisms. In fact, at the beginning of Section 2 Nietzsche summarizes this argument by stating that 'as artistic powers' the drives 'erupt from nature itself, *without the mediation of any human artist*'. This does not mean, however, that they do not also manifest themselves individually. And, to be sure, Nietzsche will also talk about individual artists: Homer, Aeschylus, Wagner and so forth. But the extent of activity of the 'drives' goes far beyond the reach of individual, or even collective, organisms. It is truly universal and in the end encompasses whole populations, physiological types, cultures with oral and written traditions, periods in history, politics, art, philosophy, and perhaps also climate, diet, geography, and so forth. The total life of ancient Greece is understood as if it were a single organism, albeit with a complex layering of interacting forces.[33] This composite 'organism' expresses its inner drives most clearly in the work of exposed personalities, *representatives* of a particular mix of forces at work in their time. Some of them, such as Homer, Aeschylus and Sophocles, are portrayed like geniuses in an eighteenth-century sense, meaning individual vessels inspired by intrapersonal creative forces that work through them; others (as we shall see from **Section 12 onwards**), like Euripides, Socrates and Plato, are negatively drawn; they strike Nietzsche as admirable for their energy, single-mindedness and accomplishments, but ultimately dishonest and in some sense 'diseased'. However, moral character judgements are not central to Nietzsche's argument, which has moved away from eighteenth- century positions of *Genieaesthetik*. Nietzsche's thinking is already on its way towards a position beyond binary moral imperatives. What is important to Nietzsche is the impact of the activities of different forces upon the developmental dynamics of cultural history. The different personalities of his historical gallery of types (including

Apollo and Dionysus) are simply the bearers of these activities. Culture understands and defines itself through the work of these representatives, who stand as nametags for cultural and artistic 'tendencies'. Recall the quotation given above: 'The philosopher [and the artist] is a self-revelation of nature's workshop'[34] – the 'self' that reveals and is revealed there is *nature*, not the philosopher or the artist. The same point is made at the **beginning of Section 2**.

The remainder of this section supports a main contention introduced in **paragraph 1**, that the art-drives originate at the level of the body. The opposition between the Apolline and the Dionysiac corresponds with the two 'physiological phenomena' of dream and intoxication which we are also asked to think of as two separate 'art-worlds'. When we are dreaming, Nietzsche holds, 'every human being is fully an artist'. Dreams are one, and the most immediate and universal, manifestation of the Apolline, but also the most important way of characterizing the essence of the Apolline. This Apolline dream world of art covers, as we will see in more detail later, strongly formal arts such as sculpture or architecture – clear images and strong lines or surfaces predominate. Apolline music is highly metrical and rhythmic; Apolline poetry is of the epic variety (Homer). This 'lovely semblance' is of no less a reality – and indeed of greater value (see **Section 4**) – than that 'in which we live and have our being'. Thus, although Nietzsche's focus here is on the drives as art-drives, he is not forgetting their wider human significance. So, for example, in **Section 21**, Apollo is the 'state founding' god (clarity and order in the organization of individuals, spaces and institutions), and most at home with other political instincts. The Apolline addresses itself not just to dreams and fictions, but also to real things around us *insofar as they can be made like dreams*.

However, there is another reason Nietzsche compares the 'lovely semblance' with everyday reality. Following Schopenhauer he asks: what if the reality in which we live is in itself the dream semblance of a 'second, quite different reality' that lies beneath the reality we experience? 'A person with artistic sensibility relates to the reality of dream in the same way as a philosopher relates to the reality of existence.' Thus, in their different metiers they both belong to the world of Apolline image-making, an important insight into Nietzsche's self-evaluation as philosopher. The artist like the philosopher is constitutionally required to sense, beneath everyday reality, what truly is. Nietzsche thus importantly claims that a dream *qua* dream entails an awareness of itself as appearance with respect to something else. With this notion of a constant awareness of appearance *qua* appearance, Nietzsche's initial account of the Apolline is complete, and his account of the Dionysiac commences.

The Dionysiac intoxicated world of art includes above all music, dance and some types at least of poetry (the dithyrambic or lyrical; the poet Archilochus is discussed in **Section 5**). Here, the aim is a blurring of images, loss of clear line (which in musical terms means an emphasis on melody and above all harmony), and an ecstatic loss of self-identity and conscious control. Nietzsche is speaking of impulses towards types of cultural production, but equally importantly, he is claiming that each of these drives has a metaphysical meaning, an inherent commitment to a certain way of understanding reality. What are the metaphysical commitments of these drives? The first hint comes in Nietzsche reporting a certain self-consciousness of dreaming. In dreaming, he says, I often know I am dreaming, that it is only a 'semblance'. What makes Apolline art beautiful, and gives us pleasure, is not just its formal qualities as such (e.g. aesthetic qualities such as balance or proportion), but rather also the constant sense that this form is only an illusion. The dream must not lose this sense of semblance and become 'pathological': thus the art of Apollo must be 'measured', free from wilder impulses, and calm. We will return below in more detail to the metaphysical notions that the Apolline and Dionysiac express in practice.

Nietzsche mentions Dante's great fourteenth-century poem *The Divine Comedy* in support of a Schopenhauerian philosophical reading of reality. This great work of literature at the threshold of modern culture figures as one of Nietzsche's artistic role models. Nietzsche is like Dante the traveller. Dante is lead by Virgil into the theatre of pain for some of the way and learns to explain the meaning of the images they are passing. For Nietzsche, the poem takes on Virgil's role; it is a guide for the philosopher as a reader of the image parade of life. It is also relevant as an aid of reinforcing Nietzsche's rewriting of Platonism: 'the reality in which we live and have our being' is not one of 'some mere shadow play' (a reference to the allegory of the cave in the *Republic*) from which one should stay aloof. For Nietzsche it is this dreamlike life-reality to which the philosopher also physically belongs. He is himself implicated in its 'scenes' (Nietzsche deliberately uses the language of the theatre here, in line with Dante's *Commedia* project). Like Dante, the philosopher involves himself in the scenes on his journey to *Paradiso* through *Inferno* and *Purgatorio*, 'and shares in the suffering'.[35] On the level of the building of allegories Nietzsche's gallery of historical representatives follows the same rules according to which Dante operates in the *Commedia*: Socrates, Zarathustra and Virgil are all both real as historical 'personalities', and more than real as living representatives of drives and of patterns of their manifestation.[36]

In **paragraph 3**, he meditates upon the meaning of the name 'Apollo'. Nietzsche plays on a pun here that works in German but gets lost in translation. The etymological root of the word Apollo in the German *Scheinen* implies 'the luminous one' (*der Scheinende*)[37] – thus the sun god is associated with light, clarity and sharp definition of lines and surfaces. However, another meaning of *Schein* or *Erscheinung* is 'appearance' or 'phenomenon', in the straightforward sense of 'that which appears before us'. Schiller uses the phrase 'schöner Schein' for art (meaning: 'beautiful appearance of being'); Schiller thinks of art as a translucent veil through which the image of being shines or appears. Who uses 'Schein', always implies as its counterpart 'Sein' (being): the two are fused together analogously to how Nietzsche thinks the Apollonian belongs together with the Dionysian. Who mentions Apollo also always implies Dionysus. But there is a third layer of meaning also implied in the word and significant for an understanding of the intentions of *The Birth of Tragedy*: apart from 'luminosity' and 'appearance', 'Schein' can also mean 'semblance', 'illusion' or 'deception'. Marx speaks of ideology as 'falscher Schein' (wrong appearance of being).[38]

These three meanings are employed throughout the text. Nietzsche enters the philosophical debate of 'Sein and Schein', 'being and appearance', which occupies a prominent position in modern German philosophy, particularly in German Idealism, including Kant.[39] In the positive sense of appearance, Schein *is* *being* insofar as it comes to appear or 'shines forth'; thus, appearance is the real, in an ordinary sense. It is not so much opposed to being, as correlated to it, as the manner in which that which is manifests itself. However, in the third and negative sense, Schein is mere illusion or deception, as opposed to true being or the truth about being; this is the Platonic view against which Nietzsche struggles. Nietzsche's metaphysics tries to navigate between these, keeping both the positive and negative senses of Schein.[40] In any case, appearance must know that it is appearance, unless it 'is . . . to become pathological'. This is Nietzsche's version of 'wrong consciousness', of ideology, where appearance is taken to be being itself, without depth, without further meaning. In this third meaning, as wrong, pathological semblance, *The Birth of Tragedy* introduces the 'Socration tendency' (cf. **Section 13 onwards**). As we will see, Nietzsche makes frequent use of the deceptive qualities of pathological appearance (the Freudian concept of 'neurosis' is under construction here). The term 'pathological' carries special significance for this book. Nietzsche uses it to mean, most broadly, a disease with respect to the art-drives, and particularly one that results in some form of metaphysical blindness. More specifically, however, it is a disease of the passions or affects (thus the 'pathos' in the term), which locates them in the wrong place – in the individual as such as opposed to the characteristic displacement and calmness of the Apolline or the de-individuated ecstasy of the Dionysiac (this is made clear in **Section 12**).

The most important aspect of the 'appearance' side of the Apolline lies in its link with 'individuation'. In some manner that which is appears as that which is, individuated in itself and separated from other appearances of being. Nietzsche identifies the metaphysical commitment of Apolline art with the *principium individuationis* discussed by Schopenhauer. This principle states that individual entities are the basic form of existence, prior to combinations or relationships among entities. Entity 'A' can be isolated and exists independently from 'B', and can be understood separately from B. A and B are things *first*, and may enter into a relationship (e.g. of causation) *second*. Thus, both separately and together, everything is ordered and intelligible. The relationship of causation (one of the 'modes' of the principle of sufficient reason), for example, can be studied as science under controlled conditions, where 'controlled conditions' means precisely the individuation of entities and their various physical values. General laws are formulated that govern the necessity of events so that no event is without a reason. Likewise, respect for individual limit and measure, both in oneself and in others, is the basic ethical law. The emphasis on separation corresponds with the emphasis on clear images and forms, strong lines and surfaces, and bright light in Apolline art. In the analogy from Schopenhauer that Nietzsche quotes, A is the man, the little boat his 'separateness', B is the surrounding ocean. The man can feel safe only insofar as he believes in his original and inviolable separation from the ocean. The 'veil of Maya' refers to Schopenhauer's assertion that this principle is an illusion, but the fact *that* it is an illusion is veiled from us. However, Apolline art – and the metaphysical meaning of the drive towards this art – is not simply an art of illusion, behind this veil. Rather, Nietzsche repeatedly insists, it is aware of this fact (the dreamer who knows she is dreaming), and the order, intelligibility and beauty of the illusion justifies it (the dreamer wants to continue dreaming). Thus, properly understood, the metaphysical commitment of the Apolline is not merely about the *nature* of reality but also about its *value*: reality as appearance is justified only through the beauty of illusion (the point is made most clearly at the **end of Section 5**).[41]

We must not miss that discussing art in terms of image and illusion will call to mind Plato.[42] Plato argues that all art is based upon illusion, for art generates images of things which, with respect to the true reality of the ideas, are already mere images. These illusory images are dangerous, insofar as they tempt us further away from truth rather than bringing us closer to it. Nietzsche will argue for a different metaphysical truth to Plato, to be sure, but agrees at least with the narrow point, which is that there is something wrong in taking the image as if it were fundamental or true being. Thus, he is subtly rewriting Plato's evaluation. Nietzsche asks, 'what is the value or purpose of this temptation?' Plato could see no value to it since appearance is not where man truly dwells, and later in the book when Nietzsche writes about Socrates (Plato's teacher) he will make much of this difference in how appearance is *valued*. More generally, Nietzsche here shows a career-long philosophical concern, not so much with the truth or otherwise of concepts, but with their function and value within historical cultures.

If the Apolline is related to the *principium individuationis* (although importantly *aware* of it as illusion), the Dionysiac dedicates itself to expressing or achieving the metaphysical counterpoint. This is outlined in **paragraph 4** of section 1. Nature is originally one (*das Ureine*), without real differentiation in time, space or concept. All 'things' are originally related in this oneness, and their differences or separations are secondary and illusory; all things are merely momentary concretions of this underlying, surging 'will'. Since the applicability of number is based upon space and time – a thing is said to be one if it is not found separately in different places or times – this original nature is not 'one' in that sense. The will is not an individual, even if we said there were only one individual. Rather, the will is 'one' in the sense of a continuous whole.[43] This conception of the underlying nature or will comes from Schopenhauer (although there is also an influence from philosophers as diverse as the Stoics and Neo-Platonists, Spinoza and Nietzsche's American contemporary Emerson). Dionysiac culture seeks to submerge the individual in this oneness. This is, from the point of view of the Apolline, a threat to individuation, and dangerous, because it implies the breakdown of the faculties of differentiation and evaluation, just as metaphorically in intoxication one loses identity and control, or in 'ecstasy' one is literally 'outside of oneself'. Reciprocally, the Apolline is dangerous as it involves the 'dismemberment' of being into individuals. Thus the Dionysiac renews the natural 'bond' among human beings, who no longer see themselves as separate individuals, constrained and isolated by artificial laws or customs; it is also associated with a celebration of nature (in the sense of plants and non-human animals) reconciled with the human world which, previously, had considered itself apart. A person in the Dionysiac state cannot be an artist producing dream images of the divine, because in the grip of this drive he is not an individual producing separate images as expressions of (and thus separate from) some metaphysical truth. Rather, he or she *is the expression, living that truth*, and thus is the work of art crafted by the *Ureine*. However, this pure Dionysiac state of artistic expression is not favoured as ideal in *The Birth of Tragedy*. As we will see (**Section 16**) 'absolute music' is the direct artistic expression of the 'Ureine', and its importance is decidedly second to the 'mixed' mode of tragedy and Wagernian musical drama. The main idea of Nietzsche's book is to propose, as the highest state of human existence and likewise the highest product of human culture, a heightened state achieved by the constant interplay between the two drives. Although Nietzsche is taking the metaphysics of the will or *Ureine* from Schopenhauer, he is committed to showing that the pessimism which, for Schopenhauer, follows from this is mistaken. Schopenhauer argues that what Nietzsche calls the Dionysiac insight is a world of constant suffering and valuelessness for the individual; it will only exist if it is never satisfied but constantly pained by the absence of satisfaction. The condition of suffering is relieved only insofar as we can *quiet* the will. (Schopenhauer talks about it as a 'salvation from the world'.[44]) Nietzsche responds in two ways. First, that the Apolline world of beauty is not *merely* an illusion but a 'theodicy' (it justifies existence), and not merely a quieting (in the sense of annulling or cancelling) of the will, but an existence that although 'calm' or 'serene' is overflowing with joy and life. Secondly, entering the Dionysiac state indeed involves the destruction of the individual, but more than compensates with the ecstatic joy of a reunion with nature. Moreover, counterpointed to the suffering of constant absence of satisfaction is the joy of the constant creation of forms. The modification of Schopenhauer's metaphysics is one of the key philosophical projects in this book.[45]

Section 1 ends with the odd combination of pagan allusions from all ages, Judeo-Christian language (covenant, gospel), and references to Schiller and Beethoven. (Note for further reference that Beethoven's *Ninth Symphony* gets a special mention, because this is not a 'pure' symphony. It is rather a mixed, hybrid form of music drama: unusual for a symphony, it contains a setting in its fourth movement of Schiller's ode *To Joy*.) This mishmash of references is deliberate, of course, as Nietzsche is telling us that the Dionysiac drive is universal, to be found underlying all discrete cultures and celebrated in a barely disguised fashion in art. The enthusiasm of Nietzsche's writing on the Dionysiac is infectious; and it is well known that while the figure of Dionysus figures prominently in his later work, the figure of Apollo seems to disappear. It is thus tempting (but mistaken) to read *The Birth of Tragedy* as if these two drives within human culture were not equally potent and important. Nietzsche discusses the productivity and meaning of the two drives separately, but the central thesis of the first third of his book is never far away: these drives are deeply linked, and it is the 'reconciliation' or cooperation of them that is responsible for the highest achievement of Greek (or any) culture, namely tragedy.

SECTION 2

The Drives at Work in Pre-Socratic Greece; Three Types of Symbolization; Psychogenesis of the Dionysian in Asia and in Greek Culture

Section 2 launches *The Birth of Tragedy's* historical dimension. As we have indicated in connection with Hegel, the book has an underlying agenda critical of recent modern German philosophy. We have attempted to describe provisionally the difference between concepts in the tradition of idealist metaphysics, and Nietzsche's attempt to redefine this approach by envisaging 'drives' that could be called 'living concepts' because they are rooted in the body, and manifest themselves variously in historical cultures. As we will see in greater detail shortly (**Section 5**), Nietzsche too is seeking to justify the world metaphysically. Superficially, the two god-concepts map onto the Kantian distinction between appearances (representation in Schopenhauer) and the thing-in-itself (will in Schopenhauer). However, his approach to metaphysics is a paradoxical or at least ironical one. Perhaps we could call him a 'metaphysical empiricist', because following Herder and other thinkers (critical of Kant and idealist metaphysics) in the line of German development theory, the crucial question Nietzsche seeks to answer in his work, from *The Birth of Tragedy* onwards, is this: how can metaphysical principles be demonstrated as physically manifest in the phenomena of the empirical world? Nietzsche's answer here is that only in art does genuine metaphysics become manifest. He sees the developments in culture, which he thinks of as largely determined through developments in the arts, as indicators of metaphysical tendencies. In a radical extension of the traditional domain of philology, *The Birth of Tragedy* is to illustrate that and how it is possible to read metaphysics as text. Or, phrased differently, what concrete shape and form do the Apolline and Dionysian (either separately or together, or alongside other non-artistic drives) assume when they are in action in cultural history? The remainder of the book is devoted to investigating this question. Up to **Section 12** the book is a case study of

Greek tragedy, in its formal aspects as a composite literary form made up of music, myth and drama, its historical development as a specific cultural phenomenon, and finally, as indicator of the metaphysical meaning of the state of civilization within the pre-Socratic period.

The section begins by making clear the point that Nietzsche is not speaking about the deliberate or conscious decisions of individuals or artists, but about general drives. He calls them 'artistic states of nature' which 'erupt from nature itself'. Although the Apollonian fulfils itself in the artist and generally generates individuation as it impacts upon culture, it is not itself born from an individual source. The same holds with regard to the Dionysian which, as the drive generating 'intoxicated reality', is not just equally independent in its origins – it has 'just as little regard for the individual' as the Apollonian – but, what is more, it is outright opposed to the individual: it even seeks 'to annihilate, redeem and release him by imparting a mystical sense of oneness'. Human beings merely 'imitate', as conscious, individual artists (Nietzsche would love to be able to include philosophers), the 'immediate' realizations of the drives. (The notion of 'imitation' is meant to call to mind both Plato of the *Republic*, and Aristotle's *Poetics*.) The artistic states of nature act like *Urbilder* (original images) upon which the artist draws. Thus, Nietzsche arrives at a typology of the artist and of artistic production, according to which artistic state of nature is its primary inspiration. In the expression *imitatio naturae*, the nature in question is not (as it is for Aristotle) the essential features of natural forms or human types. Rather, nature here is the first and most immediate realization (dreams or intoxication) of the various drives that make up the single and constantly developing system of the *Ureine*.

But there is also a third type of artist who commands Nietzsche's special attention in this book. This is the *tragic artist* in whom both drives come together. In him, two operations are intertwined; in fact they are sequenced: first he breaks down in 'Dionysiac drunkenness and mystical self-abandon' [. . .] 'at which point, under the Apolline influence of dream, his own condition, which is to say, his oneness with the innermost ground of the world, reveals itself to him *in a symbolic dream-image*'. This is Nietzsche's first, cryptic sketch of his 'solution' to the problem of the nature of tragedy. He will continue to develop the elements of this solution for several sections to come.

Nietzsche introduces here the notion of symbolization. This is one of the centrepieces of his theory of the relationship between the art-drives and cultural forms. It is part of his broader theory of representation, human perception and expressivity – or, more specifically, his theory of language – that unfortunately is left relatively undeveloped in *The Birth of Tragedy*. We have to turn to other texts from this period for further insight. In our commentary, we will try to sketch out this theory in the context of **Section 8 (Note: Philosophy of Language in Nietzsche)**. However, for the moment, by 'symbolization' Nietzsche means the transformation of the drives into something which, in its meaning, brings to the here and now, and in the concrete, the characteristic metaphysical principle of that drive. A symbol or metaphor functions insofar as it makes immediately present, here and now, that which is symbolized; this is the 'magic' or 'transformation' that Nietzsche writes about with respect to both the Apolline and the Dionysiac. By way of contrast, a mere representation and especially a concept is always separate from its origin. It may or may not be an accurate representation, but accuracy designates a quality of a copy of some other *original* thing. A metaphor or symbol could not be described as 'accurate', only as *effective* (or 'magical') in bringing into the here and now the meaning of the drive. Certainly, a symbol is also a mere representation when viewed *from outside* – that is, by someone without an aesthetic sensibility, for whom the magic falls flat (see the comments on criticism below, in **Sections 5 and 11**). Thus, Nietzsche will discuss how the tragic poet Euripides misinterprets tragedy in terms of psychology, rather than as art.

According to the three types of art and artist, there are three types of symbolization. **Paragraph 3** of this section deals with the Dionysian one; the next section with the Apollonian forms of the symbolic; the third type will not be fully developed until **Section 8**. The key quality of Apolline art is image (*Bild,* though Nietzsche, as we have seen, will also talk of the Apolline in terms of 'appearance', *Schein* or *Erscheinung*). Through the Apolline magic, image (which is otherwise mere representation) becomes symbol. This is contrasted with a set of symbolic forms associated with Dionysiac productions. At the heart of Dionysiac art lies a certain type of music which, in the combinations it enters into with other forms of art, is fundamentally different from 'the music of Apollo' which was 'Doric architectonics in sound'. In comparison to this transparent Apolline music, 'Dionysiac music in particular elicited terror and horror' from the listener. Dionysiac music disorientates and intoxicates. Nietzsche is particularly interested in dance as a Dionysiac form of symbolization, and in the 'Dionysiac dithyramb', a special hymnic form of musicalized poetic language.[46]

Nietzsche's real interest in *The Birth of Tragedy* lies in the third type of symbolization, as indicated by the long last sentence of **paragraph 1**. What is happening in tragedy is that the Apollonian symbolizes the Dionysian *ur*-experience. This is the nature of the cooperation of the two drives in tragedy, which is therefore unique as a metaphysical artistic genre.

This section continues with three brief discussions meant to flesh out the accounts of the Apolline and Dionysiac, now no longer as metaphysical generalities, but in historical operation in ancient Greece. The main emphasis of **this section** is to provide an illustration of the Dionysian in its geographical spread, its functions and its role in the interplay with the Apolline; the following **third section** is given over to a closer investigation of the roles of the Apolline. There first follows an avowedly speculative passage, covering **paragraph 2,** on the nature of Greek dreams. Again, dreams are the first, immediate realization of the Apolline drive. Nietzsche here argues that there is a difference between the ancient and the modern period in terms of the imagery, logic and structure of dreams. We can observe a close unity in pre-Socratic Greek culture between dream and art ('Homer as a dreaming Greek'), whereas in the modern world a rift springs open between the two spheres. 'A modern' could not really compare his dreaming to Shakespeare – modernity has had an effect even on the capacity to dream. Nietzsche's claim is that human anthropology is in itself subjected to historical processes of development. We know that ideas and beliefs change; but here, human nature itself at some level is understood as *historical*. Culture, in both the narrow and broad senses, has a retroactive effect upon the human. Thus, Nietzsche is interested here in what we could call a 'history of the human'.[47] This is not an isolated passage on what we call historical cultural anthropology. Nietzsche develops a similar idea more thoroughly in later work, most consistently in the *Genealogy of Morality*.

In the second discussion, by way of contrast to indigenous Greek dreaming, Nietzsche provides an account of ancient non-Greek Dionysiac festivals. These are in turn contrasted with Greek Dionysiac festivals. Although Nietzsche continues to assert that the Apolline and Dionysiac are general principles of cultural production, there is something special about Greece. The Apolline is highly refined in the Greek's 'incredibly definite and assured ability to see things in a plastic way' ('plastic' is applied to the creation or manipulation of forms). So prominent was the Apolline that the Greeks themselves 'appear' to have been protected from the Dionysiac, *as if* the latter came from the outside (from the East, borne perhaps by the invading Persian army), but was held at bay (see also the end of **Section 4**). The 'barbarian' Dionysiac is characterized by 'sexual indiscipline', a 'repulsive mixture of sensuality and cruelty' (note the pseudo-Darwinian reference to a regression to monkeys). Narrowly, here, 'barbarian' simply means non-Greek. However, throughout the book the term is used to indicate a culture in thrall of non-artistic drives. In short, barbarian means unaesthetic.

However, the Greek Dionysiac did in fact not mainly arrive from abroad and across the sea, but rather sprang from the 'deepest roots' of Greek culture itself. Thus, it is not so much that the Apolline protected the Greeks from the external 'barbaric' Dionysian, but it also hid 'their' own indigenous sense of the Dionysian 'from them like a veil'. The Greeks' own inherent sense of the Dionysian shared peaceably the cultural space with Apollo, and was of a different character from the barbarian type. The Greek Dionysiac, for the first time in the ancient world, 'achieves expression as art', resembling the barbarian counterpart only in its strange mixture of pleasure and pain. The pleasure of the Apolline is submerged into universal pain (the Schopenhauerian suffering of the will); more importantly here, the equally primordial joy of relentless creativity and of the reunion with nature is counterposed with the memory of the *Ureine's* 'dismemberment' into individuals behind the veil of Maya. Nietzsche calls this second aspect 'sentimental' (the reference is to Schiller's categories; we will discuss this fully in the context of **Section 3**). As we have

seen, the mixture of pleasure and pain is also one of the compo-
nents of Nietzsche's critique of Schopenhauer. Dance, and especially the music of Greek Dionysiac festivals, interests Nietzsche. Music, he claims, for the first time came into its own here, and a Dionysiac spirit of music permeated all other art forms. Its power, identified with rhythm, dynamics and above all harmony (as opposed to the merely rhythmic quality of Apolline music), is to 'shake us to our very foundations'. Under Dionysian influence 'a complete unchaining of all symbolic powers' occurs. Thus, dance includes the symbolism of the entire body, 'the full gesture', no longer limited to mouth, face and word. New literary forms inspired by this new Dionysian music spring up. Note out of interest here that Nietzsche calls his final collection of poems *Dionysus Dithyrambs*, and that he regards Richard Wagner as a 'dithyrambic dramatist'.[48] This combination of dance, music and literature is not a pure artistic form; it is a hybrid, and we will return to the significance of this later in our commentary (see for example **Section 18**). The comprehension of this new symbolic world, Nietzsche claims, is possible only for someone in that 'height of self-abandonment'. Thus the Dionysiac must have been incomprehensible and full of terror for the Apolline individual, who (and this is both the essential feature of the Apolline and also the true horror) even recognizes it as the occluded foundation of the calm and beautiful image world he has constructed.

SECTION 3

The Origins of 'Genealogy': Psychogenesis of the Apollonian in the Greek 'Character'. Note: Nietzsche, German 'Hellenism', and Hölderlin

This section is an account of the origin and meaning of the Apolline. It is particularly important, not only for Nietzsche's argument here in *The Birth of Tragedy*, but also because the pro-
cedure of 'dismantling' the Apolline 'edifice' is an example of a methodological strategy Nietzsche will employ for the rest of his career. This strategy is most often known as 'genealogy'. So, for example, more than a decade later Nietzsche performs a *Genealogy of Morality*. Speaking very generally, this strategy has five parts. It attempts to show (1) that some feature, concept or

value that appears to be fundamental, immediate, simple and
'naïve' (Nietzsche here again refers to Schiller in **paragraph 4**), is
(2) actually an illusion, aggregate of disparate elements or otherwise derivative, (3) which has been developed over time and with
a degree of inevitability by a specific human culture to (4) mask
(even from themselves), compensate for or protect themselves
from (5) something entirely different, especially with a different
conventional value. For Nietzsche as a cultural critic, this method
allows him to puncture the self-assurance and innocence of
widely held values. Nietzsche the historian is enabled to give an
account of the nature and significance of previously unnoticed
cultural undercurrents behind historical headlines. As a philosopher, Nietzsche uses this procedure to demonstrate the explanatory
power of his basic conceptions (e.g. here the concept of drive).
Moreover, he argues that such a genealogical account is not just
a philosophical tool but is itself an important philosophical
result: values, beliefs and even truths have their origin in, and
receive their apparent validity through, history and culture (in
the broadest sense). The brief genealogy of Apolline culture is
followed, starting in **Section 11**, by a much more elaborate and
far-reaching genealogy of 'Socratic culture' and of science.

This also helps us account for the difficulty Nietzsche has been
having with Schiller's categories. 'Naïve' poetry (or art more
generally) is the representation of immediate responses to nature;
'sentimental' poetry involves a meditation upon a prior (often
irrevocably lost) state. Nietzsche here calls the Apolline 'naïve'
because it is enthralled to beauty and depicts a state of harmony
with nature. However, at the same moment he notes that this state
had to be won by overthrowing 'titans' and emerging victorious
over a 'terrifyingly profound view of the world'. This supposed
spontaneousness is thus, in fact, a *derivative* effect. In the previous section, Nietzsche called the Dionysiac 'sentimental' insofar
as it involves mourning for its past (or future) dismemberment
into individuals, for the end of Dionysiac ecstasy. However, at the
same time the Dionysiac is also a joyful 'reunion' with nature –
and thus sounds like the naïve. In so far as cultural products are
always arrived at through a struggle between drives, the genealogical account of them can never simply rest with an 'immediate'
or 'simple' response. Nietzsche tries to borrow Schiller's concepts
here, but ultimately his position undermines them.

Here, in **paragraph 1**, the geneological method is put to work on Apolline culture. The beautiful, calm and happy sphere of Greek culture and its Olympian gods, overflowing with life, is in the eighteenth and nineteenth centuries a common classicist view of ancient Greeks. Nietzsche turns this inside-out by claiming to have discovered that this image is a mask, the whole metaphysical meaning of which is to hide and indeed protect the Greeks from a deep awareness of universal suffering and the dissolution of the *principium individuationis*. Nietzsche's evidence for this is the story of Midas and Silenus (**paragraph 2**) – the truth that would be 'most profitable' for humans not to hear is that they would be better off not existing at all. The phrase 'most profitable' Nietzsche sees as referring to the function or value of the mask. However, as additional evidence, there is in the background the traditional problem of how an audience could get *pleasure* from watching a *tragedy* (a problem to which Nietzsche returns frequently throughout). Thus, Nietzsche lists the cruellest and most horrifying myths – Prometheus, Oedipus, Orestes – which also happen to be the plots of tragedies.

The Apolline mask justifies existence, giving it *value*, by portraying the gods as living an idealized image of human existence. This is 'the only satisfactory theodicy!' (**paragraph 4**) Nietzsche says – that is, the only possible proof that life and the world are *good*. This is the Apolline symbolic function: the Olympian gods make present to humans the beautiful and pleasurable value of their *own* existence, which is in no way devalued by the constant awareness of its precarious position with respect to the underlying *Ureine*. This illusion is not deliberate, not a choice on anyone's part. Rather it grows out of the whole culture's need to respond to the underlying Dionysiac view. The culture needed to find a way of 'being able to live'. The development of Apolline *culture* happens in response to the Dionysic vision, but happens through the no less original Apolline *drive* (or 'instinct') for beauty. Or, expressed in Schopenhauer's language: in the Greek context, for the Will (nature itself) to glorify itself 'its creatures too had to feel themselves to be worthy of glorification'. This illusion is so successful that within the Apolline culture the wisdom of Silenus is reversed, and life – any life – is coveted. Nevertheless, we must keep in view one of the first things Nietzsche said about the Apolline: it is aware that its dream-images are only images. The beauty may only be appearance and not being itself, but *that is already enough*. Thus, here the genealogical method only discovered what the Greeks already knew (or at least sensed); this will not be the case when Nietzsche puts it to work on science.

Notice that in this section Nietzsche makes pretence of discretion in the comparison with Christianity ('another religion'). The Christian who views the Apolline sees no proper asceticism, spirituality or *moral* value in this celebration of life; the Christian in fact *does* experience the perfected world of its vision as an imperative or a reproach, as Nietzsche suggests at the end of the section. There are veiled critical references to Jesus and Christian ethics further down the line (cf. **Section 13**). This way of viewing Christianity as comprizing an ascetic moral core, which is founded upon a sense of reproach or inadequacy, is again a constant feature of Nietzsche's later work.

Note: Nietzsche, German 'Hellenism' and Hölderlin

At the beginning of his career, infatuated with the idea of the tragic, Nietzsche still shows an enthusiasm for Greek culture, soon to be shed and later (cf. for example **Section 6** of **'Attempt'**) fully replaced with an anthropological, 'scientific' take on culture as a phenomenon of general study. *The Birth of Tragedy* can be located at the very end of a German tradition of aesthetic theory centred on an idealization of the Hellenic. In the final section of *The Twilight of the Gods* (1888), under the title 'What I owe to the Ancients', Nietzsche adopts a positively anti-Greek stance when he says that 'one does not learn from the Greeks – their manner is too strange'.[49] By this stage, he thinks of the Romans as exemplary, like Goethe. But also in *The Birth of Tragedy* Nietzsche's attempt is already well under way of cutting himself loose from the normative, idealized notions of Greece in the tradition of Winckelmann, Lessing and Schiller. In the spirit of Winckelmann's much quoted adage in characterization of Greek plastic art: 'noble simplicity and quiet grandeur',[50] Greek culture was predominantly considered as an expression of 'serenity', in turn identified as a central national feature of 'the Greek character'. Although in a much defused form, *The Birth of Tragedy* still builds upon the historical contrast between Ancients and Moderns that, since Winckelmann around 1750, forms a central ingredient of German aesthetic critiques of modernity. (To an extent, the debate was imported from France where the *Querelle des Anciens et des Moderns* had been raging since the beginning of the century initiating a new phase in the French Enlightenment project.) From Winckelmann on (including Lessing, Schiller, Goethe, and to an extent Hegel, whose view of ancient history is more process-oriented than Schiller's, for example), Classical Antiquity, particularly Greek culture, is identified with unified wholeness of life as opposed to its broken-up non-identity in modern times. To use Schiller's dyad of contrasting terms: antiquity as an historical age of 'naive' unity of life, culture and spirit is set in stark opposition to the 'sentimental' age of life in modern times. Modernity lives off the inheritance of Greek culture by consciously and nostalgically imitating, re-evoking or emulating it. This figure of diametrically opposed ages is used for over a century in German thought as a lever to support and legitimize the agenda for a critique of modernity.

Ironically, it is through seemingly adopting the German tradition of Hellenism that Nietzsche undermines it and substantially contributes to bringing about its demise. Thus, for example, he espouses the classicist notion of 'serenity', but only to expand its meaning, to such depths that it is no longer the cliché that a hundred years of overuse have turned it into: serenity in *The Birth of Tragedy* is one psychological cultural function in an ensemble of many others, like pessimism, for example, or 'scientific optimism', not an absolute state of ideal being. It is one specific, though highly visible, outcome in a process of continuously shifting and constantly clashing forces that can be identified psychologically, historically and geographically. By researching the historical and psychological conditions that made it possible in the first place, *The Birth of Tragedy* thus uniquely historicizes and scientifically de-idealizes the notion of serenity. In fact, Nietzsche looks at it genealogically. This means that it is regarded not as unique, but as a derivative phenomenon that points to the existence of other underlying factors with their own independent developmental histories, metaphysical commitments and values. In this way 'serenity' marks a transitional stage in a process that leads from rapturous unity of man and nature in the pre-civilized, iron-age era (cf. **Section 4**) to civilized man of the modern European societies, far detached from nature and barred from adequately corresponding with it or even understanding it.

Through the central role ascribed by Nietzsche to the 'aesthetic of the tragic', Greek culture of necessity features prominently at this early stage in Nietzsche's development, and the way it does this bears superficial resemblance with traditional classicist notions. But even here Nietzsche is not primarily interested in what he later calls, with ironical self-distance, 'the grandiose Greek problem' as such (cf. **'Attempt', Section 6**). It is tragedy he is primarily involved with as a modern art form (Wagner's music drama) with an ancient pedigree. This confirms what we are arguing throughout, that Nietzsche is concerned first and foremost with the problem of modern culture.

The traditionally prefigured contrast between Ancients and Moderns is evident in Nietzsche's *The Birth of Tragedy*, even though we can also see how Nietzsche is eroding it. The text still uses Greek culture as a mirror (itself fractured by now) for the reflection of modernity; Schiller's preconscious/consciousness divide between 'naive' and 'sentimental' is still intact (although Nietzsche employs it not as a master template, but as a flexible analytical tool). But the focus has shifted, almost imperceptibly but irrevocably, to the dark side of Greek preconscious culture, no longer to be identified with naive unity and childlike playfulness: tragedy, as Nietzsche sees it, is a more complex, elemental topic of critical investigation than sculpture, the predominant art form of classicist Hellenist criticism. Tragedy is about how not to go mad when with sudden shock the realization occurs what nature is all about and what man's place is in it.

By focusing on culture as forms of mental stabilization and madness-avoidance, the book has triggered a paradigm shift in cultural theory.[51] The direction is set for future research agendas into early Greek culture and early cultural history in general: from now on these dark phases form part of theories of the civilizing process, henceforth conceived of as multilayered and open-ended. In having achieved this, *The Birth of Tragedy* also represents an important first step on the way to realizing Nietzsche's genealogical method of critique. A new psychologically anchored 'genealogical' perspective on Greece opens up, no longer concomitant with the rigid classicist dichotomy of ancient and modern.

In his attempt to free himself from the stranglehold of classicist German Hellenism, Nietzsche finds support in the work by the poet and philosopher Friedrich Hölderlin, contemporary of the German Idealists and on the fringe of the circle of writers who constituted Weimar Classicism. As the favourite author of his *Schulpforta* boarding school days, Nietzsche was intimately familiar with Hölderlin's work and his personal circumstances. Like Nietzsche, Hölderlin remains an outsider, in spite of the many cross links with the two circles mentioned above: he is one of the most erratic individuals amongst this generation of artists and philosophers. In fact, Nietzsche and Hölderlin have in common personal isolation, being misunderstood by their contemporaries (an important feature in their lives), and both also suffered a breakdown from which neither of them recovered. The parallels between them extend so far that the question has arisen as to whether Nietzsche's madness could be in any way 'explained' by linking or comparing it with that of Hölderlin, or even whether there might be any element of Nietzsche 'modelling' his own madness on that of his revered compatriot.[52] Hölderlin, though isolated amongst his contemporaries, spearheads the endeavour to reconcile some of the contradictions that had arisen from what were widely seen as unpalatable conclusions of Kantian philosophy (amongst others, Schiller, Goethe, the Romantics and Kleist worked on this). For Hölderlin a solution lies in elevating art to a position of mediator between instinct and reason. He regards art as a historical barometer for the success of human correspondence with nature, a notion built upon by Nietzsche.

Amongst his contemporaries, Hölderlin's view of Greece is unique. He 'is, almost a century before Nietzsche, engaged in resurrecting tragic vision against the Platonic heritage.'[53] For both, the experience of the tragic, akin to that of madness, blasts through the veneer of philosophical reasoning, scientific logic and civilized surface patterns and opens up a hidden world of chthonic forces and maenadic raving. In a re-evaluation of the tragic, Hölderlin was ahead of his time. He was also the first amongst the post-Winckelmann generation to contextualize the achievements of Greek culture by setting it within an anthropological backdrop of conflicting human forces manifest as geocultural phenomena. It is particularly through this pioneering correction of the image of Greece in the direction of 'scientific' historical investigation that Hölderlin's is attractive to Nietzsche. The schematicism of the binary divide between ancients and moderns upheld in classicist, idealist notions of antiquity is beginning to evaporate in Hölderlin's historical gradations. Like later Nietzsche's in *The Birth of Tragedy*, Hölderlin's perception of the Greeks is based on the notion of fragility of cultural equilibrium, to be hard fought for and prone to collapse: serenity conceived of as the result of a bitter struggle to keep a check on harmful, foreign Dionysian intoxication. To Françoise Dastur Hölderlin is a pioneer because he has started to regard Greek culture as an element in a wider whole of geo-cultural forces. He has 'orientalized' the Greeks: they fought back dangerous Asian influences by adopting and taming them in a fusion with indigenous cultural stock. Hölderlin's approach is to explain Greek culture contextually as a result of clashes of foreign and indigenous cultural influences. Nietzsche to a large extent follows Hölderlin when he seeks to embed Greek culture as a phase in a process which consists of migration, adaptation and assimilation of constitutive forces (cf. **Section 4**). This changes the value of the Greek experience as a formative phase of European cultural history. Hölderlin, Dastur claims, distinguishes between the Greeks as a model and as an example. This distinction is extraordinarily important for *The Birth of Tragedy*. A model is something to be copied; an example is an achievement of a certain type which cannot be copied but can be *repeated* in the unique circumstances of the present.[54] For both Hölderlin and Nietzsche (at this stage) the Greeks are exemplary because they are 'an inverted mirror image of ourselves, they do not represent something of a bygone past'.[55]

Nietzsche builds on Hölderlin's pioneering forays in the area of cultural history, by consolidating as a 'methodology' with developed theoretical principles and terminologies what had remained fragmentary and embryonic in Hölderlin's thought, more that of a tragedian and poet. We can also see Nietzsche still following Hölderlin in his attempt to replace the language of Kantian philosophy deemed insufficient to cater for the redefined tasks of philosophy in the post-Kantian era, with a new symbolic language more adequate for capturing life in its elusive aspects that are only instinctively perceivable. Both are poets,[56] even though for Hölderlin poetry is more central as a medium of philosophical discourse than for Nietzsche, in whose work philosophical analysis, albeit metaphorically converted and poetically tinged, proportionally outweighs the element of 'pure' poetry.

* * *

SECTION 4

Necessity of Relationship between the Drives: their 'Reciprocal Intensification'; the 'Ethics' of the Drives; the Five Periods of Greek Culture; Introduction of 'Attic Tragedy'

This section elaborates on the relation between Apolline and Dionysiac. Although in everyday thought we think of dreams as unreal and of secondary importance with respect to our waking lives, from a true metaphysical point of view (which is revealed through the Dionysiac drive), this is reversed. Our waking lives are only valuable and worthy of being lived to the extent they can become more like dreams; dreams are the original image 'imitated' by the Apolline artist. So, the relation of Apollo to Dionysus is described as one of absolute mutual need, a position already suggested by the notion of 'duality' used in the first sentence of the book. '[T]hat which truly exists . . . needs, for its constant release and redemption . . . intensely pleasurable semblance [*Schein*]', Nietzsche writes here. It desires to objectify itself and appear, and in a form worthy of itself. And, reciprocally: 'And behold! Apollo could not live without Dionysos'.

Why is this important? Let us restrict ourselves to only four reasons. First of all, as we have seen, this is an important claim in Nietzsche's attempt to rewrite Schopenhauer's pessimism of weakness. Secondly, it entails that if one of these drives is fundamentally modified or repressed, then the other too will be changed. As we will see, this is precisely what happens immediately after the brief blossoming of tragedy. Thirdly, we have already noted Nietzsche's historical interest in what is at work behind the famous events of history; now we see that the nature of human cultures (in both narrow and broad senses) and their historical development is and must be built upon antagonism, on a see-sawing conflict between the basic drives. This notion gives Nietzsche what he considers powerful conceptual tools for the understanding of historical *change* (such as the 'four great artistic stages' – tragedy makes five – in **paragraph 4**).

However, it also provides powerful 'weapons' for *precipitating* change in the present. Finally, Nietzsche can now claim that the advent of tragedy (an art form that requires both drives) may be an accident insofar as it happened in precisely such-and-such a place and time, but nevertheless should be seen as the 'pinnacle and goal' of both drives, and indeed of the will that underlies both drives.

The *Ureine*, as is expounded in **paragraph 1**, demands semblance, and all our waking life is (under the influence of the *principium individuationis*) just such a semblance. It follows that our dreaming life (the original domain of the Apolline) is the semblance of semblance and so is a 'yet higher satisfaction' of that demand. Again, Nietzsche borrows the structure of Plato's analysis (in the *Republic*) but re-evaluates it. Art is indeed the copy of a copy, and for Plato that is precisely its metaphysical danger. However, for Nietzsche this is neither mere representation nor semblance in the merely negative sense, but transfiguring, magical symbol. Nietzsche uses Raphael's *Transfiguration* to illustrate. His reading is not entirely convincing since much of the power of that painting has to do with the sudden revelatory recognition of the transfigured Christ by several figures in the lower half; in any case, Nietzsche's use of the painting is more significant for the decidedly non-Christian interpretation he gives of an iconic Christian image.

Notice the broadly ethical dimension of the Apolline that Nietzsche discusses in **paragraph 2**. By 'ethics' we mean the principles by which we should conduct ourselves and relate to others. Within Apolline culture, the basic ethical rule is 'respect for the limits of the individual, *measure* in the Hellenic sense'. This is contrasted in **paragraph 3** with the lack of measure (a lack of the possibility of measure) and thus excess of the Dionysiac. But to the Dionysiac too there is an ethics: the 'gospel of universal harmony' and of liberation from the barriers and shackles of law and custom, as Nietzsche described it in the first section. As we saw in **Section 1**, that discussion of Dionysiac ethics referenced Schiller's *To Joy* and Beethoven's Ninth Symphony that sets it to music. There are two contrasting ethical systems corresponding to the two cultural modes: one based upon the basic difference of human beings from one another, autonomy and value-in-themselves as individuals; the second based upon the essential commonness we share, and indeed the metaphysical assertion that all are one. In recent philosophy, the former is probably meant by Nietzsche to remind his reader of Kant (the term 'respect' is the clue), and perhaps Nietzsche has in mind various theories of individual rights. The explicit ancient references, though, are to the idea of restraint of the passions in Plato and 'measure' or 'moderation' in Aristotle. An ethics based upon commonness Nietzsche gets in part from Schopenhauer: for Schopenhauer, violence against the other person is, in fact, violence against oneself – it is the will perversely self-harming.[57] Although Nietzsche has other reasons for not wanting to make these connections, the idea also has some resemblance to contemporary Utilitarianism (for which the question '*who* has happiness?' is irrelevant) and Marxism (and ethics based upon the common interests of social groups). These two ethical positions are not put forward with any detail, clearly; Nietzsche is not taking sides, but rather providing a broad classificatory instrument.

In **paragraph 4,** it looks as though Nietzsche is finally ready to launch the book's narrower subject matter, Athenian tragedy in the end of the sixth and first few decades of the fifth century BC. In fact, though, we will wait till **Section 9** for all to be revealed. Nietzsche is more interested in the process of development that leads to Athenian tragedy – and the metaphysical significance of that process – than in the particularities of the finished product as such. Attic tragedy is positioned as the 'later' artistic paradigm at the end of and emerging from a process of 'earlier Hellenic history'. The material manifestations in artistic styles of the two drives serve as indicators for a historical periodization of Greek culture. (A similar programme of historical sequencing is followed in the second half of the book for the modern period.) Nietzsche maps the fourfold 'to-ing and fro-ing' between the two drives onto a historical scale, prior to tragedy's fifth stage.

Nietzsche suggests that it is the inherent *telos* [goal or purpose] of this whole early era in Greek history to conflagrate in this final period and to enter into a 'mysterious marriage'. The teleology of the drives smacks of Hegelianism, but in Nietzsche we have a potentially endless to-ing and fro-ing between them; in Nietzsche's grand historical periodization at the end of the section, this happens four times before they join up and reproduce. Clearly, an Hegelian triadic scheme of dialectical evolution is not adhered to. What is more, after the brief period of Attic tragedy (even as a consequence of it?) not only is their successful 'marriage' over, but so too is the swinging of this pendulum – the Apolline and Dionysian no longer occupy the centre stage of European culture. There will be a 'rebirth', perhaps, if Wagner can be relied upon. In other words, the Hegelian elements of necessity and progress are no longer part of Nietzsche's equation of historical development. They have been replaced by a logic of history that follows an evolutionary pattern characterized by erratic jumps, repetition, deviation, and regressive events – 'degeneracy,' a new concern in the wake of Darwin's theory. The 'common goal' does not *govern* the process, leading it forward, but is rather a description of the implicit highest possibilities of the constituent drives.

Nietzsche returns here to the analogy between culture and biological reproduction introduced in the first sentence in **Section 1**. We are further encouraged to regard the drives as gendered here, when we learn that the reproductive effort was 'crowned with . . . a child'. The child's name is, of course, tragedy, bearing features in which both parents are recognizable, and who is 'both Antigone and Cassandra at once'. Antigone is the eponymous heroine of Sophocles' play, who is doomed by an insoluble conflict; Cassandra is in Aeschylus' *Agamemnon* (among other plays), a prophetess of Troy fated always to be disbelieved or misunderstood. They are thus prominent tragic characters and royal children (so that fits), but more importantly are *already* an image of tragedy's downfall, as described starting in **Section 11**.[58]

SECTION 5

Historical Manifestation of the 'Third Type' of Symbolization: Archilochus, the 'Father' of Tragedy; The Fusion of the Drives in Lyric Poetry

Section 5 begins the treatment of the Apolline and Dionysiac in combination, rather than separately. Here, Nietzsche is putting forward ideas that are distinctively his own. The explicit rebuttal of Schopenhauer's treatment of lyric poetry (**paragraph 4**) shows this. The **first four paragraphs** focus on the figure of Archilochus, an early Greek poet whose work survives only in fragments, together with a number of colourful biographical stories. Nietzsche regards the work of this poet as the first manifestation of a new type of poetry that is characterized through its lyrically subjective qualities. This new style of poetry is also significant to Nietzsche for its musical qualities, both with regard to the musicality of its 'dithyrambic' language and the musical style in which it was likely to be performed. An interesting paradox opens up for Nietzsche here. He argues that even though the lyrical reflexivity of Archilochus projects the subject of an 'I' into the centre, this kind of poetry is more in touch with the 'objective' ur-ground of all being than the epic poetry of Homer, normally categorized as objective. How can this be?

There is a distinction common in Idealist Philosophy between subjective and objective art, poets and poetry. By 'subjective' is meant a poet who writes about and from their own feelings – lyric poets, Nietzsche claims, would appear to fall into this category. By 'objective' is meant a poet (like Homer) who writes about other people and places (whether real or imagined). The distrust of the *merely* subjective element of artistic creation can be traced back to a basic principle of disinterest found in Kant, Hegel and Schopenhauer in connection with the aesthetic experience.[59] Nietzsche accordingly writes, 'the prime demand we make of every kind and level of art is the conquest of subjectivity, release and redemption from the I'. The subjective poet would appear to be an oxymoron, or at least a bad poet. Nietzsche argues that in an artist like Archilochus, the 'I' or 'subject' is not, despite appearances, Archilochus himself, not any 'empirically real human being' – but instead the 'genius of the world'. The subject in Archilochus has become symbolic. For reasons that have already been discussed (at the beginning of **Section 2**), Nietzsche is therefore not interested in Archilochus *per se* or the personality of the new lyrical ego that speaks from his poetry. Like all the other figures in his historical gallery of personified concepts, Archilochus is a representative of new configurations of the cultural drives.

Archilochus has been to the depth of the Dionysiac abyss, where he has glimpsed the *Ureine*, but rather than being destroyed by it, or hiding it from himself, he has re-emerged from this shattering experience to tell the tale, the tale of a journey to the mothers of being expressed in symbolic images and language.[60] Thus, in Archilochus the subjective has the deepest ring of objectivity. In fact, Nietzsche thinks that these two categories do not achieve much as tools of critical analysis of art and culture any more, because his work has revealed that both the subject of the artist and the object of the art are to be understood quite differently and are not in an oppositional relation. The artist's subjectivity is a means for the drive to achieve symbolization; and the object is the first and most immediate realization of the drive. 'Let me shine until I may become being' as Goethe says in a poem.[61]

'Compared with Homer', Nietzsche says, 'Archilochus frankly terrifies us with his cries of hatred and scorn'. He is not an artist conforming to conventional criteria of beauty. We are provided with the first indication here of what we could regard as Nietzsche's aesthetics of the ugly (see **Sections 16, 21** and **24**). The work of the lyrical artist does not shudder back from that which is despicable, horrifying and ugly. It encompasses the world in all its dimensions. Homer can be identified as Apolline artist *par excellance*, (a 'pure' Apolline symbolization) whilst in Archilochus the Apolline becomes significant as a function of the Dionysiac (the third type of symbol, see our discussion in **Section 2**).

Nietzsche's interpretation of the lyric poet is based upon two clues: first, the comment from Schiller, dealt with in **paragraph 2**, about the origin of his poetry being a 'musical mood'; secondly, the purported fact that early lyric poets were also musicians and not just writers of words. Nietzsche then describes the lyric poet in two stages: first, as Dionysiac artist 'at one with the *Ureine*, with its pain and contradiction' producing an 'image-less and concept-less' 'copy' of this unity in music; and secondly, in the Apolline mode this music generates a second reflection, a 'symbolic dream-image'. Music is the direct manner in which the *Ureine* finds expression (the idea is straight-forward Schopenhauer, see **Section 16**). The source of Apolline imagistic material is the lyric poet ('the tangle of subjective passions'), but this material is not used representationally (of the subjective states of the poet) but symbolically (as the expression of the *Ureine*). Dionysiac truth reaches 'sensuous expression' in a manner no longer merely Dionysiac or Apolline, separately. Thus, such lyric poems 'unfolded to their fullest extent, are called tragedies and dramatic dithyrambs'. The problem of how lyric poetry is possible at all turns out to be the preliminary solution to how tragedy happens. In tragedy, however, the source of symbolic imagery need not be the individual who happens to be the poet, but is much broader, taken from myth.

Sometimes, Nietzsche adds, the artist catches a glimpse of his or herself in the union with the world-genius. This glimpse does not just yield symbolic content for poetry, but contributes to an account of the nature of art; only in this way can the essence of art be understood. Otherwise, all philosophizing about art, and even theories and observations on art *by artists* (i.e. those artists who have not 'fully merged' with the 'original artist' and have comprehended themselves as such), is 'at bottom entirely illusory'. 'Illusory' because the observations cannot understand subjective images as symbols, for example, or indeed that the theories misunderstand 'who' is the artist. This comment is very important, for two reasons. First, as a claim within philosophical aesthetics – and a claim with a deliberately paradoxical or 'fairy-tale' air about it – that analysis or any other understanding of art is doomed to failure unless crafted by the Dionysiac (or Dionysiac/Apolline) artist. Nietzsche, who was himself deemed to be a talented though amateur composer, and also a poet, could claim privileged insight. Thus, this is a more finessed and detailed version of the claim about an aesthetic sense being required for criticism, which we discussed in the context of **Section 1**. Secondly, because this 'fairy-tale' situation of the poet being also, simultaneously and essentially, an actor and spectator, becomes an enormously important moment in the full account of tragedy that Nietzsche will give shortly.

This then is the fourfold significance of the inclusion of this seemingly obscure figure of Archilochus whom Nietzsche iconoclastically seems to elevate even above Homer (the hero of generations of classical philologists). First, through Archilochus, Nietzsche distances himself from Schopenhauer's version of will-metaphysics. By upgrading the underrated status of lyrical poetry he arrives at a new model of an integrated relationship between appearance and being (*Schein* and *Sein*); in the lyrical artist, being corresponds *symbolically* with appearance. Secondly therefore, the lyrical poet is the historical paradigm of tragedy and introduces the phenomenon in a model way. Archilochus can be called the father of tragedy; that is why Nietzsche puts him here, as a historical ur-type of the tragic artistic experience. Thirdly, the analysis of Archilocus reveals the ground of the only possible aesthetic analysis or theory – only the artist who catches sight of him or herself returning from ecstatic submergence in the *Ureine*, and thus understands the true symbolic function of art, is fully capable of understanding art. Section 5 ends with one of the deepest, most enigmatic statements of the whole book, recapitulated in part two in **Section 24**, that 'only as an *aesthetic phenomenon* is existence and the world eternally *justified*'. Fourthly, then, Archilochus's work explains Nietzsche's metaphysics of art thus: it stands for the moment when the drives in their struggle become simultaneously productive, and for once the shining forth of appearance truly symbolizes, makes possible insight into and justifies all of being (existence and the world).

SECTION 6

Folk Song; Fusion of Language and Music

Section 6 elaborates on the new material from Section 5, showing the two drives engaged in symbiotic collaboration in a 'new' artistic genre, of extreme interest to Nietzsche because in it music combines with poetry. Archilochus is praised for the achievement of 'having introduced the folk song into literature.' Thus, of the many things Nietzsche is attempting with *The Birth of Tragedy*, this is a further concern: to uncover the origins of this hybrid artistic form as one of the historical stems from which tragedy branches off. The nineteenth century saw a fashion for collecting traditional music, with an emphasis on the anthropological or nationalistic (or both). Examples include Chopin's musical connection with his Polish roots in the numerous mazurkas, polonaises etc.. At the beginning of the century, the German Romantic novelist Achim von Arnim collected the seminal folk-song anthology *Des Knaben Wunderhorn* (The Youth's Magic Horn) which Nietzsche mentions in **paragraph 2**; the Austro/German *Kunstlied* (art-song) of Schubert and Schumann builds on imagined folk roots, imitating folk songs through the device of artful simplicity; and many of Nietzsche's own compositions are in this genre.[62] In any case, in a German context, particularly in the second half of the nineteenth century, the search is on for national roots in folklore, at a time of national identity crisis. Again, Nietzsche is working here in the wake of Herder whose forays into cultural anthropology had pioneered this area at the end of the eighteenth century; and he can refer, apart from a variety of more recent examples (Liszt for instance), to Haydn's and especially Beethoven's pioneering initiative in the field of musical ethnography.[63] In the light of these developments, Nietzsche regards the folk song as a vestige of the original Dionysiac/Apolline double drive which he sees at work behind lyric poetry.

For reasons Nietzsche will elaborate later, after the period of Greek tragedy, such arts and related practices either died out or had to go 'underground', into marginal forms. The folk song, presumably, is one of these 'underground' art forms – hidden far from the mainstream, and its nature hidden *even from practitioners*. From **paragraph 2** onwards Nietzsche repeats points about lyric poetry from the previous section: its origin lies in music and, specifically, that the textual dimension of poetry is an 'objectification' of *melody*. ('Objectification' is Schopenhauer's term for describing how the underlying will appears: that is, how it will manifest itself at a certain level of individuation, from broad types of things, e.g. matter, or species of plants, up to individual human beings.) A similar objectification happens when a listener (or, indeed, composer) feels compelled to describe musical passages with concrete images. Not just deluded contemporary critics, but Beethoven himself did so, controversially in Nietzsche's view, in his 'Pastoral' symphony. It distorts the depth of symbolic significance when the music is merely seen as an imitation of some countryside scene. The reverse should be the case: the music speaks first and the images are, at best, *symbolic* expressions of the underlying Dionysiac truth of that music. This is why there is an undertone of suspicion in Nietzsche's discussion of this, perhaps his least favourite, Beethoven symphony, which he seems to charge implicitly with what Schopenhauer dismissively calls 'imitative music' (**Section 16**); Nietzsche himself uses the term 'tone painting' (**Sections 17** and **19**) for music unduly influenced by concepts or images. The other side of this argument is that *The Birth of Tragedy* makes a case for a form of art, tragedy, which combines pure music and its poetic objectification.

Music can speak for itself and stand on its own. But, like Schopenhauer, as we will see in **Section 16**, Nietzsche is more interested in forms of objectification of music in poetry or drama than in 'absolute' music on its own. As we know by now, Nietzsche has a deep interest in Wagner's music drama, not in the symphony,[64] to him a comparatively exhausted classical form of 'pure' music. And as we have already mentioned, Beethoven's Ninth captured his special attention precisely because it is an hybrid piece of music. The investigation of this idea of a musical-poetic mix is a key aim of this book, as the originally intended title of the book makes clear. 'Melody gives birth to poetry, and does so over and over again, in ever new ways'. The 'dramatic dithyramb', a key poetic ingredient of tragedy, is the chief example of a literary objectification of music targeted in *The Birth of Tragedy*.

The section ends by dismissing the claim that language could ever 'externalize' the 'innermost' meaning of music. Nietzsche insists that music has priority over poetry, in the same way as the Dionysian is the basis for Apollonian symbolic dream imagery. The language of lyric poetry 'depends utterly on the spirit of music'; and Nietzsche likes the idea that this poetic language is strained to its very limits in its encounter with music. The attainment of language to symbolization is the outcome of this 'straining'; we will discuss this more fully in the context of **Section 8**. This symbolization is not an externalization; the metaphor Nietzsche prefers is illumination *from within* (**Section 24**). In tragedy, as will become clear shortly, the relationship between music and language is different from that in lyrical poetry: both are more independent and they free each other up by granting the other the possibility of an optimum realization (see **Section 21**).

It is worth noting in passing the preponderance of metaphors of energy (and especially electricity) in Nietzsche's writing, particularly obvious in **paragraph 4**. Several times already we have encountered figures such as 'intensification', 'discharge' – here we have 'sparks' and 'energy utterly alien'. As the list of textbooks covering these areas in Nietzsche's home library shows,[65] often imbued with extensive marginalia, he was widely read in contemporary sciences. Notions of polarity and physical or indeed spiritual attraction or repulsion of objects derived from the theories of electromagnetism were frequently used as metaphors in nineteenth-century European works of art and non-fiction.

Think of the popular 'Gothic' novel Frankenstein where recent theories of electricity (Galvanism) feature as an essential ingredient of the plot. Thus, Nietzsche is not on his own in attempting to utilize new scientific findings as metaphors to illustrate philosophical points. We can observe, however, that this fascination with current thought models in the sciences in *The Birth of Tragedy* goes very deep and beyond the occasional term borrowed from science. The principle of bipolarity is the central structuring device of Nietzsche's ideas of developmental processes. These are initiated and maintained through the varying activities of antagonizing forces.[66] Arguably, the analogy of electromagnetic fields forms a compositional basis upon which rests *The Birth of Tragedy*'s very style of writing. In this way the book circles around its rather than directly focusing on them, repeatedly experimenting with the configurations and contexts of the drives, observing the changes in 'atmosphere'.

SECTION 7

The Chorus as Historical Nucleus of Tragedy; Nietzsche's Critique of Hegel

Nietzsche now turns to one of tragedy's nuclear elements, the chorus. This section asserts it to be a matter of historical fact that tragedy arose from the chorus alone. We are probably more familiar with the chorus as a relatively secondary feature of drama (or opera), a group of citizens of a city, for example, commenting on the action of the lead characters. Moreover, we are used to the chorus being on the stage and faced by an audience of spectators. All these features (individual actors playing lead roles, and having an audience at all) are later additions to the original nucleus of the chorus. Accordingly, Nietzsche is able to dismiss claims that (1) the chorus represents the democratic instincts and wisdom of Greek society or (2) the chorus is the ideal spectator, responding to the action the way the real spectators ought to (August Wilhem Schlegel). The absurdity of the later position, Nietzsche claims, is shown by the fact that spectators (unlike the role of the chorus) know the difference between reality and the stage fiction, and thus do not, for example, run onto the stage to free Prometheus from his torment.

Nietzsche gets more help here (from **paragraph 4** onwards) from Schiller: with Schiller's aid, Nietzsche can claim that the chorus is a living wall that protects the tragic space from 'naturalism'. Nietzsche refers here to the fashionable nineteenth and early-twentieth-century demand that characters, actions, setting and so forth not only be 'believable', but be as if taken without modification straight from reality. The manifesto of naturalism is contained in a preface Emile Zola added in explanation to his novel *Thérèse Raquin* (1862).[67] The movement that identifies with this programme, one of exaggerated realism, operates on the (supposedly) scientific principle of the predominance of social environments or biological factors (poverty and disease) over morality and individual choice. The idea of a 'war' on naturalism attracts Nietzsche, and we are reminded of the 'battle' image in Nietzsche's **Foreword**. In passing, we should note that, dispositionally, Nietzsche feels uncomfortable with whatever ideas are 'fashionable'. Popular culture is a system of forms and tendencies that often seem to represent underlying diseases very clearly. His next publications will be collected as '*Untimely* [or 'Unfashionable'] *Meditations*; and the first of these meditations are clearly targeted at more 'popular' culture. (The opposition may be disingenuous, since Wagner, Schopenhauer and Darwin are hardly sideshows. But we will let it pass.) This opposition is more than just stubbornness: it is on principle a rare and difficult thing to understand one's culture, and its metaphysical foundations. For example, we have just seen in **Section 5** why no philosophers and few artists understand the nature of art. 'The sphere of the philosopher and the artist exists above the tumult of contemporary history, beyond need [. . .] But they are thrown far ahead of their time, because they only gain the attention of their contemporaries very slowly'[68]. Throughout his career, Nietzsche sticks with this notion of working on a philosophy that could only ever be 'for the future', and perhaps even then only for the few.

Let us return to the problem of tragedy's origin. The Greek chorus protects itself from naturalism by residing on a 'platform' of fictitious creatures (the satyr) in a fictitious nature. However, this fiction is not a 'mere caprice', but a world 'just as real and credible to the believing Greek as Olympus and its inhabitants'. This is akin to the 'middle world' Nietzsche has spoken of before: not our everyday, empirical world, but also not something simply fantastic, for the middle world occupies a religiously and mythically sanctioned ground. Again, Nietzsche is here commentating on Plato, but perhaps by way of Aristotle's *Poetics*. Plato had argued that the imitative nature of art makes it metaphysically and thus also morally dubious, because it takes us away from ideal truths. Aristotle responds by rethinking the nature of 'imitation' (*mimesis* in Greek, see also the discussion of Aristotle and artistic *imitatio naturea* in **Section 2**). 'Mimesis' is no longer the formation of a (more or less deficient) copy of reality, but the *construction* of plot, character and language.[69] Thus, to some extent, for Aristotle, *that which is imitated* has to be seen as a *product* of the activity of mimesis. Moreover, this fictitiousness is not understood as incompatible with, or the opposite of, truth or insight. On these points, with his notion of 'middle world', Nietzsche has clear affinities with Aristotle. A key difference, however, is that Nietzsche is telling this story from the point of view of the chorus, from *inside*, so to speak, whereas for Aristotle it is told from the point of view of the dramatic poet or the spectator.

The Dionysiac chorus has, as its first effect, the 'overwhelming feeling of unity' that shows 'all divisions between one human being and another' to be illusory. The verb Nietzsche uses here is *aufheben*; we will return below to the significance of this term. But the middle world of the chorus of satyrs is nevertheless a 'metaphysical solace [*Trost*]'. Despite the never-ending and always changing succession of appearances, the chorus, held as it is above everyday reality and as symbolic of Dionysiac insight into the *Ureine*, consoles us with the feeling that 'life is indestructibly mighty and pleasurable'. This solace is necessary because while the Dionysiac state is 'lethargic' – Nietzsche clearly intends this in the meaning of its Greek root, from Lethe, the river of forget-fulness or oblivion – the return from the Dionysiac state is experi-enced as pain. The pain arises not just from what he earlier called the 'dismemberment' of the individual from the unity, but also because of the sense of terrible and meaningless destructiveness of the world of appearances (things come into and go *out of* existence), along with the realization of the futility of any belief or action within that world, for that belief or action cannot alter the underlying reality. (Nietzsche illustrates this with a nice and not unconvincing interpretation of Hamlet.) There is a 'danger of longing to deny the will as the Buddhist does', Nietzsche writes, and this is directed also at Schopenhauer. But 'art saves him, and through art life saves him – for itself'. That is to say, the representation of the 'middle world' of the satyr chorus – itself not a product of culture directly but of a living art-drive – serves as a healing or consolation to this terrible insight. That is its function; that is why life (the *Ureine* and its basic currents towards realization) required the chorus to exist at all. This account of metaphysical solace has taken us one-step further to Nietzsche's yet fuller account of tragedy, which is finally provided in the next section.

Let us return to **paragraph 6** and the term *aufheben*. We have already discussed *aufheben* briefly in connection with duplicity in **Section 1**. It is usually rendered simply as 'to sublate', but translators have trouble with it, often (as in the Cambridge edition of *The Birth of Tragedy*) substituting half a sentence. The difficulty stems from the fact that it was such an important, but very complex, concept for Hegel. (Although Nietzsche mischievously cites Wagner, as if Hegel did not exist.) Hegel uses the term to refer to the manner in which the logical conflict between two mutually negating concepts is overcome in a synthesis. In the process of *Aufhebung* the individual component in an antagonism is both annihilated and also preserved and elevated. 'Preserved and elevated' in so far as the new synthesis carries forward what is true or significant, without the conflict which was shown to be an illusion based upon an insufficiently elevated viewpoint; 'annihilated' because the conflict and both separate components which were defined in part by conflict, have been cancelled. The synthesis can itself be one part of a new antagonistic divide. Thus, Hegelian 'sublation' means to abolish and overcome through elevation or transcendence. But, as we have seen since the opening sentences of the book, Nietzsche is concerned to distance himself from the Hegelian account of the logic of development of conscious states, beliefs or cultural forms. So, why use so inescapably Hegelian a word at all? Just as Nietzsche (following Aristotle and Schiller) has here turned upside down Plato's notion of mimesis, so he (following Schopenhauer and Wagner) will here do the same with Hegel and *Aufhebung*.

Civilization is *aufgehoben* in Dionysiac music – let us say it is *overrun* ('as lamplight is superseded by the light of day'), just as the individual Greek was overrun by what achieved symbolization in the satyr chorus. What we were dimly aware of suddenly submerges us. Wagner uses the Hegelian term in a deliberate act of provocation; Nietzsche does likewise. The most obvious point of divergence from Hegel is that the sublation is only half (or less) of the story – there must also be a de-sublation as one emerges from the ecstatic state (Nietzsche turns to this in the **penultimate paragraph** of the section). This back-and-forth movement, exemplified in any individual instance of tragic drama, is also another clue to Nietzsche's more general critique of Hegel. The key point at this important juncture, still near the beginning of the book, is that the Apolline and Dionysiac are 'permanent' (beneath innumerable combinations and inflections) drives that are, in some way, a part of any culture (although, as we shall see, there may be other drives). *Aufheben* here means the realization of the drives together with the effect of this realization upon human beings or culture; it does not mean anything like the drives' reconciliation or cancellation. Moreover, earlier and later realizations overlap, without a clear progression (see also our discussion in **Section 4**). The chorus, for example, is *still there* in the new phenomenon and later developments of tragedy; it has not disappeared. The rest of the ingredients that make Attic tragedy have grown arabesque-like around the chorus as its nucleus. In this way the chorus sticks out as the oldest and core element of tragedy. It can be identified as a relic essential to but not unified with the rest of the ingredients. This idea expresses the anti-classicist nature of Nietzsche's aesthetics, in which works of art are not envisaged as uniquely rounded artefacts based on the integration of each detail into the compositional whole. In Nietzsche's reckoning, art is like a palimpsest of historical layers. These are piled on top of each other with time and can be peeled back, isolated and made transparent again later in operations of archaeological uncovering. Thus, foreshadowing Adorno's 'negative dialectics',[70] in this new approach the true is no longer the whole, as Hegel proclaims, but precisely the false, inasmuch as in it the Hegelian *aufheben* makes the individual feature fit, to an extent that it is annihilated in the whole. Thus, it is possible with the principles laid down by Nietzsche in this earliest of his books already, to recognize 'permanent' difference rather than unity as the central ingredient not just of art, but of historical and cultural development in general: a new principle of philosophical logic derived from the critique of Hegel.

SECTION 8

The Chorus as Earliest Cell of Tragedy; Modern Poetry and Theory of Language. Note: Philosophy of Language in Nietzsche

This section continues the investigation of the chorus as the oldest element of tragedy. We can catch another glimpse of what Nietzsche later turns into a fully-fledged methodology of critical-historical analysis of culture: 'genealogy' (see discussion in **Section 3**). What we just called 'cultural factors', genealogy artificially separates for the purposes of investigation. By tracing back individual elements to their various contexts of origin – and 'origin' here always means a drive (or drives) realizing itself in a specific historical manner – it throws new light on a given present state. This is how it works with regard to the chorus: **Section 7** showed how the chorus as a primeval rudiment survived as part of the more 'modern' mix of ingredients that form the historically later Attic tragedy. This section now shows us where the chorus itself originates. As it turns out, it is the embryonic cell of all tragedy. Nietzsche takes us back to 'the primitive state of its development' in what he calls 'original tragedy' (**paragraph 2**). We learn that it initially fulfils a specific psychological function 'as a self-mirroring of Dionysiac man' in the first periods of traceable history. In the uncharacteristically short paragraph, about half way through (**paragraph 5**), Nietzsche puts the pieces back together again and states his solution to the problem of how to evaluate the chorus as a primeval ingredient element of modern Greek tragedy.

The section is organized around three contrasts we have seen several times before already: the modern and the Greek; the cultural and the natural; and appearance and thing-in-itself. Nietzsche also allows himself to comment critically here on the problematic position of the poetic wedged in between the different demands made on it by the spheres of culture and nature. Thus **paragraph 1**, by way of an example, contrasts the modern, and for Nietzsche clichéd, figure of the shepherd (see also **Section 16**) – since the sixteenth century a common poetic or dramatic figure of pastoral nostalgia for ancient origins, a hankering for rural, later even pre-industrial idyll – with the Greek figure of the satyr. Modern culture suffers in the comparison, appearing superficial and inauthentic, as it does also later in the passage when Nietzsche speaks of the role of the chorus in modern opera (**paragraph 7**), and especially in the scathingly funny dismissal of modern poets and poetry (**paragraph 3**). Nietzsche speaks of this modern contrast as that between 'genuine truth of nature and the cultural lie', the latter we can equate with our discussion of 'wrong appearance' (see **Section 1** and also **Section 13** onwards). The satyr was 'nature, untouched by knowledge', and the original image (*Urbild*) of man. The 'ur' here, as elsewhere, does not mean original in a straightforward chronological sense (thus, in a reference again to Darwin, the *Urbild* is not a 'monkey'). Rather, it means something in its most basic essence, or least-veiled truth. In the symbolism of the satyr this modern rift between 'true nature' and 'false culture' has not yet opened up and is very far away on the future horizon of history. On the contrary, 'the symbolism of the chorus of satyrs is in itself a metaphorical expression of that original relationship between thing-in-itself and phenomenon' which has been lost. Thus, in an act of preconscious transference, it is an ideal ancient example to modern poetry for reform and revitalization.

Paragraph 2 goes back to Schlegel's idea of the chorus as ideal spectator, refuted in the previous section in Schlegel's sense of democratic representation on stage, but here upheld in its 'deeper meaning'. As the chorus actor transforms into the satyr, the chorus' vision is transferred upon the 'spectator'. 'Spectator' is an inappropriate term, Nietzsche holds, because there is not really a segregation in Greek theatre between spectators and actors. Thus, aided by its peculiar architecture with its special place of the chorus in the orchestra, mediating between action and spectator, the ecstatic vision of the chorus transformed the actors. It then jumps infectiously across onto the spectator who, in terms of the architecture at least, are already almost part of the chorus. Thus, a 'self-mirroring of Dionysian man' occurs.

Note: Philosophy of Language in Nietzsche

The **next paragraph** is an excursion into the theory of metaphor and ultimately a theory of poetic language. We will take this opportunity to sketch out Nietzsche's early account of language and its relation to the underlying movements of the will. This is based upon a number of sources, but three are of particular significance: first, of course, the scattered discussions in *The Birth of Tragedy*; secondly, a preparatory sketch for that book entitled 'The Dionysiac World-View'; and finally, a famous fragment from 1873 called 'On Truth and Lies in an Extra-Moral Sense'. All three of these are conveniently collected in the Cambridge edition. Only the first, however, is an authorized publication of Nietzsche's. The others are sketches or abandoned projects. So, we need to be careful not to ascribe too much significance to something Nietzsche might have been merely trying out.[71]

Here in this section, Nietzsche combines the discussion of metaphor with a broadside rebuke of modern poetry. We complicated, abstract-minded and generally talentless moderns have lost the faculty of appropriately contemplating an 'original aesthetic phenomenon' when we see one. Two of *The Birth of Tragedy*'s aims are to construct a theory of symbolization, together with a theory of what it means to be able to 'see' aesthetically. Nietzsche writes, 'for the genuine poet metaphor is no rhetorical figure, but an image which takes the place of something else, something he can really see before him as a substitute for a concept.' Metaphor is not essentially a phenomenon of language (a rhetorical figure) nor of thought ('substitute for a concept'). Metaphor, which we will take here as a species of symbolization, raises the act of language to the level of a symbol which 'makes present' ('he can really see before him'). Importantly, Nietzsche is speaking of both Apolline (he mentions Homer) and Dionysiac as well as tragic (the next paragraph turns to the tragic chorus) poetic effects. Thus, all three types of symbolization (see **Section 2**) are under discussion here. Poetry overcomes, at least to this extent and in this way, the limits of language, which is to merely represent, and perhaps only represent, something that is already abstract – that is, already *dead*, for we should not miss the repeated use of the word 'live' and its cognates in this paragraph. To be sure, even poetry is not in itself music, but with the aid of musicality and under 'strain' (see **Section 6**) it can attain symbolization.

The central thrust of Nietzsche's account of language and perception is in the realization, and this is only seemingly paradoxical, that the rationality of systematic philosophy and the reasoning of mathematics and formal logic lead us *away* from insight into the nature of things, and not towards it. In the great rational systems of modern Western philosophy a hardening of linguistic (and conceptual) expression has occurred, so that ideas and methods have become disconnected from the forces of life – while in 'ordinary' life a parallel deadening has occurred (thus the observations about modern poets and modern dreams). Modern thought systems bear no resemblance to the insights of the pre-Socratics and to what originally inspired the 'dithyrambic dramatists' of the early Greek musical culture. In 'On Truth and Lies', Nietzsche supposes a hierarchy of forms of human expression in terms of their proximity to a direct sensory stimulation of the body (movements of the will towards satisfaction or realization). This hierarchy ascends from the prelinguistic 'nervous stimulation', through immediate metaphors (images) that retain a vital connection to perception partly because we are aware of them as metaphors, and then to the solidified and abstract language of 'positive' science and 'systematic' philosophy. Each stage is a higher objectification of the will (in Schopenhauerian language), but also a loss of connection to the body, nature and to existence. Each stage is also a 'creative' or 'artistic' achievement of semblance. These stages can be broadly identified with the Dionysian, Apollonian and Socratic. The last, highly civilized forms are furthest removed from the authentic expression – the latter Nietzsche, not surprisingly, finds preserved only in music. Section 4 of 'The Dionysiac World-View' tells a similar story, although it is expressed in more orthodox Schopenhauerian language of will and feeling. After music, poetry belongs to a relatively early stage in the process of the subjective appropriation of the movements of the will. 'Free' poetic expression precedes the stage of linguistic hardening of statements of philosophical truths. In poetry the metaphor or symbol reconnects with sensations, with the basic physiological stirrings of the sensitive body, reactivating the original metaphor that led away from them.

In late cultural products, the outside world has turned into colourless shadows expressed in a language of 'metaphors which have become worn by frequent use and have lost all sensuous vigour, coins which, having lost their stamp, are now regarded as metal and no longer as coins' (p. 146).[72] In our modern scientific age we no longer possess the ability of existing at the level of sensual perception. Instead we are adhering to

the obligation to be truthful which society imposes in order to exist, i.e. the obligation to use the customary metaphors, or to put it in moral terms, the obligation to lie in accordance with firmly established convention. (p. 146)

Nietzsche concedes in *On Truth and Lying* that it is human nature to turn sensuous impressions into metaphors and metaphors into an abstract grammar that orders the world. Such abstraction makes something possible that could 'never be achieved in the realm of those sensuous first impressions, namely the construction of a pyramidal order based on castes and degrees, the creation of a new world of laws, privileges, subordinations, definitions of borders' (p. 146). The problem starts when our abstractions turn into substitutes for or denials of life – as in the scientific 'optimism' of Socratic culture. Our systems turn into something so artificial and at the same time so powerful that they not only get in the way of, but also deny either the possibility of or even the value of a genuine experience of the world via sensuous perception. 'Touched by that cool breath', we forget that

concepts too, which are as bony and eight-cornered as a dice and just as capable of being shifted around, are only the leftover residue of a metaphor, and that the illusion produced by the artistic translation of a nervous stimulus into images is, if not the mother, then at least the grandmother of each and every concept. (p. 147)

Modern poetry, Nietzsche claims, operates entirely at the level of language and concepts, having somehow lost the ability to transform language into symbolic image so that poet and reader are 'surrounded by crowds of spirits'. We are not Apolline poets, we are incapable of being as 'vivid' as Homer; the situation is still more hopeless with respect to the Dionysiac. There is no longer the capacity to relate to a 'primal artistic phenomenon', of which the tragic chorus is an example. The chorus, in its projection of the vision, and in its condition of viewing itself as 'surrounded by spirits', generates the 'artistic gift' of the poet. The true poet sees himself surrounded by figures, not merely thinking them through concepts, but envisaging them through metaphor or symbol. The Dionysiac chorus is poetic in this sense, one that is shared with Apolline poetry. However, the chorus member does not merely contemplate the external image, but is also himself transformed and projected in becoming the chorus. As the phenomenon of Greek tragedy develops historically, this vision is reinforced by the use of increasing numbers of masked actors upon the stage – which is located behind the chorus, as if it were the vision of the chorus – who portray the 'action'.

* * *

Returning to **Section 8** of *The Birth of Tragedy*, **paragraph 4** gives a fuller account of the specific poetic from of choral musical speech, the 'dramatic dithyramb'. The dithyrambic dramatist differs from the Homeric rhapsode by entering right inside the world of the imagery he presents, 'as if one had really entered another body'. The rhapsode does not merge with the images he presents, but remains outside of them. This explains the intoxicating impact of dithyrambic performance: 'this phenomenon occurs as an epidemic: an entire crowd feels itself magically transformed like this.' Thus, in this state of Dionysian ecstasy a community is created of unconscious, or perhaps better: preconscious actors. This passage from *The Birth of Tragedy* has gone straight into Antonin Artaud's *Theatre of Cruelty*,[73] a seminal text on modernist theatre, which aims at resurrecting the preconscious ecstatic community of actors and spectators on the modernist stage.

Paragraph 5 leads us back to thinking of early Greek theatre in terms of the presence of both of the art-drives. It combines the Dionysian principle of 'enchantment' with that of Apollonian 'vision', or epiphany, with the transformation from one to the other occurring in the mythic 'middle world' of the satyr. This paves the way for a discussion**, in paragraph 6**, of theatrical stage activity as a metaphor, namely, as Apolline symbolization of Dionysian experience. Nietzsche has come back to this specific type of benevolent cooperation between the drives and the equivalent (third) type of symbolization that involves them both. The

last two paragraphs take us back to tragedy in the narrower sense of the word. Whilst the ur-drama presents itself as a vision of the satyr chorus that depicts the sufferings of the god Dionysus (**paragraph 7**), later more fully evolved tragedy adds another layer of artistic planning, or perhaps consciousness: it becomes the 'representation' (*Darstellung*[74]) of the original vision. The 'tragic hero' enters the scene. The sufferings of Dionysus are now symbolized in the fate of this individualized representative.

The chorus was considered enormously important (despite being made up of 'lowly, serving creatures') even with respect to the 'action' on stage. In this 'enchantment' the chorus member 'sees himself as a satyr' – that is, he loses his civic identity, his cultural existence is 'overrun' by the Dionysiac, and he becomes the *Urbild*. The satyr is wise insofar as he speaks from nature. Moreover, 'as a satyr he in turn sees the god'. The ideal perfection of his state is projected as an Apolline image *upon the stage*. (Recall that the projection of the Olympian gods as idealized and justifying possibilities of the human is a key function of the Apolline.) The chorus must be made up of serving creatures because its function is to serve its master, Dionysus, by creating the vision and watching the suffering. The wise satyr is also the 'fool' because he is a symbol of the impulses of nature, 'untouched by knowledge' and always the mere servant of the god. 'With this new vision the drama is complete.'

A key metaphor Nietzsche employs in this passage is that of illness. The enchantment 'infects' the audience, indeed causes an 'epidemic' (since the Dionysiac vision is a *mass* phenomenon). Moreover, in Nietzsche, the vision itself is described as 'trembling', as if hallucinated in a fever. In accordance with this metaphor, although the vision is Apolline – 'clearer, more comprehensible' – it is also at the same time more 'shadow-like' (this latter image also anticipates the playful account of Plato's allegory of the cave in the next section). And, again, although the poetic form employed by the actors is Apolline, it is only '*almost* in the language of Homer' (our emphasis), 'almost' because this is not Apolline symbolization independent of Dionysian impulses, but an Apolline language of symbolic dream-images in the form of the dramatic dithyramb which has willingly taken on the task of the Dionysiac.

SECTION 9

The Double Meaning of Sophoclean and Aeschylean Tragedy

Nietzsche has so far used more than one third of the full text of *The Birth of Tragedy* for isolating tragedy's conditions and elements in analytical and historical order before he finally touches upon the 'mature' form. We can see in this procedure an application of a Kantian critical principle in the area of cultural and historical anthropology: Nietzsche asks what the *anthropological* and *historical conditions* are that made tragedy *possible*, indeed which makes it in a certain sense *necessary*. Even now, Nietzsche does not present us in this section with an integrated picture of tragedy as a rounded or completed from, but rather as a form continually in development. This process-oriented approach to art and culture is the key feature of Nietzsche's burgeoning genealogical methodology. It investigates a subject matter by means of analytically isolating its ingredient elements and then maps their changes in meaning, form and value as they evolve in combinations with various other elements.

Tragedy has now, however, grown beyond the stage of anonymous collective utterance. It has achieved the status of documented literary text, associated with names of specific tragic artists and centred on the portrayal of a symbolic individuality, a 'hero' whose downfall creates the tragic transfiguration. In reverse historical order, Nietzsche highlights the work of two Athenian tragedians, first Sophocles, then Aeschylus. But, as we saw above in our discussion of **Sections 1** and **2**, 'Sophocles' and 'Aeschylus' are still merely names for particular instruments by which the Apolline cultural force satisfies its creative drive in serving his Dionysiac partner drive. Sophocles writes a play, and may even be conscious of the meaning or message he believes his play to have (although, of course, the idea that a literary work has a 'meaning' or 'message' in the sense of which we think of this today, might be an anachronism). However, whatever this conscious meaning is (at least in its broad outlines), and especially the *necessity* Sophocles felt to give the myth *this type of meaning*, are part of the drives operating through individual vessels in Greek culture. Nietzsche looks at three seminal tragedies: Sophocles' *Oedipus at Colonus, Oedipus the King*, and Aeschylus' *Prometheus*.

Section 9 is among the book's richest. The section is built around two comparisons. First, a contrast is set up between the Apolline interpretation of a tragedy, and its underlying Dionysiac meaning rooted in myth; secondly, a comparison between two spheres of meaning within the 'classical' tragedies of Sophocles and Aeschylus, centred on the figure of Oedipus (in two of Sophocles' plays, *Oedipus the King* and *Oedipus at Colonus*) and of Prometheus in Aeschylus' *Prometheus*. But Nietzsche is not content with just that level of complexity. The section also contains – and not incidentally but centrally – references to Plato, Christ, Goethe, justice, and criminality. Moreover, there are at least four other comparisons in this text which, as we know by now, is thriving on the play of interconnected 'opposites'. These are at least partially coordinated with each other: the feminine and masculine, Olympians and Titans, the nature of sainthood and artists, and the Semitic and Aryan cultural traditions.

The focus is less on the nature of art (or of the artist) as narrowly conceived than on the *meaning* of specific art works. There are two significant comments that should be made already. First, this discussion reinforces the idea that for Nietzsche art comprises the whole cultural system on production and consumption. For example, as we saw in the last section, spectators are not separate from the work, (this will be further reinforced in **Section 22**) they form an essential part of it. Secondly, the meaning of the work is not some message consciously placed in it by the artist (although it might *also* be that). For Nietzsche, the manner in which the particular work serves to bring out the significance of the *original* mythic structure, either in itself or for the culture, is what should be called the meaning of the work. This meaning is a historically specific variation on the basic metaphysical meaning of the underlying drives. The meaning in turn is brought out by interpretation. Interpretation, therefore, is more an act of cultural history than attention to this or that specific work in itself.

An implied critical thrust of this section is the refutation of Winckelmannian notions of Greek serenity which have influenced generations of European literary, artistic and philosophical classicists far into the nineteenth century. Nietzsche's conception of high Greek literary and plastic culture as serene sublimation of raw primeval energy is influenced by Hölderlin, the only one of the German classicists to highlight the dualism of dark mythological underground and light surface imagery of Greek cultural forms (see our discussion **Section 3, Note: Nietzsche, German 'Hellenism', and Hölderlin**). The basis of Greek serenity is pain, sublimated and transfigured. In the dialogue of characters, which Nietzsche calls 'the Apolline part of Greek tragedy', the Greek disposition to serenity shows itself. 'The language of Sophocles's heroes surprises us by its Apolline definiteness and clarity'. Behind this image of light (*Lichtbild*), 'projected on to a dark wall' (yet another allusion to Plato, but it also seems possible to see an allusion to photographic image projection), we go deeper into the myth 'which projects itself in these bright reflections'. Thus, Dionysiac myth is represented as its Apolline sublimation in the individualizing interpretative treatment of the tragic artist.

Paragraphs 2 and **3** are Nietzsche's comparative readings of the Oedipus and Prometheus myths in the treatment they receive in Sophocles' and Aeschylus' tragedies. In essence, Nietzsche reads tragedy, in the texts of this temporary and unstable 'classic' period, as allegorical interpretations of myths, or to put it in his own terminology: as Apolline symbolizations of Dionysiac experience. But the symbolization can be read in two ways: in tragedy, myth is speaking its Dionysiac wisdom, even if the explicit 'message' of the play is an Apolline shield. We can think of tragedy as the transparent Apolline top layer of meaning (we will call it the Apolline interpretation) built upon two Dionysian layers below that only become present on the surface through the magic of symbol. Deepest down is the experience of the *Ureine* which has no equivalent in any form of linguistic or visual representation, followed by tragic myth, the (historically) first medium for processing the Ur-experience. Tragic myth tells the story of the confrontation of man with primeval nature. 'Modern' Greek tragedy works as an allegory in that it feeds off the underlying layer of tragic myth by at the same time hiding it within its surface symbolism. The tragic myth could never have been explicit in the play, since the play exists precisely to bring us in proximity to, but also shield us from, it. Nietzsche explicates the relation between the two meanings by a playful use of Plato's allegories of the sun and the cave. Here, light appears as the illusion, hiding from us (or indeed healing us of – recall the infection metaphor of the previous section) the true darkness.

The figure provided tries to correlate the various contrasts Nietzsche makes in this section.

The Apolline interpretation of the Oedipus myth observes his suffering through the unravelling of the 'knot' that is his fate, and watching the plot's 'dialectical solution' is, as Aristotle also appreciated, one of the great thrills of the theatre. But the gods have a 'matching piece of divine dialectic', whereby the same plot that was the undoing of Oedipus (in the first play: *Oedipus the King*) is achieving a broader and higher end (in the next play, *Oedipus in Colonus*) that will last long after Oedipus' death. The passivity of Oedipus' suffering (the etymological meaning of 'passion') is shown to be the highest activity. Clearly, Nietzsche sees Sophocles' Oedipus in some relation to Christ, or at least to the idea of 'sainthood', as is made clear in **paragraph 3**. We encounter more implied references to Jesus and Christianity in the second half of the book (cf. **Section 13**) in connection with Socrates and Plato. Thus, Nietzsche's genealogical programme already contains, still in brackets at this early stage, the project of delineating the descent of the idea of Christianity from its sources in classical antiquity.

Underlying this surface, though, is the Dionysiac meaning of the Oedipus myth: Nature is incommensurable with humanity and 'wisdom is an offence against nature'. The Apolline beauty of the unravelling plot, and the serenity evoked by that beauty, serves to mask not only the hideousness of Oedipus' crimes, but also the fact that they are consequences of his wisdom. Wisdom is only to be had at the cost of 'some enormous offence against nature', and, moreover, a natural consequence of that cost is the 'dissolution' of the wise person. This notion is by now familiar to us. These types of tragedies therefore point in their Apollonian forms of representation to the Dionysian depth of being, the real subject matter of tragic myths, of which the tragedies are symbolic readings. 'The poet's whole interpretation of the story is nothing other than one of those images of light held out to us by healing nature after we have gazed into the abyss.' In fact, Nietzsche detects a very poignant rebuke of wisdom and knowledge in the essence of what he identifies as the tragic in the Oedipus tragedies. No wonder then that Socrates and Plato eyed tragedy suspiciously. In Nietzsche's reading the Oedipus myth culminates in the tragic realization that 'whoever plunges nature into the abyss of destruction by what he knows must in turn experience the dissolution of nature in his own person.' This is of importance for an understanding of Nietzsche's critique of modern knowledge after Socrates' arrival. Modern scientific man has systematically misinterpreted nature so as to prevent exposure to Dionysian experience of being, or even to recognize the *Schein/ Sein* distinction as anything other than a distinction between false and true; he has lost the ability to realize that 'wisdom is an offence against nature'. The rebirth of tragedy will re-establish that direct link between *Sein* and *Schein*, and put the artist back in his place as the only true mediator between the two.

As with the Oedipus plays, so there are two different meanings to be found in *Prometheus*. In **paragraph 3** Nietzsche moves to an interpretation of Aeschylus, using Goethe's 1774 *Sturm und Drang* poem (fragment of a never completed drama) of the same story as a clue. The Apolline interpretation (though notice that Nietzsche does not so clearly identify it as such in this case: indeed, he senses an 'un-Apolline quality' of Aeschylus 'pessimistic view of things') begins with Prometheus, the titan, defying the gods to create a race of humans who command fire and who can then likewise defy the gods. Subject to eternal justice, Prometheus must suffer eternally for his crimes, but this price is accepted. Compared to Oedipus the saint-like ascetic, Prometheus is the prototype of the artist, with the typical character features of relentless creativity and 'bitter pride'. This interpretation shows itself to be broadly Apolline insofar as Apollo is the god of 'individuation and of the boundaries of justice'. As before, however, the meaning that may have been conscious to Aeschylus does not reach the Dionysiac depths of the myth represented in this tragedy. To further study these depths, Nietzsche uses a contrast between the 'Aryan' myth of Prometheus and the 'Semitic' myth of the Fall, thus pursuing his side-project of a genealogy of Christianity by demonstrating the descent of a Christian form of mythology from primeval models.

Now, given the appropriation of Nietzsche's name by fascist anti-semitism in the twentieth century, readers often become uncomfortable at such passages. It is worth pointing out, first, that even as late as the 1870s, the primary usage of the concept 'Aryan' is as an anthropological category in wide usage across European universities; it was only beginning to acquire the nationalist baggage it would have later. Note also that Nietzsche compares the relationship between the two types to that between 'brother and sister', thus demonstrating that rather than following a line of racial segregation he is interested in relation and interdependence. Finally, the racial denomination of difference is in fact an account of the metaphysical meaning of *gender roles*. The racially based analysis does not go away in his later work (how could it, given Nietzsche's basic thesis that cultural life is rooted, at least in part, in physiology), but it does become more nuanced and balanced.[75] Such observations are of real importance for a serious assessment of the link between Nietzsche and Fascism, both Italian and German.

Nietzsche demonstrates how the original myth of the Fall changes and acquires the ethical features in the Old Testament that makes it foundational for the Christian movement. The Dionysiac interpretation of the Promethean myth sees fire as the essential possession of a rising culture, but also sees its possession as a theft from the divine. Man and god are in conflict; their worlds are individuated; this is the 'contradiction hidden within the heart of things'. The Promethean heroic impulse is to 'reach out towards the general', to take single beings on its back like Atlas and to cross these boundaries (to steal fire). The hero must accept the punishment of this hidden contradiction. It is, Nietzsche says, the essential activity and the dignity of the theft (both of which he terms 'masculine') that contrasts with the myth of the Fall. In the former, sin is a virtue; in the latter, the crime (the transgression of Adam and Eve) is something to which one is seduced and is undignified; it is something 'feminine'. In fact, the subtext is clear here of *The Birth of Tragedy* as a critique of Judeo-Christian morality as life denying: Prometheus as Dionysian representative is pitched ultimately against Jesus. Thus, Prometheus is a 'rather un-Apolline' symbolization of a tragic Dionysus myth, and in Aeschylus' tragedy, the figure of Prometheus is a 'Dionysiac mask' (p. 51) of the god.

SECTION 10

The Revival of Myth in Tragedy as its Death Throes: The End of the Mythological Age and the Dawning Age of Logic

Section 9 introduced the notion of the mask. Despite an ever-increasing presence of Apollo, who makes himself felt in the tightly woven network of surface symbolism and the focus on the symbolism of the individual tragic hero or heroine, the sufferings of Dionysus are the true subject matter of all Greek tragedy. This is true right from its earliest origins to its highest forms (at which point it is already beginning 'to turn in on itself'). In the accomplished tragedies of the Athenian period Dionysus hides behind a mask of heroic individuality. Here he is present not, of course, as an individual being behind the mask of an individual, but rather as the mythic emblem of insight into the *Ureine*. Thus the god, already strangely 'ideal' or 'universal', a de-individuated being, lies behind a variety of masks. Notice that Nietzsche turns to Platonist vocabulary to express the notion that the one manifests itself in a multiplicity of subordinate forms, an 'effect of Apollo, the interpreter of dreams, who interprets to the chorus its Dionysiac condition by means of this symbolic appearance'.

The passage that follows explicates all too briefly Nietzsche's interpretation of the various myths of Dionysus, focusing especially on two aspects. First, the late myth of him being torn apart and then remade, which Nietzsche sees as both the painful rending from the One that happens in individuation, and then also the promise of a return. Secondly, the double nature of the god, both cruel and gentle, which reflects the double-sidedness of Dionysiac wisdom, depending upon whether one views the principle of the *Ureine* as the individual submerged and destroyed or as the joyful and loving reunion with the ground of nature. In both of these aspects of the myth, doubleness promises a 'third Dionysus' that could be realized only in and as *art*, in the brief but all-important phenomenon of tragedy. The destruction of the symbolic heroic individual is both terrible and promising because it releases the temporary vision of a homecoming of humanity returning into the bosom of nature.

In **paragraph 2,** Nietzsche introduces an additional complexity in the mythically staged conflict between the Dionysian levels of the titans (the first gods, for example Prometheus) and the broadly Apolline level of the Olympians (descendants of the titans who defeated those earlier gods). The victory of the latter, Nietzsche had claimed, was the basis of the Homeric epic (**Section 3**). In a circular movement, the titans now rise again. That is, the drive and metaphysical meaning of Prometheus/Dionysus becomes operative in Greek culture, especially as tragedy. But they rise again not to form new myths – Dionysiac truth is 'always under the old cloak of myth' – but through the power of music to reinterpret these myths, giving them new meanings. Any given mythic image is always only one of many possible with respect to the insight of music – thus we can say here what Nietzsche does not: it is the function of music to reinterpret Dionysiacally. Significantly, Nietzsche sees this reinterpretation not as an appropriation of the past such that the new meanings are anachronistic; rather he sees it as a restoration of myth's living *youth*. The titans arise again, at least in Apolline symbolic form, because the historical culture that thrived on the Homeric epic and Olympian myths had become exhausted.

One condition of tragedy is that myth had previously been in its death throes. In tragedy myth gets a new lease of life, but overall is dying, and the decline of tragedy as an artistic form marks the true end of the age of myth. The significance of this idea cannot be over-estimated. This circular or reverse movement of historical succession is an important theme throughout the book: for, as we shall see, starting in **Section 15**, it is precisely the exhaustion of modern culture that Nietzsche believes or hopes will bring about a rebirth of tragedy as a first step to start the cycle in the other direction. What is meant by myth having become exhausted here? Nietzsche describes it as the point when the mythic presuppositions of a religion become dogmatically systematized as a completed set of historical events. The middle world of symbolic myths or idealized human possibilities is flattened, so to speak, so that it is represented as being on the same level of existence as human events. The tendency then is to see such myths as merely in the past and without 'living' significance. Moreover, the tendency is to see them as even originally without transcendent meaning; this Nietzsche has already defined as the 'pathological' failure to grasp appearance as appearance. Even Aristotle thought that history (in that sense of a record of events) must be less insightful than poetic narrative.[76] '[T]his is usually how religions die [. . .] when the feeling for myth dies'. This discussion represents the beginning of Nietzsche's treatment of what he calls Socratism. We should also note that Nietzsche returns to the nature of myth in much greater depth in the corresponding sections towards the end of the book.

Euripides (the topic of **paragraph 3**), the third in the sequence of great tragic playwrights of ancient Greece, tried to force this dying figure (myth) to do 'slave's work . . . once more'. Nietzsche identifies 'wicked' Euripides as the epicentre of the death of tragedy. The 'once more', however, is very significant. Myth and religion – the life of Greek culture – was already doomed and dying when tragedy first arrived, and the cultural force that had been the Apolline art of Homeric epic was already yielding to something new. Tragedy delayed the inevitable for a brief moment, and even made of the situation something extraordinary; but then Euripides finished it off. Accordingly, by 'deserting' Dionysus, Euripides is also deserted by Apollo. The next two sections of the book will explain what Nietzsche means by a 'copied, masked' myth or music, as well as detailing this exhaustion of Homeric culture and specifically how it manifested itself in the period of Euripides.

SECTION 11

Euripides as Critic rather than Poet

Section 11 investigates the conditions that led to the 'death' of Attic Tragedy. Nietzsche claims that in comparison to the other arts of the Greek culture period which 'died serene and natural deaths at advanced ages', tragedy 'died by suicide' owing to an 'insoluble conflict'. Nietzsche does not explicitly name this inner conflict here, but he means two things. First, 'suicide' because the chief instrument of its death was the foremost practitioner in the later classic period, Euripides. Secondly, 'insoluble conflict' because tragedy is founded upon the struggle of the art-drives, not their unity, and this made the phenomena of tragedy vulnerable to misunderstanding (see the 'incommensurable' in **paragraph 7**).

From **paragraph 2** onwards Nietzsche looks back on the end of the great period of Greek tragedy from the point of view of the 'New Attic Comedy', a later dramatic tradition or movement that Nietzsche considers degenerate, and which, importantly, saw Euripides as its hero. The key feature of New Attic Comedy (and for that matter of Euripides), is its naturalism. The clearest evidence for this trait is Euripides's endeavour at bringing the spectator onto the stage (which is a metaphorical way of saying that characters in the drama talk and act realistically, like real individuals). The preconscious unity in pre-Attic drama between actors and spectators (cf. **Section 7**) is being destroyed in the conscious effort to make the spectators 'participate' as real empirical individuals. Curiously, this naturalism was not simply a mirror image of life, but in fact an ideal or normative image. Euripides was teaching his audience how to speak and think, he was transforming the audience through education **(paragraph 3)**. So, as Nietzsche remarks only a page later **(paragraph 4)**, there is something contemptuous in Euripides treatment of his audience: he saw them as needing education in order to be proper, real human beings.[77] A certain conception of the purpose and effect of proper oratory – enabling 'slyness and cunning' – becomes the dominant virtue celebrated in this drama. Neither drama nor its audiences were able to conceive of any weightier concerns than the present. We have seen in Section 10 how Nietzsche discusses the reduction of religious myth to history. Myth bears upon the present in no other way than as the past; no longer as the 'immortal'. The 'ideal' past and future of tragedy, its universality and its profound glimpse into metaphysical truths, are absent. Accordingly, Nietzsche agrees with early Christian critics who saw such a 'cheerful' drama – and by extension such a culture – as shallow and 'womanish'. However, these critics' broadly accurate characterization of *later* Greek culture was inappropriately extended so as to also cover the *earlier* period (the period of tragedy, the Mysteries of Dionysus and so forth). This resulted in a centuries-long denigration, or at least profound misunderstanding, of Greece as a culture built on straightforward cheerfulness and serenity. The eighteenth- and nineteenth-century classicist misunderstanding of the Greek culture period originates here: it is the tail end of the Platonic and Christian misunderstanding of tragedy.

In order to understand Euripides' odd contempt for his audience, Nietzsche engages in a fanciful reconstruction (in **paragraphs 5** and **6**) of the dramatist's intellectual biography. This is a pretty common Nietzschean device in later work, but here is the first time we have seen a sustained example in *The Birth of Tragedy*. (Socrates will receive similar attention in **Section 13**.) Euripides feels superior to the great mass of the public, but not to two spectators in particular. The first is Euripides himself **(paragraph 7)**, but not as a poet, rather precisely as a thinking spectator or *critic*. Euripides is thus a poet in name only – he uses literary forms and language, and perhaps even uses them very well, but the result is not artistic in the sense Nietzsche has been developing. Nietzsche avoids naming the second spectator for some time, in a playful attempt to create suspense. (This too is a common device in his writing; notice also that it is precisely suspense that Euripides tries to *eliminate* in these tragedies.) Nietzsche imagines Euripides the critic being entirely unable to understand the work of Aeschylus or Sophocles. He saw something 'incommensurable' (which Nietzsche has identified as the tension of the Apolline and Dionysiac) in these tragedies, as if otherwise clear figures 'trailed a comet's tail' which points towards darkness (indeed, it points towards the Dionysiac).[78] Nor could Euripides understand (1) the antiquated role of the chorus in the overall structure, (2) the 'dubious' resolution of ethical or political problems and (3) the 'pomp' of the language. The chorus Nietzsche has explained to us as a vestige of earlier forms, but one that is the essential core of the nature of the tragic; the ethical or political problems take us back to the notions of justice operative in the interpretations and meanings of myth which Nietzsche outlines in **Section 9**; finally, the 'pomp' of the language has to do with the non-naturalistic de-individualized hero, Dionysus wearing a mask (**Section 10**). Euripides was discomfited, Nietzsche imagines, neither able to understand these plays' features, nor receive from anyone else a satisfactory rationale for them. Until, that is, he found another spectator who agreed with him.

SECTION 12

The Misunderstanding and Repression of the Art-Drives

Into **Section 12**, Nietzsche coyly still refuses to reveal the other spectator, and instead reviews the 'incommensurable' essence of tragedy which so confused Euripides. Without an understanding of the Apolline and Dionysiac as mythically coded artistic forces that were coessential in tragedy, tragedy would have then indeed seemed a jumble of disparate forms, and lacking a coherent view of the world. Buoyed by the other spectator, Euripides undertakes to put in its place a new tragedy that conveys a fully 'coherent' and non-Dionysiac conception of art, morality and reality. Again, though, Nietzsche chooses to examine this change in **paragraph 2** from a later point of view; in this case, the point of view of Euripides' *Bacchae*, written at the end of his career. The play concerns the disastrous consequences that ensue when the whole of Thebes does not welcome the arrival of Dionysus. Nietzsche reads this as a late confession by Euripides that his non-Dionysiac conception of tragedy was a mistake, perhaps realizing that he himself had been merely a mask, not of Dionysus nor Apollo but of 'an altogether newborn daemon called *Socrates*'. This realization was too late – tragically so, since it is a convention of tragedy that the hero or heroine comes in agony and horror to a realization of his or her fate.

For the earlier Euripides, then, the key struggle is Dionysus versus Socrates. In this slightly odd way, the figure of the philosopher Socrates arrives on the scene in **paragraphs 3** and **4**. Euripides is imagined above all as a Socratic thinker. Indeed, a few pages later towards the end of **paragraph 6**, the 'other spectator' who agrees with Euripides' confusion with earlier tragedy and who supplies the new, non-Dionysiac conceptions upon which the new tragedy will be based, turns out to have been Socrates.

In **paragraph 3**, Nietzsche returns to Apolline, Homeric epic, in order to contrast it with Euripides' new 'tragedy'. As we have seen, one of its key features is the delight in and release through semblance; the poet and also the actor remain calm and distant from the images, not identifying with or entering them, even when they are terrifying or emotionally charged. In Euripidean tragedy, however, the poet and actor both merge with what is portrayed. They do not see it as semblance, but feel it directly and in themselves as affect. This is decidedly not Apolline; but the new tragedy is to be non-Dionysiac also. How then is it to have any effect upon the audience – that is, with what 'stimulants' is it to work? First, through thoughts, the coolness of which might resemble Apolline images, but are otherwise entirely different. Secondly, through emotional affects, which again might resemble Dionysiac 'ecstasies' but are felt by individuals *as* individuals rather than as the dissolution of the individual into the *Ureine*. Because their ideal is immediate realism (or naturalism), neither of these 'stimulants', Nietzsche stresses, are in any way genuinely artistic. The new tragedy, then, takes as its principle that 'in order to be beautiful, everything must be reasonable'; this is an aesthetic manifestation of the basic Socratic principle that virtue is tied to knowledge. In both the aesthetic and the ethical domains, these are powerful new ideas. Nietzsche, however, can barely disguise his feeling that they represent a newly arisen drive, the operative metaphysical principle of which is deluded.

The key features of Euripidean tragedy stem from the Socratic requirement of reasonableness or coherence, and are devised to serve the new poetic devices (thought and affect) that have replaced the modes of realization typical of artistic drives of the Apolline and Dionysiac. Of these features, we have already seen the new 'realistic' language, character types and plots revolving around cunning 'games of chess'. In addition, Nietzsche now discusses the necessity of supplying a prologue, preferably in the mouth of a reliable source like a god, so the audience would not be so busy working out the plot that they missed the pathos (again, the emphasis is on the emotion of the immediate present). Likewise, the endings have to have a similar definiteness, to remove ambiguity about character's fate or the significance of the action. Clearly, Nietzsche is uninterested in a detailed analysis of the structure and style of Euripides' new tragedy. He is much more concerned with what these changes mean, for Euripides and Socrates as individuals, but more importantly as exemplars of a new (and dangerous) system of cultural forces that (expressed as metaphysical principles) involve a distinct way of understanding the nature of knowledge, reality and art. An analysis of this new system of cultural forces occupies the **next few sections** of the book.

Section 12 ends with the identification of Socrates as the other spectator, and with a discussion of *consciousness*. Euripides, Nietzsche imagines, sees his superiority over earlier tragedians in that everything is done consciously or deliberately (instead of instinctively or by allowing the preconscious drives to act through him), where this means also that all the elements of the tragedy have that quality of reasonableness. It is as if he is the first sober artist in a tradition of drunks. The dominance of reason in the ordered mind is the basic principle of both the good (in Socrates) and of the beautiful (in the 'aesthetic Socratism' of Euripides). From this idea of reason and reasonableness, Nietzsche increasingly stresses 'logic' and 'dialectics' in the later discussions of Socrates, having used these terms sparingly thus far. (*Logos* means not only reason but also language insofar as it is imbued with knowledge or truth.) Socrates causes Dionysus to flee. That is, the drive or 'daemon' of thought and action represented by Socrates represses the Dionysiac drive, only allowing it to appear in an attenuated form as mere affect, or to realize itself partially in a widely distributed set of marginalized cults. With it, too, the Apolline is repressed, its place taken by logic, thought, consciousness, and reasonableness, its full expression and metaphysical significance nowhere permitted.

SECTION 13

Socrates – The Axis of Cultural History

Section 13 stands out. Numerically, it is the exact centre of the book, and in the representative figure of Socrates, the Greek and the modern half of *The Birth of Tragedy* is joined together. To Nietzsche the emergence of Socrates marks the moment of changeover in Western history from classical antiquity to modernity. Nietzsche's role as critic changes now from that of classical philologist of the first half, who led us onto the high plateau of the Greek period, to cultural critic of modernity, who presents to us a new age of deficiency and crisis. This section focuses on Socrates, and, at the very end of the section, the revulsion Nietzsche shows for Socrates and what he calls the 'Socratic tendency' is shot through with astonishment, even admiration, for the 'daemonic force' of this one man trying to understand the world solely by means of abstract concepts and logical ordering. In Plato, the life-denying disease of abstract logic of the Socratic tendency catches on and spreads.

Nietzsche claims, in **paragraph 1**, that initially the modern 'tendencies of Socrates and Euripides were closely related'. We learn of the personal affinity of these two representative figures. Socrates as 'an opponent of the tragic art' here made an exception and 'would only join the spectators when a new play by Euripides was being performed'. From Aristophanes comedy *The Clouds* can be gleaned that the cultural conservatives of the time, 'the supporters of the "good old days"', '. . . would mention both names in one breath'. These two are high on the list of 'seducers of the people': at the end of the section Nietzsche calls Socrates 'the true eroticist', a kind of Don Juan, of knowledge, compulsively driven for more, who leaves the 'lovers' in the *Symposium* (a dialogue precisely about the nature of love) asleep, striding out ready for the next conquest. These two bring about a progressive physical and spiritual atrophy in the name of a 'dubious enlightenment'. The contrast is being set up here, broadly speaking, between a modern attitude of life-denying knowledge and life lived according to its organic nature – a *leitmotif* in all of Nietzsche's work. Nietzsche uses the term 'Enlightenment' [*Aufklärung*)] here pejoratively: to Nietzsche, Socrates is the first major representative of this movement, often more narrowly associated only with European thought of the seventeenth and eighteenth centuries.[79] The modern-minded contemporary spectators of *The Clouds*, however, 'could not get over their surprise that Socrates should figure in Aristophanes' plays as the first and leading Sophist'. 'The Sophists' is a collective name for a certain kind of teacher in ancient Greece. The term becomes pejorative later, partly because of Plato, who uses it as a term of abuse, directed against these often well-paid teachers in Greece who he accused of professing wisdom while actually merely employing rhetorical and logical tricks to bamboozle their students. Thus the 'surprise': Aristophanes suggests (and Nietzsche approves) that Socrates' opposition to the Sophists is ironic and itself a mere ploy.

A pronouncement of the Delphian oracle shows the importance of Socrates in his time for Nietzsche. It also permits him to release the name of Sophocles into the ring once more. Sophocles is ranked in the oracle's pronouncement in position three in a hierarchy of wise men (Nietzsche calls them the 'knowing ones'). The mention of Sophocles in this context makes explicit what Nietzsche only implies in **Section 9**, namely, that with Sophocles the height of perfection of tragedy already coincides with the beginning of its downfall. Thus, as Nietzsche says at the beginning of **Section 11**, tragedy died of suicide. Sophocles is already consciously *aware* of the use of the artistic means at his disposal, and he deliberately uses them. Consciousness that shows, for example, in the dramatization of ethical or political issues, or in the form of stagecraft (e.g. in a clearly outlined dramaturgy for the chorus), undermines tragic art. This reaches its point of culmination in Euripides' dramatic engineering. Nietzsche uses the Latin technical term *deus ex machina* (god from the machine). This refers both to the use of behind-the-scenes machinery as part of productions, and also to the manner in which Euripides' plots and especially their resolutions are 'authorized' by some divine presence. With Sophocles, a knowledge-based ethics of artistic creation enters Greek culture, displacing Aeschylus' still more instinctive art. The prescriptive awareness of dramatic rules starts with Sophocles and culminates in Aristotle's *Poetics*, which derives its aesthetic categories for drama with particular reference to *King Oedipus*. The same spirit of methodological awareness is found in Socrates' dialectics. Amongst his contemporaries, Socrates' is the most obsessively inquisitional of minds, and with him self-questioning is turned into a profession. His curiosity is directed at the very foundations of knowledge, thus opening up the line of philosophical *critique* that culminates in Kant. Nietzsche acknowledges Socrates' honesty. He was his own sternest critic, 'when he said that he was the only man of his acquaintance who confessed to *knowing nothing'*. This negative self assessment is the precondition for his voracious hunger to find 'the same illusion of knowledge anywhere'. Socrates turns his realization that he does not know into a methodology for questioning existing knowledge; indeed, a whole ethics ensues of how to live as a questing individual. The crux of the problem Nietzsche has with Socrates lies in his ignorance of the instinctive predetermination of his own intellectual drive. '"Only by instinct": the phrase goes to the heart and the centre of the Socratic tendency.' Socrates has fallen victim to powers beyond his intellectual control whose plaything he is, precisely when he assumes a superiority of consciousness over instinct. He thus lacks any capacity for the mystical. Nietzsche explains this by referring to what Plato called the '"daimonion of Socrates"'. Plato uses the term to mean an 'inner mystical voice'. Nietzsche argues, however, that in Socrates the relationship between instinct and consciousness is pathologically turned on its head, because instinct is denied its leading, formative role: it only intervenes negatively. Socrates' instinctive voice is one that denies, that 'blocks', his understanding; Nietzsche objects that 'in the case of all productive people' it is instinct that is the 'creative-affirmative force' and conscious reflection that gives out warnings. Nietzsche says that 'the logical drive which appeared in Socrates was completely incapable of turning against itself.' Here this means: both incapable of understanding itself (or at least, as in the Apolline, aware of itself as appearance), and also incapable of limiting itself, of knowing its proper sphere. If the logical drive had knowledge of its partiality it could no longer set itself as absolute against what it does not, and of necessity cannot, understand. The critical account of the foundations of knowledge is structurally incapable of interrogating its own foundations – until, as we shall see in **Section 18**, Kant. Kant represents not only a pinnacle of critical philosophy but also the beginning of the end of Socratism (just as Sophocles was both a pinnacle and crisis point for tragedy). This turning upside-down of nature leads Nietzsche to call Socrates *eine gänzlich abnorme Natur*. With *Natur* Nietzsche uses an older German word for character, person, figure – whilst also punning on 'nature' in the now familiar, broader sense of natural forces. What Nietzsche is saying here is that Socrates is an exceptional *denaturierte Natur*, a monstrous degenerate that was nevertheless allowed to breed.

In the 'person' of Socrates the principles of Nietzsche's anthropology of natural and cultural forces are presented exemplified in terms of individual psychology. Nietzsche stresses the individualness of Socrates often; here is a new, modern type of individual, quite different from the Apolline which in no way had a 'disintegrative influence on the instincts'. Intellectual obsessiveness denies the possibility of a multiple and instinctual foundation of the self. We are only a hairsbreadth away here from Freud's 'discovery' of the unconscious as the driving force of personal identity. We must look *through* Socrates and see the 'enormous drive-wheel' of a new, natural force or instinct: the logical drive, that manifests itself through him. In this wider regard Socrates can be linked as an exemplary type with cultural theory from Rousseau to Freud, Jung and beyond, that employs some notion of a 'collective unconscious' and investigates the suffering from the pressures of developed civilization. If we extrapolate from Socrates to modern culture, the possibility opens up for a diagnosis of the disease of modernity as the 'neurosis of modern culture' resulting from repression of instinctual drives.

Nietzsche ends this short chapter with an implied comparison between Socrates and Jesus. (The comparison begins at least as early as the 'hem of its robe' remark at the end of paragraph 3; cf. Mark 5:25ff.) In Nietzsche's later work Jesus assumes central significance as the other prime target of his critique of modernity, a representative initiator like Socrates, in this case of Christian ethics.[80] Jesus' name is not mentioned; for a first publication there are sufficient contentious issues already here, without Nietzsche exposing himself to the additional charge of blasphemy or atheism. (See also **Section 9** [myth of the Fall], and

'**Attempt**'; Nietzsche there explains the conundrum that *The Birth of Tragedy's* main critical thrust is directed towards life-denying Christian morality without ever openly mentioning it). An implied similarity between the two types seems obvious. Both are driven by a blind ascetic pursuit; both have sacrificed their lives for principles fanatically followed. Indeed, Socrates manufactured his own death sentence. The 'appropriate' outcome of his trial[81] would have been banishment: Socrates is a martyr on the altar of knowledge. There is nothing of the 'natural dread' of death in Socrates, and by extension in Jesus and Christianity; the instincts have become perverted to that extent. Both have managed to perpetuate what they stand for through disciples (indeed, both leave them asleep, cf. Mark 14:32ff). Finally, both are representatives or prototypes of new modes of human being: one founded upon a logical drive to understand, the other on a system of life-denying ethics; a common denominator for both is the pathology of what Nietzsche later calls *ressentiment*.[82]

SECTION 14

Death of Tragedy; Birth of Modern Art

The portrayal of Socrates in **Section 13** is the commencement of Nietzsche's critique of modernity detailed in **Sections 14** to **25**. There, Nietzsche discusses a number of zones of conflict in modern culture, all of which are derived from the original hegemony of consciousness over instinct. In many of the areas of strife the instinctive will reasserts itself surreptitiously against the rule of consciousness, undermining and taunting it. In this section, Nietzsche deals with Socratic and Platonic aesthetics as one of the most important factors involved in the destruction of tragedy.

In **paragraph 1**, Nietzsche addresses Socrates' or Plato's aversion to tragedy. As we already know from **Section 13**, Socrates does not appreciate tragedy. Socrates' 'Cyclopean eye [. . .] was debarred from ever looking with pleasure into the abysses of the Dionysiac'. (Part of the joke here is that a Cyclops would have no depth of perception; the metaphor of surface and what lies behind it runs throughout the passage.) Tragedy is unreasonable, that is, things happen for no reason (there is no cause and effect); everything is 'multifarious' and thus lacking order and clarity; and it can have a dangerous effect upon sensitive or feeble intellects in the audience. Moreover, it is untruthful, representing only what is pleasant rather than what is real or useful, and 'like Plato he thought it belonged to the flattering arts'. The only genre of poetry Socrates understood 'was the *Aesopian fable*'. As **paragraph 2** informs us, this idea of the 'untruthful' becomes particularly clear in Plato, who famously decries tragic poetry – and all the old forms of art, including especially Homer – for being imitations of 'an illusory image' and thus without relation to knowledge. Philosophical inquiry attempts instead 'to find the reality of ideas behind the empirical.' Nietzsche emphasizes the irony that Plato, starting with a complete misunderstanding of tragedy, ended up as a philosopher where he started as a poet. As 'irrepressible predispositions' struggle with 'Socratic maxims' (notice the metaphors of pushing or forcing throughout), Plato arrives without intending to do so at a new *artistic* form, the dialogue.

Dialogue means a conversation; in Plato's writings we have 'records' of mostly fictional conversations, generally between Socrates and a handful of others, most often some of the young men who were Socrates' students.[83] From 'dialogue' we have the term 'dialectics'. In Socrates, the idea seemed to be that the proper method of philosophy was a process of question and answer, governed by the rules of logical analysis and inference, which aimed (though often explicitly failing) at the mutual uncovering of a universal definition of something (e.g. knowledge, the just, the good, the beautiful). The term dialectic or dialectics then has a long philosophical history, from Plato himself and Aristotle, through Kant and German idealism. (In attacking dialectics, Nietzsche is again also attacking Hegel, cf. commentary **Section 1** and **4**.)

The Platonic dialogue is the vehicle for the new *philosophical* project of eidetic critique. Surprisingly, it resembles the rejected form of tragedy. For, tragedy is not the imitation of the empirical, but the projection of Dionysiac truths that lie 'behind the empirical'. However, tragedy does this not through dialectic, but through Apolline symbolic forms. Moreover, tragedy 'absorbed' all the other artistic genres (music, poetry, dance, etc.), and the same can be said of the dialogue. But whereas the fusion of tragedy occurs within 'the law of the unity of linguistic form' (strangely, Nietzsche does not mention music here), Platonic dialogue is a synthetic monstrosity, which 'hovers somewhere midway between narrative, lyric, and drama, between prose and poetry', distrusting them all. Against the philosophical will of Socrates and Plato the banished art seeks refuge in Platonic dialogue and manages to survive in bastardized form in this hostile medium. In Platonic dialogue it is transmitted into the modern period where it assumes a new transmogrified form – the modern novel.

Linking the modern novel thus with Platonic dialogue and the Aesopian fable as its precursors can be regarded as an astonishingly advanced insight into the origins of this art form. In twentieth- century literary criticism the novel is defined as a modern form because of its eclectic openness to include all other literary forms.[84] Held together by the biography of an individual journeying through life, it is a mixed composite of diverse formal elements all loosely fused together to serve a moralistic or didactic purpose, to provide orientation. Nietzsche is attracted to forms of art (ancient and modern) precisely when they are blended together from various constituent ingredients. In a way different from the novel, as we have seen (**Sections 8** and **9**) and will see again (**Section 21**), tragedy is also such a mixed form of divergent elements. In this paragraph we also find a good example of Nietzsche thinking of the relationships between things as their defining feature: he draws a parallel of power relations between neo-platonic philosophy as a discipline subordinate to theology, and poetry as merely ancillary to dialectics in the novel.

In **paragraph 3,** Nietzsche further clarifies what happens to 'modern' art by reference to the main dualism of the text. The Apolline drive – which always aimed at clarity of form – has 'cocooned' [*sich verpuppt*] itself in logical schematism. (Notice the biological metaphors: 'overgrown' and 'cocooned' – Greek culture imagined as a garden but never an Eden.) The idea is of going into hiding, protecting itself with the cocoon as with a mask, awaiting a metamorphic re-emergence (which, indeed, happens on the last page of the book).[85] The spinning of the cocoon is yet another image of the veil, and in the next section, the 'net'. The joke is on Plato's account of art: it is *science*, not art, that is doubly veiled, twice removed from reality. It is not only unaware that the forms it creates are only appearances, but is also unaware of the *second* veil that the Apolline here draws over itself. Relative to the Apolline, the Socratic drive is 'pathological' (see **Section 1**) – meaning it is diseased insofar as it is determined by immediate, phenomenal affects, and considers such affects to be fundamentally important – insofar as it fails to see the dream as dream and maintain its affective distance (see also **Section 12**). In this change, *muthos* (myth, which becomes an increasingly important theme in the remainder of the book) is misinterpreted as *logos* (discursive language, logic, knowledge). Similarly, Nietzsche refers us back to his discussion of Euripides for the observation that the Dionysiac – which always aimed at ecstasy, and at nature, broadly speaking, is 'translated' as naturalistic, emotional affects. This too, relative to the Dionysiac, is pathological (see discussion of Aristotle and Goethe in **Section 22**), insofar as the ecstatic nature of the Dionysiac is misinterpreted as the affects of an individual. Eventually, the Dionysiac takes a 'death leap into domestic tragedy' (what today we might call 'kitchen sink dramas' or 'soap operas').

So, not surprisingly, Nietzsche sees the figure of Socrates as the 'dialectical hero in Platonic drama', and very similar to 'the Euripidean hero who must defend his actions with reasons and counter-reasons'. In both cases there is a pervasive optimism, an optimism that acts like a defence against the world of nature and the pain inflicted in the exposure to it. In Socrates, this optimism asserts implicitly that knowledge is possible, and explicitly that knowledge governs virtue, sin is ignorance, and that virtue leads to happiness. Because of this optimism, tragedy dies. The moral content of the art-drives is replaced by an epistemological imperative to know thyself; more specifically, the 'transcendental justice' in Aeschylus is replaced by the god from the machine, and the show of dialectic reasoning on the theatre stage drives out the divine mystery of human fate.

The chorus and 'whole musical-Dionysiac' foundation of tragedy is understood from this new Socratic point of view as a dispensable relic. However, 'we have recognized that the only way the chorus can be understood at all is as the *cause* of tragedy and the tragic.' Once again Nietzsche clarifies that with Sophocles – who 'recommended' changes in how the chorus was to be employed – tragedy already is in the first stage of its decline. This changing in the portrayal of Sophocles from hero (in **Section 9**) to agent of decomposition might be seen as Nietzsche contradicting himself. However, that could only be the case if we assumed that each figure Nietzsche discusses is, as such, a homogeneous expression of a univocal cultural tendency. But we know from the first sentence of the book that this is not the case, that Nietzsche's conception of cultural development and history is more broadly one of an interplay of forces. In later work, this complex model becomes Nietzsche's famous concept of 'perspectivism', wherein the value of something depends upon what power- or value-relationships it is viewed in.

Through the devaluation of Sophocles, Nietzsche prepares the ground for a re-evaluation of Socrates in **paragraph 5**, because Sophocles shows that 'the anti-Dionysiac tendency was already at work before Socrates and was only expressed by him with unheard-of grandeur.' In other words, as we have noted before, the case of Socrates is not just the case of an aberrant individual but of a whole aberrant (and by now dominant) mode of natural instinct and cultural production. Moreover, the Platonic dialogues – as influential and even great works of art – 'do not permit us to view him solely as a disintegrative, negative force'. Nietzsche wonders rhetorically whether 'the relationship between Socrates and art is *necessarily* and exclusively antithetical'. Just as there is a changing, perspectival, characterization of Sophocles, so there will be of Socrates. Here Nietzsche is laying the foundations for an argument concerning the problem of culture in the post-Socratic modern age. For Nietzsche, Socrates' 'achievement' cannot be undone; one cannot simply reverse history and become Aeschylus. The Greeks are not models to be imitated, but exemplary in what they achieved under their conditions (see **Section 3**). The question is rather whether the Socratic logical drive can be combined again with an artistic one, whether 'an artistic Socrates' is conceivable. The 'artistic Socrates' here, and the 'music making Socrates' in the next paragraph, are provisional formulae for a reunification of humanity with itself under conditions of modernity.

Nietzsche refers to a dream in **paragraph 6** that – very similarly to the warning voice, the daimonion, discussed previously – repeatedly tells a guilty-feeling Socrates to 'make music'. Nietzsche sees this as an 'Apolline insight', as if Socrates were about to commit sacrilege like a barbarian king. (Of course, being in some relations so un-Greek, and misunderstanding the Apolline and Dionysiac artistic forces so thoroughly, Socrates *is* a sacrilegious barbarian. The term 'barbarian' is used throughout the book to mean 'dominated by non-artistic drives'.) The words of Socrates' dream-voice 'are the only hint of any scruples in him about the limits of logical nature.' With this notion, we are returning to the idea that critical dialectics is incapable of grasping its own limits, foundations, and its relation to instinct. Nietzsche concludes with a couple of rhetorical questions through which he states that the logician and the scientist require artistic insights as a 'corrective.' The main task for the modern period thus comes into view: the complementation of science with art. If we were wondering in part 1 where Nietzsche's interest in the Greek culture period was leading, from now on it is evident that this is a book about the difficulties of life in the modern period. Socrates is the book's second starting point, leading up to the new paradigm of cultural production in Wagner's *Tristan*.

SECTION 15

Science as a Deficient Mode of Art; Socrates at the Gates of Modernity

Socrates was not simply a historical event, but the clearest expression of a new cultural force that stands in opposition to the artistic drives, and which changed and formed history thereafter. Socratic culture casts a shadow into the future. Note the use of metaphors here. First, again, the Platonic metaphor of the cave is turned around against Socrates. Secondly, history is envisaged as a day, late modernity is 'evening' and the setting sun as symbolic of the dwindling of cultural substance. Similar metaphors, where individual perception of time in terms of the times of day are transposed as images for the whole of history, are a particularly frequently used stylistic device in Nietzsche.[86] (Here, the metaphor is strained, for the evening and shadows are 'unending'.) Because, as the last 'prophetic' question of the previous section suggested, art is 'a necessary corrective' to science, Socratic culture requires that art is perpetually created anew – beginning straight away, as we have seen, with Socrates in prison, and with the proto novels that were the Platonic dialogues. Nietzsche conceives of an almost self-regulating process of regeneration and correction of the drives involved in the making of cultural history. In this way, contemporary Enlightenment culture – the latest and perhaps the last expression of Socratic culture – will be complemented, almost automatically now, by a new artistic culture. In this way also, all art depends upon the Greeks.

To see this, one must be the 'one individual who reveres truth' and (metaphorically) imprison and execute the whole late Greek cultural inheritance in the same way Athens did Socrates – as something deeply opposed to the *health* of contemporary culture. (Notice also the cyclical motif: we have to 'experience' and try to overcome the past in a mirror image of how the Athenians tried to overcome the future.) Attempting to copy Greek art, or even compare oneself to it, is doomed. The Greeks are like mischievous chariot drivers that aim the whole towards destruction. Indeed, why attempt to copy such a 'presumptuous little people', whose remarkable culture was ephemeral and indeed simply an accident of history? Again, history is irreversible; the task in the present could not be to 'imitate' the Greeks if this meant turning back the clock. Instead, Nietzsche will argue that the contemporary task is to *repeat* the Greek invention of tragedy but in our own time and with the resources available to us.

Socrates too is an unwitting part of this artistic pantheon, because the science he inaugurates is either itself a form of art or at least inevitably produces art as correlate and corrective. This is an extraordinary turn of argument. Science accords with the 'deepest and already metaphysical sense' of art, which is the justification of existence. Like art, it is infinitely contented with existence, even though science typically suffers under the delusion that existence requires correction and can be corrected (Nietzsche explicated this idea most clearly in the case of Euripides 'correcting' his audience). Like art, this contentment defends against pessimism. The pessimism arises from, among other things, the futility of scientific discovery as such. Thus, Nietzsche's digging a hole through the earth analogy later: even if one *could* dig down to the depths, one would only arrive at a different surface! Accordingly, science continually reaches its limits and must transform itself, more or less unconsciously, into art – which, Nietzsche claims, was the goal of the underlying cultural drives all along. Like art, finally, science is more concerned with the veil than with what is veiled (the reference is back to Schopenhauer's veil of Maya, introduced in **Section 1**). Nietzsche cites the leading Enlightenment figure Lessing, for whom the unveiling was more important – a greater stimulant – than the unveiled. For that latter reason, too, science finds its optimism borne out because its success is guaranteed – science does not see that it does not matter if what is unveiled is really unveiled, that is whether science has actually uncovered the truth of things. One key difference between science and art is that the former is unwitting. So unwitting, indeed, that Socratic science often manifests itself as a hostility to art (as in Plato). By contrast, the Apolline contentment with existence is accompanied by and indeed predicated upon an awareness of the appearing quality of existence and the beautiful forms that grant such contentment. In the next section, Nietzsche thus claims that only through the Apolline can contentment with existence as appearance 'truly' be found.

This optimism leads Socrates to accept death ('without the natural dread') based upon reasoning. The 'dying Socrates' is the 'heraldic shield' for all science. Socratic culture suffers from an excessive belief in the truth of appearances. Truth is idolized. Thus, in the next paragraph, Nietzsche identifies art (in this broad sense), the unwitting aim of Socratic science, with myth – and it is myth that at the end of the book becomes a key concept. Here, the reference is to Plato. In many dialogues, when the Socrates character's dialectical reasoning leads to a dead end, a mythical story is told.[87] Nietzsche's observation is that, unbeknownst to Plato, this is not a substitute for dialectic, but rather its essence and its goal.

All these are the budding motifs of Nietzsche's critique of the prejudiced nature of modern science, applied here for the first time and fully developed in *Thus Spoke Zarathustra* and *Beyond Good and Evil*. (See also **'Attempt'**.) Also prefigured here is the idea that science will eventually have to realize the incompleteness and contingency of its own epistemological foundations, for in its approach to nature it is based upon a misunderstanding of its own instinctive basis. It is the sciences' instinctual foundation which it has in common with art (and religion). One consequence of this idea is Nietzsche's own ambition to expand the possibilities of philosophical investigation by infusing it with artistic elements.

The notion of Socrates as the founder of modern philosophy is expounded here. After him, 'one school of philosophy follows another, like wave upon wave'. Since the days of Socrates we have reached a high degree of universality of knowledge, not only across the globe but also across previously separate disciplines. So, even the phenomena of morality, virtue and affection are to be studied and derived from dialectical reasoning and therefore are also 'teachable' (again, recall the discussion of Euripides and his audience). Thus, 'one cannot do other than regard Socrates as the vortex and turning-point of so-called world history.' The construction of this global Enlightenment project, Nietzsche argues, has absorbed vast human energies that would have otherwise, had they been allowed to roam freely, caused the equivalent of hell on earth bringing with it a 'horrifying ethic of genocide out of pity'. Again, science like art serves to defend life against the destructive impulses that are a part of life itself. Science is a tool for sublimation.

Socrates teaches 'a new form of Greek serenity', contrasted with the Greek cheerfulness that Nietzsche analysed in the opening sections of the book. It seeks to discharge itself in actions (the correcting of existence) and being the 'midwife' to new Socratic geniuses.[88] Notice the metaphor of the 'net' of Socratic insight, attempting to encompass all appearances, and to weave itself 'impenetrably close'. The notion is a variation on the veil, with two new ideas: first, that of capturing and holding. This is the universalizing tendency of the Socratic. Everything falls under the dialectical method; everything can and will be understood. Secondly, in this case, it is not a question of finding and perhaps removing a veil, but of setting out to manufacture one, under the guise of truth, to create an ever more perfect, 'corrected' appearance.[89] The veil is art, as Nietzsche in the last paragraph of the section reminds us. But it is an art that, having misunderstood and misused the art-drives, is unconscious of its limits, towards which its optimism is hurrying. Indeed, it has already happened; a 'noble and gifted' scientist will have pursued a problem to the point where the essentially ungrounded nature of both the problem and its pursuit is revealed. The circle of science, although containing an infinite number of points, is nevertheless finite with respect to the *Ureine* that encloses and determines it and which makes of the centre of the circle (dialectical reasoning) not an authentic origin of truth, but an arbitrary mode of cultural production. Only towards the end of the

Enlightenment in Kant and Schopenhauer, does science itself become an object of scientific knowledge (see **Section 18**). Then, 'logic curls up around itself and finally bites its own tail': knowledge recognizes the circle of its own possibilities.[90] In *The Birth of Tragedy* the completion of the circle of knowledge signifies knowledge becoming knowledgeable about itself; it thus turns *tragic*. This is in fact the same knowledge that it was the purpose of tragedy to reveal in protective symbolic form. Tragic knowledge needs *art* simply to be endured. Such modernity that comes up against its own limitations Nietzsche regards as tragic culture, tragedy enacted on the historical level of imploding cultural paradigms, whose catastrophic collapse both reveals the true nature of things again and demands tragic art.

The Birth of Tragedy is now, with the Greek past behind it, standing 'at the gates of the present and the future.' Here we encounter another set of metaphors constantly employed later: 'gate' and 'gateway' are important images in *Zarathustra*, for example.[91] This is the moment where the argument of *The Birth of Tragedy* changes from an investigation informed by methodologies of classical philology and historical anthropology into a revolutionary polemic with the openly stated purpose of intervening into the cultural-political matters of the day. To be sure, Socratic science was always only fully realizing itself in art, but always as a lower form predicated on unwitting blindness and not insight. But Nietzsche's contemporary cultural landscape is different: it is in crisis, and because the limits of science have become a part of science, that distinctive kind of blindness is no longer possible. Like Schiller and Kleist, Nietzsche is having his own Kant-crisis here. Will an art emerge (the famous image of the *music making Socrates*) capable of comforting and healing even this contemporary form of life, pessimistic, rootless and barbaric as it is? We try to observe the struggle, but 'Alas! The magic of these struggles is such, that he who sees them must also take part in them!'[92] Nietzsche envisages a form of engagement here that bears resemblance to how he defined the role of the chorus in classical Greek tragedy: the bystander who is taken up and into the tragic community (**Section 7**). It is interesting to note that Nietzsche derives a vision of contemporary political commitment of a revolutionary kind from the model of ancient tragedy itself.

SECTION 16

Aesthetics of Modern Music Drama. Note: Nietzsche, Music and Style

This section marks the beginning of what we could call Nietzsche's aesthetics of modern art, particularly his theory of music. This modern theory of art forms a substantial part of the overall achievement of *The Birth of Tragedy*, and much of the remainder of the last ten sections is devoted to it. One key feature of this new aesthetics is that the aesthetics of tragedy in the first half of the book is recast with the concepts of myth and music firmly at its centre, something anticipated but not fully realized earlier (e.g. **Section 10**).[93] Nietzsche states that it is the musical 'spirit alone' that 'can give birth to tragedy'. The phrase 'rebirth of tragedy' is now introduced. An investigation of the conditions that lead to a rebirth of tragedy determines the agenda for the remainder of *The Birth of Tragedy*. He intends 'to name the forces which seem to me to guarantee a *rebirth of tragedy* – and some other blissful hopes for the German character.'

Nietzsche recapitulates the nature of the combative relationship between the two forces symbolized in Apollo and Dionysus – emphasizing that instead of tracing aesthetic phenomena to a single principle, there are two. Two properly *artistic* drives or forces, we should emphasize, since the previous sections made it clear there are other drives, including the Socratic-scientific which interact with the artistic drives, often with hostility, to form the overall cultural landscape. Nietzsche then also recapitulates the approving citation of Schopenhauer and Wagner, seeming to credit them with his having 'the magic at my command' to write the present book. Notice the elaboration on the notion of physical form: the Apolline concerns physical nature (appearance); the Dionysian, metaphysical reality. Wagner criticizes aesthetics for applying the criteria of the former (beautiful forms) to the art of the latter (music). Nietzsche, however, is writing philosophy; so, he must employ the 'magic' to bring the original problem before his soul 'corporeally' (*leibhaft*) – that is, as a *form*. This should be compared with the account of poetic 'image' in **Section 8**. This bringing forth of forms is more productive than traditional aesthetics which, just like Socratic science, is contented with mere 'shadow-play'. The point is that, *methodologically*, Nietzsche has to re-enact the *metaphysics* of the topic under investigation. So, one contribution Nietzsche makes to the 'science of aesthetics' (mentioned at the beginning of **Section 1**) is that science is not only given a new content, but must proceed in at least Apolline (perhaps also Dionysiac) instead of Socratic terms.

Note: Nietzsche, Music and Style
We have already observed Nietzsche's debt to Schopenhauer's overall metaphysics, and how this relates to the broad conception of tragedy. What is new in this section is the problem of the aesthetics of modern music *per se*. The key idea is that music directly expresses the underlying reality of the will (the *Ureine*), and is not a representation, image or concept of it.[94] This claim permeates the argument of *The Birth of Tragedy* as one of the fundamentals of Nietzsche's new philosophy of language and expression (see **Section 8, Note: Philosophy of Language in Nietzsche**), and serves as a yardstick not only for his critique of other forms of less effective mimesis but also as an epistemological and moral imperative for his own philosophy. Duly, Nietzsche translates Schopenhauer's definition of music as 'a direct copy of the Will' into a demand for himself (we must not forget that he has some ambition also as a musical composer). Nietzsche endeavours to leave behind Schopenhauer's pessimism based on resignation and express his affirmation of life in 'a new style' that takes him beyond the conventional language of philosophy (see **'Attempt'**). Paradoxically, perhaps, this endeavour has its origins in Schopenhauer. Nietzsche is so much indebted to his role models that he struggles to surpass them: the same is true with Wagner.

In the second part of *The Birth of Tragedy* Nietzsche identifies the model for this new writing. He derives it from Wagner, or more precisely, from Wagner's opera *Tristan and Isolde*. One of the most musically innovative and advanced of Wagner's works, it helps kick-start the Modernist revolution in musical composition. One of the musical devices that Nietzsche favours is Wagner's idea of 'Leitmotiv' or 'leading motif' which Nietzsche translates into a device of linguistic composition. In fact, the boat/sea/helmsman motif is one of those leitmotifs taken directly from opera into text. The light/darkness metaphors derived from the mythological God-pair is another, and likewise images of the veil, tissue, net, fabric, and so forth. The leitmotif device serves

Wagner in structuring the vastly dimensioned musical canvases. As in the opera's music, motifs appear and reappear also in Nietzsche's text at different strategic moments of development of the argument, underpinning it metaphorically and structurally by forming recognizable landmarks of meaning during the shifts in proceedings.

Another key musical element of *Tristan* is a single, harmonically hybrid chromatic chord. It has entered the literature under the name of the *Tristan-chord*, and it is reverentially quoted in a number of compositions central as manifestos to the modernist movement (for example, in Arnold Schönberg's *Three Piano Pieces* Op. 11, 1909, and Alban Berg's *Lyrical Suite*, 1926). Nietzsche therefore had his ear on the ground when he elevated Wagner's opera to the status of an aesthetic-philosophical paradigm of a new era.[95] Schönberg's Chamber Symphony No. 1 of 1906 opens up a stream of compositional experiments that lead from 'free atonality' to serial twelve-tone composition. The developmental arch of *Tristan* is built on this harmonically unresolved chord, which features as a minimalist harmonic symbol of the opera as a whole: from this musical seed that the harmonic and dramatic structure of the opera's vast architecture germinates. Resolution is delayed by the device of a discord followed by another discord. The *Tristan-chord* is constructed in this way: it contains two dissonances. At each resolution, only one dissonance gets resolved, leaving the other dissonance open. By delaying the full release of tension for the duration of the 4-hour opera, Wagner manages to turn the audience experience into a prolonged building of desire for resolution, thus musically heightening the sensual impact of the final tragic destruction of the couple in their climax of illicit love. In this way Wagner not only revives tragedy through binding it into a new musical context; his operas also render philosophical insight as musical expression: in *Tristan* longing (*sehnen*) is directly translated into musical form: longing is symbolized musically.

The chord treats dissonance differently from the way it had hitherto been applied in 'classical' (e.g. the first Viennese school of Haydn, Mozart and Beethoven) and Romantic music, down to Brahms and Bruckner. Traditionally, dissonance featured as a device for portraying exceptional, extreme moments, either musical or extra-musical (e.g. psychological). For example,

Mozart's String Quartet no. 19 KV 465 (1785) in C, the last in a series of six dedicated to Haydn, has become known as the *Dissonanzenquartett*, because the basic key of c-major in the first movement is arrived at after a long slow introduction (22 bars) entirely built on harmonic friction and juxtaposition that torturously meanders towards the harmonic balance in the dominant key. The Classical Tradition features dissonance as an extraneous device and mainly for contrast to sanction the inevitability of harmonic stability, 'extensive chromaticism' is used as 'a disturbance of the sense of harmonic stability that, nevertheless, lies on the surface of the fundamental harmonic structure'.[96] Examples could be drawn from various works leading up to Wagner's time, for instance from Brahms' or Bruckner's (particularly the 3rd movement of the Ninth) or even from Mahler's symphonies at least up to the Eighth, where dissonance is used more extensively, even centrally, but still for contrast and as a delaying stratagem. What Adorno with reference to Mahler calls *Durchbruch*[97] (breakthrough) inevitably finally occurs; harmonic stability always in the end prevails, in spite and because of dissonance. Wagner's *Tristan-chord* is radically different because it turns dissonance itself into the centre of musical activity. In this way it can be said that Wagner has liberated dissonance. From here on the edifice of classical and romantic harmony is crumbling. The search is on for the widening of the scope of musical expression that first, based on chromaticism, leads beyond the restriction of fixed tonality and later to new 'disharmonic' structuring principles like Schönberg's twelve tone technique.

Nietzsche's book seeks to apply Wagner's musical ideas in the way it is constructed as a text. It 'translates' Wagner's new melodic and harmonic principles into the principles of an aesthetically resonating new style of philosophical critique. In parallel to Wagner's operatic experiment we could call Nietzsche's style 'chromatic': it is based on friction and montage of parts of ideas (leitmotifs), juxtaposed differently, forever entering into new combinations, as terms and images build into sentences, paragraphs and longer units of writing.[98] The secret of the text's stylistic specificity lies in the tension caused in it by using repetition to induce variation (of ideas, motifs, terminologies, etc). Rather than along the line of stringent logical explication, the development of ideas occurs through slight shifts of nuance and angle, so that the argument forms one long and 'undulating line' (cf. Nietzsche's description of Wagner's melodic lines **Section 21**), with recurring *leitmotifs* thrown in as landmarks of meaning. With this writing we therefore do not experience the unfolding of a rationally dissected subject matter; instead, the text opens up a 'web of complex relations' (the phrase is Darwin's) between ingredient components: 'a tissue being woven on a rising and falling loom' (Nietzsche with reference to *Tristan*, **Section 21**). As Wagner in *Tristan* musically defers harmonic resolution for as long as possible, Nietzsche endlessly defers logical resolution to the conflicts he constructs until the very last moment. Ironically, Nietzsche finally 'resolves' the argument of *The Birth of Tragedy* with a discussion of dissonance as an aesthetic category with anthropological significance (see **Section 25**), thus ending his first work with an apotheosis of the artistic device with which Wagner's music drama begins and out of which the opera's long arch of tragic suspense unfolds. Thus, *The Birth of Tragedy* could be read as a dyed-in-the-wool piece of Wagnerite writing. Chromaticism and deferred resolution of dissonance are the main stylistic devices employed in both media. Cosima Wagner's thank-you letter to Nietzsche for expediting a copy of *The Birth of Tragedy* after publication says that she did not think it possible that effects such as they are evoked in the book could have been produced by anybody other than 'the master'.[99] Nietzsche will further discuss Wagner's compositional practices in **Sections 21** and **24**.

* * *

To move forward towards a specific aesthetics of modern music, Nietzsche recasts the Greek problem of the temporary cooperation of the Apolline and Dionysian in tragedy in the following question: 'how does music relate to image and concept?' To answer his question, Nietzsche first examines the detail of Schopenhauer's musical theory through an excessively long quotation from *The World as Will and Representation*. Another important reason for Nietzsche to cite Schopenhauer is the aspect of *admixture* of the two drives. Here Nietzsche finds prompts in the second major strand of Schopenhauer's argument, the first one being that music interprets the world of physical phenomena by intuitive analogy 'to the inner spirit' of phenomena. Music is universal language, not in the sense of universality of an abstract concept, but rather insofar as it expresses the 'innermost kernel' of the underlying will. Music is genuinely expressive if it is an immediate, intuitive analogy, and not some kind of sonorous image of the particular things or actions in a poem, and still less in concepts. The latter are highly mediated, even arbitrary, representations of the same 'kernel'. Schopenhauer thus opens up the prospect of judging a piece of music unsuccessful if it is based on 'an imitation brought about with conscious intention by means of concepts.'

Music can represent the 'thing-in-itself of every phenomenon' in two ways: Schopenhauer implicitly distinguishes between absolute music – he provides the example of the symphony with its possibilities of infinite, un-representable presentation – and what could be called 'applied' or 'concrete' music. It is possible to combine the universality of musical composition with a concrete representation of a 'perceptive expression', such as a poem, because 'the two are simply quite different expressions of the same inner nature of the world.' This distinction is of great importance for Nietzsche's conception of musical drama which is essentially hybrid and anti-symphonic, as we will see. Music that is applied in the above sense sets specific 'individual pictures of human life [. . .] to the universal language of music.' Schopenhauer is here talking about various non-symphonic musical forms, such as the setting to music of a poem, a ballet, or opera, that combine both of these elements. Nietzsche returns to this differentiation of the forms and genres of music later (**Section 19** onwards).

Nietzsche now maps Schopenhauer's principles of musical aesthetics against his own system of artistic drives. The Dionysiac is the metaphysical undertow immediately expressive of the will. Any associated 'image and concept' 'acquires a heightened significance'. Images or concepts elevated in this manner Nietzsche defines as 'myth'. In other words, images and concepts – in themselves merely appearances or abstractions from appearance – can through the influence of music become raised to a level akin to the directly expressive. This is what Nietzsche calls the symbolic. In a way different from the composer, the poet and the poetic philosopher, if musicality is embraced, may also achieve some kind of access to the 'the same inner nature of the world'. This is the theoretical foundation of modern opera as a hybrid form in which music aligns itself with myth; it is also the foundation for a new form of philosophical writing.

It is interesting to note that Nietzsche is not devoting time to any discussion of absolute music (e.g. the symphony). Like Schopenhauer, Nietzsche is interested more in the type of music that forms an alliance with other, appearance-based forms of art. His interest lies in modern hybrid musical forms, and most of all in the mixed medium of opera. For one, it is his intention to underpin the Wagnerian opera project with an appropriate modern musical aesthetic. And he also has a vested interest in forms of musical hybridity as a young philosopher who regards himself at the same time as a composer and poet. Nietzsche here refers to his earlier discussion of the lyric poet (Archilochus, **Section 6**). Lyric poetry anticipates tragedy insofar as it achieves the expression of some Dionysiac wisdom through music and Apolline images. That earlier analysis thus backs up this new account of Dionysiac wisdom coming to be expressed symbolically.

We can see Nietzsche here developing his theorem of symbolization, as laid down in **Sections 1 to 3,** by re-designating it through myth as one of the cornerstones of an aesthetic theory of modernity, a groundbreaking move that reverberates in the aesthetic theories of Heidegger, Neo-Kantianism (Cassirer,), the Frankfurt School (Adorno, Kracauer, Benjamin), of Modernism and beyond. (See **Chapter 4, Reception and Influence**). Nietzsche redrafts the notion of the symbolic in accordance with what Schopenhauer calls 'perceptive expression', as a concrete material manifestation in image or artistic language of an intuition that presents the appearances of things as portrayals of the 'inner nature of the world'. The notion of symbol permits us, Nietzsche argues, to understand why a spectator feels pleasure in watching a tragedy (cf. particularly **Section 8**). The destruction of the individual in tragedy is the symbolic vehicle for an insight into the indestructible will. The section ends with another comparison with Apolline contentment with beautiful appearance which is 'in a certain sense a lie'. The Dionysiac, however, has a 'true, undisguised voice' that speaks: 'be as I am!'. This demand is significant: the Dionysiac is not simply a metaphysical truth, or an experience, or a feeling – it is a mode of existence, a long-neglected possibility of the human.

SECTION 17

Death of Myth as the Death of Tragedy

In this section, Nietzsche returns briefly to the death of tragedy in Greece in order to exemplify his modern recasting of an aesthetics of tragedy and music primarily in terms of myth.[100] The section begins with one of the clearest, most exhilarating and beautiful expressions of the Dionysiac insight. The essential procreative lust for existence makes necessary the unceasing creation and destruction of forms in appearance. ('Appearance' here does double duty: the beautiful image celebrated by Apollo; but more especially the appearances that are taken for the real object of science.) This 'makes necessary', together with the 'immeasurable, primordial delight in existence' the metaphysical solace that is the essence of all art. The reference to 'fear and pity' is to Aristotle's poetics,[101] and thus touches on the problem (which Nietzsche believes he has finally solved) of why an audience feels pleasure in watching a tragedy.

Paragraph 2 turns to myth, practised but never properly understood by the Greeks (who were 'eternal children', that is, unaware of what they were doing – even and especially those Greeks starting with Sophocles who believed that they *were* aware), nor hitherto by modern aesthetics. In ancient and more recent tragic drama, 'myth is certainly not objectified adequately in the spoken word'. Nietzsche refers to Shakespeare's *Hamlet*, who 'speaks more superficially than he acts'. Nietzsche introduces the element of music as a vital component of Greek tragedy (now though from a point of view of modern music drama), about which, he concedes, we can only conjecture. Of ancient tragedy, we have only the words; there is thus a temptation to forget that these dramatists were also (indeed, first and foremost) musicians.[102] Only in the contemplation of images, music, structure, and the whole of this layered artefact, is the true meaning of the myth revealed. This may happen 'almost', but evidently not quite, 'by scholarly means'; this is another brief reference to the fact that Nietzsche is proposing not just a new aesthetic theory, but a new method of aesthetic *enquiry*, redesigned as cultural anthropology and requiring as its condition an aesthetic sensibility. All this implies that in terms of awareness of the musical possibilities of recreating the tragic myth, the moderns are ahead of the Greeks.

Nietzsche addresses an apparent historical gap in the development of tragedy. What happens to the spirit of music and the Dionysiac world view, after its decline – after, as he says of poetry two paragraphs later, they became 'homeless'? Given these cultural phenomena rest on 'universal' artistic drives, do these drives express themselves in any way in the period of their repression? The Dionysian, at least, Nietzsche says, goes into hiding in the Christian Middle Ages in mysticism and in the mystery plays. (Recall the observation about mysticism at the end of **Section 13**.) The Dionysiac world view has occasionally 'attracted more serious natures', and Nietzsche utters the hope that it might re-emerge one day as art 'from its mystical depth' – that is, from its neglect and misunderstanding as 'mere' mysticism. The 'eternal struggle' between the theoretical and tragic views of the world can only permit the rebirth of tragedy when the former has realized its limits – this is the topic of the next section.

The remainder of the section discusses three key features of the period of the death of tragedy, interpreting these more explicitly than before in terms of the concept of myth. These paragraphs partly overlap with, and should be read alongside, the treatment of Euripides' innovations in **Section 12**. The first of these three is the 'new Attic dithyramb' (as opposed to the 'original' 'Dionysiac dithyramb' of the chorus), the forms of music and of setting words to music that replaced the admirable tragedies of Aeschylus and Sophocles, and with which Euripides 'makes free'. Here, music 'no longer expressed the inner essence, the Will itself, but simply reproduced appearances inadequately'. This is 'imitative music', as Schopenhauer called it. As an equivalent to the new dithyramb Nietzsche considers 'tone-painting'.[103] This 'makes the phenomenal world even poorer than it is' – the argument is essentially the same as Plato's concerning poetry in the *Republic*. By contrast, Dionysiac music 'enriches and expands the individual phenomenon, making it into an image of the world' – that is, it creates myth as the most significant example and bearer of symbolic insight. Another area of assault by the 'un-Dionysiac spirit' is the progressive introduction of 'psychological refinement' in tragedy from Sophocles on. (Again, notice Sophocles is both the high point, and the beginning of the end, of tragedy.) By this is meant what we might call psychological realism in characterization. For Nietzsche, it is evident that the kind of 'universality' Aristotle had in mind was the universality of concept, not the universality of the mythic symbol.[104] With Euripides and the new Attic comedy, characters have lost their capability 'of being expanded into an eternal type'. They take on characteristics of a single psychological type.

Finally Nietzsche looks at a change in the endings of tragedies, which change from providing 'metaphysical solace' (the 'purest' form of this Nietzsche finds in Sophocles' *Oedipus in Colonnus*) to suggesting 'an earthly resolution of the tragic dissonance'. 'Metaphysical solace' returns us to the theme of paragraph 1 of the section. Earthly resolution means that the resolution occurs at the same metaphysical level (appearance, understood as theoretical culture understands it) as the action of suffering. Everything in these later tragedies is on the surface and in the sphere of present concerns; the hero now receives a 'well-earned reward in the form of a handsome marriage, or in being honoured by the gods.' The section ends with a contrast between 'Greek cheerfulness' or 'serenity' (the subject of **Section 9**), which was the 'flower of Apolline culture', balming the abyss with beauty, and a new form (introduced already in **Section 11**), 'senile and unproductive'. Within the latter, some forms are more 'noble' than others, and the cheerfulness of 'theoretical man' is the most noble. By 'noble' Nietzsche here evidently means that theoretical man is not *simply* debased, degenerate or unintelligent; not simply unaware in some manner of the heaviness of being (see paragraph 1 of **Section 18**); he is after all capable of achievements, and thus not entirely 'unproductive'. (Nietzsche may have the ignoble aspects of Christianity in his sights here.) The relative nobility of theoretical man in this sense was discussed in the **sections** on Socrates, such as **14 and 15**. Nietzsche finishes by reminding us in what way this relatively noble cheerfulness is nevertheless staunchly anti-Dionysiac.

SECTION 18

The Crisis of Socratic Modernity. Note: on 'Bildung'

This section elaborates Nietzsche's theory of modernity. At this first stage in his career, Nietzsche's use of the notion 'modern' lacks precise definition. He clarifies it later on, most notably in *Beyond Good and Evil* and *Genealogy of Morality*. Though in the next section echoes are audible of Jacob Burckhardt's *Civilisation of Renaissance in Italy*,[105] on the whole Nietzsche's notion of the modern period here remains largely unaffected by the contemporary debates, especially regarding questions of the inception of the modern period in the transition from the Middle Ages to Renaissance culture in fourteenth- and fifteenth-century Italy. To Nietzsche, 'modern man' in *The Birth of Tragedy* is not affiliated mainly with modern history since the Renaissance, but rather with the Socratic or Alexandrian cultures that have dominated Western history since before the Christian era. 'Modernity' in this sense therefore begins very early indeed. Nietzsche also uses the modern in two more senses: occasionally it includes Weimar Classicism (Schiller and Goethe), German Idealism (Kant), the classical and Romantic period in music and literature (Beethoven); but the most critically loaded meaning of 'modern' in Nietzsche occurs when he refers to the special set of circumstances characterizing his own contemporary cultural situation of nineteenth-century Germany and Europe: this most recent period presents a deep crisis and new possibilities of hope, fully instantiated in Schopenhauer and especially Wagner.

The further we read into *The Birth of Tragedy* the more we realize that its general principles for a theory of culture are derived from the contemporary situation of modern culture. From the angle of this section, the first half of the book devoted to Greek culture takes on new relevance, in two ways: first, it lays down the historical and theoretical parameters for the investigation of contemporary culture of part 2; secondly, it serves as the first half of a cyclical model, whose construction, as becomes clear now, is the prime theoretical target of *The Birth of Tragedy*. Thus the book projects a modern theory of history, whose constituent principles are derived from an assessment of the immediate historical present. It thus paves the way for a methodological revolution in historiography based on the realization that the historical past cannot be interrogated independently from a specification of its input to the contemporary present.[106] In this way, *The Birth of Tragedy* lays down the foundations of Nietzsche's anti-historicist critique, directed against the 'source-based' positivism of the German Historical School since Ranke.

Nietzsche in this section produces a theory of modern mass culture, torn in all kinds of directions and in conflict with itself because the leading paradigm of an Enlightenment quest for knowledge has been undermined and is falling away without having been replaced yet by a new cultural paradigm. (In later work, Nietzsche diagnoses this condition as nihilism.) For Nietzsche, modern culture as contemporary culture has three characteristic features: first, it is impure and a hybrid of coexisting cultural forms of differing origins. This means, secondly, that contemporary culture bears the mark of 'fracture'. The 'man of action' displaces theoretical man; the artist is on the ascendency again, thus contributing his share to an undermining of the rationalistic foundations of Enlightenment culture; additionally, a class antagonism in the social realm emerges: a split occurs between 'nobler natures' and a 'slave class'; mass culture is threatening traditionally established forms of high culture; theoretical man can no longer maintain his coordinating grip. Thus, thirdly, contemporary culture turns 'illogical' because the hitherto all-powerful driving force of Enlightenment optimism is undermined by a stifling self-awareness and self-doubt; a creeping conviction is spreading that this far down the line of history all culture was built upon illusion and prejudice.[107]

Nietzsche's concept of modernity is intimately connected with a complementary notion of hybridity, already essential to the account of Greek tragedy. He detects it in the make-up of the contemporary social sphere as well as in modern art, such as the novel (discussed in **Section 14**) and the opera (dealt with in the **next section**), and most of all of course in Wagner's operas (**Section 21**). Hybridity is successful when it achieves the symbolic aim of the art-drives; it is unsuccessful when it is in the service of the Socratic. In the artistic sphere, the novel and early opera are synthetic aesthetic forms rejected by Nietzsche (here, as his later embrace of both forms shows, mainly for the sake of critical contrast and consistency of argument) as representative of a wrong type of hybridity. But, under the new name of 'music drama' (**Section 21**), Wagner's type of opera presents the acceptable, desirable face of artistic blending. Whatever the drawbacks may be of Nietzsche's often half-hearted embrace of modernity as a synthetic cultural mix of impure elements, it is important to note that any notion of return to a state of organic harmonious whole of society or culture is totally out of the question, even if in *The Birth of Tragedy* Nietzsche at times seems to get carried away with the prospect of the re-emerging unity of the 'German national character'. His is a theory of cultural history that essentially thrives on 'fracture', transitional developmental states and incomplete processes. This is an as yet nascent theory of modernity that is thus essentially equally different from the prescriptive classicism of the German idealist and Romantic tradition as from the regressive utopias devised by some of his own and Wagner's later 'followers', as, for example, in Houston Stewart Chamberlain's *The Foundations of the 19ᵗʰ Century*[108] or Oswald Spengler's *The Decline of the West*.[109] *The Birth of Tragedy* marks the beginning of Nietzsche's own increasingly refined account of modernity, and more generally of German modern cultural theory that leads into modernist aesthetics, for example, Benjamin's or Adorno's.

This section builds on the notion of 'Alexandrian' culture, as introduced in the previous section, to categorize the particular mix of cultural blending in the immediate present. The three most important drives (represented by Apollo, Socrates, Dionysus) objectify themselves as artistic, Socratic or tragic culture; using historical exemplification, these are now called Hellenic, Alexandrian and Buddhistic, respectively. This is not even to mention the many other drives and cultural types that are 'more common', 'common' both in the sense of more frequent but especially in contrast to that which is 'noble'. As cultural modes, these three are all 'illusions' – that is, they create *forms* which, as forms, are always mere objectifications of the underlying will. Likewise, they serve the 'greedy Will' in being manners in which life can be stimulated to 'carry on living', though as noble individuals we have in some way glimpsed the 'heaviness of being'. Significantly, Nietzsche seems to conceive of these forms of culture as almost always coexisting. Thus, our impure, mixed modern culture is a state of exacerbation and not something entirely new.

Notice that Nietzsche has adopted the name 'Alexandrian' as his favoured name for Socratic culture understood in its broadest sense; that is, not merely as science in any ordinary sense, but also any forms of cultural production that have a similar metaphysical basis. Key examples for Nietzsche will be opera, which he discusses in the next section, and education in the section after. 'Alexandrian' serves in two ways to denote the characteristics of modernity: in one sense it stands for the mixture of competing cultural origins and contradictory features which characterize the latest modern period. In this regard the late modern period is therefore comparable to the mixture of cultures that occurred as a result of the campaigns of Alexander the Great. The second sense of the word is that it introduces the idea of the Alexandrian library. We moderns are the librarians of life with atrophied senses, living off the substance of life by merely cataloguing past representations of it. The later idea is likely an implicit reference to the Enlightenment project of the encyclopaedia.[110] Two things are interesting to note at this juncture. First, the term 'noble'. Nietzsche's notion of 'nobility of character', a central element of his later work, is under construction here. The other revelation is in the identification of the tragic with Buddhistic. This is explained more clearly in **Section 21**. Nietzsche utilizes his predilection for non-Christian forms of religion to shape his ideas. Another example of this is the faux-Zoroastroism of *Thus Spoke Zarathustra*. The idea of rebirth itself, though no doubt derived here and in the later works from debates on the Renaissance initiated by Michelet and Burckhardt, takes on a decidedly supra-historical Buddhist aspect even in this earliest text.

The true importance of Goethe for Nietzsche becomes evident in this section. Like Kant through philosophical critique, Goethe radically challenges the validity of certain enlightenment intellectual premises. Whereas Kant demonstrated the mind-dependent nature of seemingly absolute truths of space, time and causality, Goethe questions the validity of the human quest for knowledge as such. Goethe's *Faust* makes us realize that the era of modern man is coming to an end through a sensing of its own limits. (Note yet again the sea, sailing, and shore leitmotifs.) The theme of the cognisance of limits has been developed at least since **Section 14**. Goethe, it emerges, also instilled in Nietzsche the adoration for Napoleon, a trait he shares with many other European inhabitants of the age, for example Thomas Carlyle, and his American paragon Ralph Waldo Emerson. In Napoleon, the 'man of action', Nietzsche adds another type to his gallery of historical personalities representing an idea. Napoleon stands for something 'astonishing' to modernity, the will-type of 'non-theoretical man'. Notice that both Faust and Napoleon are 'inherently understandable'; that is, they are not arbitrary or simply irrational forms of existence, as mysticism might have *appeared* to the Socratic. Like the artist, the 'man of action' is in opposition to theoretical man.

This paragraph contains the draft of Nietzsche's anti-democratic vision of modern class struggle. He argues that 'Alexandrian culture needs a slave-class in order to exist in the long term' – an observation concerning, for example, the extraordinary exclusivity and detachment of the university system that Nietzsche was in the process of leaving behind him. However, its inbuilt limitless optimism asserts that 'a general culture of knowledge is possible' where everybody can share the fruits of happiness and wealth. This is a very Kantian or Hegelian antinomy or antithesis. The result of dilution in this way must be 'extinction'. Nietzsche's critique is directed here at notions of social equality as they are being discussed in contemporary theories of Socialism and Utilitarianism. Nietzsche lampoons the vision of a socialist revolution and utopia of human equality as awakening 'a class of barbaric slaves which has learned to regard its existence as an injustice'. With myth and therefore also religion 'crippled', religion is only for the 'learned'. That is, religion too is thus opposed to the slave class and at the same time dependent on it, and 'our society's destruction' is almost complete. The least we can say here about Nietzsche's critique of contemporary culture is that it is not grounded in any deeper knowledge of economics, and his perception of political forms of social organization remains undeveloped. In *Genealogy of Morality* Nietzsche is closer to a Marxian position that ascribes to economical phenomena, for example the creation of monetary value, the power to generate moral and psychological values. In any case, we have to be clear that Nietzsche holds that equality cannot result from the exploited class revenging itself on the superior class in an act of political revolution. The way to emancipation (if indeed that is desired) for Nietzsche can only lie via the road of education and cultural revolution.

From all sides the modern age is under siege. We have already discussed Goethe; now Kant and Schopenhauer are honoured for using the tools of science to show the limits of science. Kant showed, so Nietzsche states, first, that the laws of science are not 'entirely unconditional laws' but simply a misunderstanding of appearance; the law of causality will thus not permit us to penetrate behind appearances. Secondly, Nietzsche appears to credit Kant with the insight that there is a delusional optimism built into the nature of logic or reason (he is referring to the natural illusions of reason[111]). There are two responses to these two crises (the political crisis of the 'slave class'; the intellectual crisis that has 'logic biting its own tail', cf. **Section 15**). The first is to 'dip into the store of experiences' and try out various forms of solace or protection. Thus comes about, for example, the obsession with resurrecting historical styles of cultural production, which Nietzsche pokes fun at towards the end of the section. The second response is in the formation of a new type of culture which he calls 'tragic'. By this he means that after the delusions of theoretical omnipotence of the past are stripped away, a new wisdom [*Weisheit*] can be put 'in place of science' as the highest goal. Such wisdom is characterized by turning 'its unmoved gaze' on the world as a whole, instead of a part of it which is then (illegitimately) universalized, and embracing the world as the domain of its own eternal suffering. Notice that this does not involve the repeal of science (which is impossible), but rather a science that maintains itself within critical limits, a pessimistic science if you will, and which perhaps draws sustenance from a wider and deeper wisdom. What follows is Nietzsche's very own vision of a revolution based on an education or training that one imparts to oneself (or, perhaps, that one 'rising generation' gives to itself).[112] Such a new generation, living in and being productive of tragic culture, demands a new type of art that mirrors the depth of its wisdom. Tragic culture is so named for two reasons: first of all, it *enacts tragedy*: it is in crisis and doomed to collapse; it is aware of this fact, and despite of all its achievements, it is powerless.[113] However, secondly, this is a culture that fulfils its correspondingly profound need for art with the rebirth of tragedy (rather than ever more scientific optimism). It is the culture of the music-making Socrates.[114]

Note on '*Bildung*'

In the commentary of **paragraph 3** of **Section 1**, we discussed Nietzsche's use of the etymology of name of Apollo. Apollo's identification with symbolization and image-making creates another etymological opportunity. The word *Bild* ('image') in German can be put to a wide variety of uses, many important to

The Birth of Tragedy. *Bild* does not only mean image, but also features in 'symbolic' (*bildhaft*). Another important use is made of *Bild* in the notion of *Bildung*, which – difficult to translate precisely – roughly means something like 'character training', 'education of the full person' or 'formation of the soul through education'. Two things should be noted about the term *Bildung*. First, since its root is image or figure, it means to give proper form or shape to something. Secondly, that it is the other side, so to speak, of culture understood simply as the various products of human life. *Bildung* concerns the way in which culture in that normal sense reciprocally forms human beings (through education, broadly speaking) and is formed by them. The relationship is more clear in English: culture cultivates. The other aspect of *Bildung* is that it occupies a firm place in German national ideology. Schiller for instance, in the fragmentary poem, *Deutsche Grösse* (German Greatness, 1797), maintains that the French have their politics, the British their empire, both their capital cities with national theatres, museums (he singles out the British Museum containing the loot of empire-building). All of this 'the German' can do without, because he has his inner values, intellect, morality and language. Thus, *Bildung* is a central element of German national ideology which is meant to help compensate for Western European achievements by turning them into shortcomings: *Bildung* suggests that Germans have depth of soul where other nations merely live on the surface of life. Marx uses the term *Bildungsbürgertum* to characterize a special intellectual subclass within the broader category of '*das Bürgertum* or 'the bourgeoisie'. In English the colloquial term chattering classes' comes close. Nietzsche is fundamentally critical in *The Birth of Tragedy* of the notion of the old style German humanist and narrower and more recent nationalist ideal of *Bildung* (cf. also **Sections 20** and **22**). This kind of *Bildung* cannot solve the problems of 'post-modern' mass culture, Nietzsche thinks, since it serves only to reinforce Alexandrian culture which is the disease not the cure. What is needed is a new formulation of *Bildung* that will be able to initiate the birth of a future humanity.

* * *

The paragraph ends with another evocation of the 'original ill of modern culture' – a Nietzschean version of original sin. The art of the period expresses this crisis of confidence in innovation: it has turned historicist, imitating all manner of styles and characters of bygone periods. 'Alexandrian man' has turned into 'a librarian and proof-reader, sacrificing his sight miserably to book-dust and errors'. 'Everyone' agrees on this 'fracture'. There is more than a hint of derision in the 'everyman' [*Jedermann*], for whom even a profound cultural crisis is just another thing to talk about. Only a few see to the bottom of this 'fracture', fewer still envisage a response. The 'critic', the 'librarian' (Alexandrian man), can see no response other than to 'run up and down along the shore' of existence. Anything else would be 'illogical' – nonsensical, not understandable. But we have seen from the **Foreword** on, and even here in this section, that 'astonishing' new forms of existence are not irrational, broadly speaking, but rather deny the absolute universality of the domain of *logos*.

SECTION 19

Naïve and Sentimental; Early Opera – Mismatch of Ingredient Elements

The previous section ends with a sociological perspective on art: the idea that art in its themes, techniques and styles mirrors the 'realities' of social-historical situations. This approach is carried forward into Section 19 which is a short essay on the history of opera as an indicator of modern social conditions. Nietzsche's fascination with music shines through these pages; we can feel the involvement of the critic who also speaks as a composer, absorbed with questions of musical structure, proportion and cohesion of form, practicalities of performance, questions of style and historical development. In determining the exact social and aesthetic parameters of opera as a hybrid form representative of a culturally mixed historical age, Nietzsche reaches again the heart of his critical interest in modernity: 'opera is built on the same principles as our Alexandrian culture.' Under 'opera' Nietzsche does not include Wagner, who he sees as decisively breaking with the Alexandrian culture.

This passage is an exemplary exercise of Nietzsche's idea of a new musical criticism, even if the sharp analyses of historical and theoretical musical detail are marred by the need, as it appears, for a thoroughly negative judgement of early opera:

Nietzsche builds up early Italian opera as a negative Latin foil for the glorification of Wagner's new German opera. However, Nietzsche does evidence knowledge of material only scarcely known at the time. For example, though it is not explicitly mentioned, he seems conversant with the early tradition of the form as found particularly in Claudio Monteverdi's (1567–1643) *Orfeo,* published in 1609. This was the first fully-fledged opera in the *stile rappresentativo,* and part of the revival of Greek tragedy started in the Neo-Platonist circle of humanist philosophers, artists and scientists in fifteenth-century Florence. But modern interest in *Orfeo* only started in 1881 with the publication of the Italian score by the musicologist Robert Eitner[115]; and the first modern performance of the opera did not take place before 1904 in Paris. Nietzsche's judgement may be negative, but the depth of his interest and detail of critical appreciation is in itself a positive phenomenon in the largely philistine academic and cultural environment of the early Second Reich. (Later on in his career, as Nietzsche turns away from Wagner, his valuations of Italian and French art, literature and music, including opera, change radically: Bizet's *Carmen* advances to the position of favourite.) However much clouded Nietzsche's forays into the music of the early modern period may be on occasion by the shortcomings of contemporary stereotyping, we have before us here a piece of shrewd historio-sociological critique of opera, a pioneering piece of music criticism, sometimes foreshadowing the style of music sociology of Adorno and others, developed in the 1920s in journals such as *Pult und Taktstock* (Lectern and Baton) and *Anbruch* (Dawn). Alexandrian culture dominated *all* forms of cultural production (including the 'arts'), and cannot be understood as narrowly concerned with science only. Thus, in this period, connections are opened up beyond boundaries of seemingly diametrically opposed cultural forms: the pioneering emergence of *Orfeo,* for example, coincides perfectly with the work of one of the greatest pioneers of the scientific revolution, Galileo.

Nietzsche introduces opera as the product of cultural transition from the Christian Middle Ages to the Humanist rebirth of Classical Antiquity in fifteenth- and sixteenth-century Italy. He finds it remarkable that the sublime and sacred gothic style of Palestrina (1526–94) could be appreciated alongside the *stile rappresentativio,* a theatrical style of recitative-based declamation where words and music support each other for best dramatic effect. To be sure, there is a superficial social cause in the 'amusement-hungry' audiences. However, a more sinister force is at work; 'some extra-artistic tendency in the nature of recitative' pushes for supremacy over Palestrina. In other words, this is another instance of the Socratic struggle against the art-drives. Akin to Burckhardt, Nietzsche comes close in this section to acknowledging the Renaissance as a significant new historical stage. He actually uses the term once ('The educated man of the Renaissance. . . .'). The thesis that the rise of opera represents the continuation of the Socratic tendency, however, induces Nietzsche to see more of the same behind the surface of Renaissance culture. Thus, we can identify Nietzsche's preoccupation with Socrates and Plato as one of the reasons for his comparative inflexibility in determining historically more differentiated and precise epochal categories. Moreover, the end of the previous section, with its pillorying of the Adamic naming of periods and styles, suggests Nietzsche might have seen such periodization as a symptom of modernity.

What are Nietzsche's arguments for what he considers the artistic failure of *stile rappresentativo*? Early opera is the result of a specific blending of music and text, but the admixture is wrongheaded because it is based upon a mistaken understanding of the spirit of music. Nietzsche here draws implicitly on Schopenhauer's analysis of the relationship between music and text as quoted in **Section 16**. In early opera, this relation, instead of nurturing a mutual complementation, leads to one element paralyzing the other. The singer wants to satisfy the need of the audience 'to hear the words clearly amidst the singing' by speaking more than he sings: the *recitativo* style. However, at the same time, the composer or librettist helps him to 'discharge' himself as a virtuoso singer in lyric passages. This alteration, being unstable and arbitrary, means even the timing may fail: the singer 'may allow the music to become dominant at the wrong time'. Thus, Nietzsche's first argument: this alternation between understanding and music, between epic and lyrical styles, is wholly unnatural, and nothing to do with Apolline or Dionysiac. *Stile rappresentativo* is simply inartistic. Schopenhauer's directive of the fundamental possibility of blending music and text is not fulfilled in early opera, nor indeed in the later Italian eighteenth-century recitative-based

variety from Handel to Mozart – *opera seria*, to give it its technical name. Music and text are not allowed to fuse in this mixture
and remain external to one another.

What lies behind this error of the inventors of early opera is
that they thought they had recreated with the *stile rappresentativo* the spirit of classical antiquity. In fact they had only given
expression to a powerful and decidedly non-artistic need of the
age to escape the vagaries of modern life by going back in time
to a point where mankind could be imagined to be at one with
itself and with nature in Arcadian happiness. It followed from
this popular and general misconception, Nietzsche posits, that
the 'Homeric world was the *world in its original state*'. Nietzsche
regards opera as a precursor of that very classicism against
which his book is directed. Nietzsche concedes that 'the Human-
ists of the period' used this idyllic image to oppose the medieval
theological view of original sin. Opera supplants it with an
opposing dogma, and thereby also – one of the general functions of all culture – provides a 'solace' against pessimism. But
this hardly matters since it is the same Alexandrian culture
expressing itself in both, and in each case expressing itself via
non-artistic means. What is more, here is another stage in the
book's refutation of an outdated and naive model of a political
philosophy of history which permeates thought from the
Florentine neo-Platonists down to Hobbes and Rousseau. This
model constructs an original state of human natural existence as
a lever to force a change in the present conditions of alienated
human social life. And it is thus not astonishing when Nietzsche
draws the seemingly absurd connection between opera and
socialism; the link is that both are founded on an anthropological misconception that man is intrinsically and originally good.

Nietzsche next provides a second argument for his view that the
emergence of opera is Alexandrian. Opera fulfils the entertain-
ment needs of a mass culture of laymen, who again demanded
that they be able to understand the words. Why? Because just as
spirit is held to be a 'nobler' thing than the body, so words were
elevated above harmony. Again, as with tragedy in the hands of
Euripides, there is a misconstruing of the 'Dionysiac depths of
music'; these depths are transformed into 'a reason-governed rhetoric of passion', while music is reduced to mere 'sensuous pleasure'.
(Reason-governed passion, we should note, would be a possible

literal translation of the term 'pathological'.) Because there is no ecstatic vision, 'the theatrical technician and stage decorator' assume a disproportional significance; the *deus ex machina* is back again. The non-artistic 'artist' believes that music can be reduced to a system of passions or affects, communicated by *logos* (the reason-governed rhetoric of the first argument), because he is dreaming of an idyllic, original state in which 'passion sufficed to create song and poetry'. Notice, once again, Nietzsche's point is all about the misunderstanding and mispositioning of the affects. As we saw in the first part of the book, his analysis of epic, lyric and indeed also tragedy bypasses the 'pathological' focus on individual feeling.

Nietzsche's two paths of justification (alternation of styles founded on a belief in the original state and goodness of man; the layman's belief in the nobility of words) can also be linked using terms from Schiller (see also our discussion in **Section 3**).[116] Schiller's aforementioned essay *On Naive and Sentimental Poetry* states that 'nature and the ideal' are either mourned if represented as irrevocably lost and unobtainable (the sentimental; elegiac poetry), or celebrated if imagined to be real and present (the naïve; idyllic poetry). Nietzsche claims that opera has nothing of the former, sentimental, element; opera in its Alexandrian optimism is pure idyllic tendency. The Greek idyll is not lost, at worst it merely needs to be recovered by 'removing the trappings of excessive learning'. The category of the sentimental just does not seem to be relevant to Nietzsche, except in the sense that theoretical culture replaces pre-Socratic, preconscious culture. We could then plausibly identify the modern with the sentimental only insofar as it is in crisis and has an awareness of being in it. More importantly, the memory or anticipation of the loss of individuality, or the loss of wholeness, which torment the Apolline and Dionysiac respectively, are metaphysically quite different from the concept of loss or unattainability discussed by Schiller. The latter are founded upon Kant's analysis of transcendent ideas, instead of Schopenhauer's concept of the will. Elegaic loss and mourning are replaced by the existential problem of the need to carry on living with the 'fearful gravity of nature'.

Nietzsche now prepares the scene for the counter position to opera. **Paragraph 5** is mainly an energetic summary of what he has discovered thus far. One cannot just say 'boo' and scare

Alexandrian cheerfulness away, because at its root lies a whole mode of life. In the penultimate paragraph, Nietzsche prophesies the 'reverse process' of 'the metamorphosis of Aeschylan man into the blithe spirit of the Alexandrian world', namely *the gradual awakening of the Dionysian spirit*. He reassures himself that this event is imminent when he takes stock of developments in German music 'from Bach to Beethoven, from Beethoven to Wagner'. Note that Nietzsche puzzlingly appears to condemn along with opera 'the arithmetic abacus of the fugue and the dialectic counterpoint', even though these are key elements of the compositional style of two heroes on the list: Bach and Beethoven. However, he is speaking of these as a 'formula' that critics might use in understanding music, just as later in the paragraph he speaks of beauty and sublimity. These categories or formulae are 'nets' to capture phenomena that appear as 'terrifying and inexplicable' to Alexandrian culture as Aeschylean tragedy did to Socrates; they are thus strategies of containment by an 'impoverished sensibility'. The true musical artist does not compose from formulae (the reference is to the Kant's third *Critique* and the idea of a judgement without a concept[117]). Even the Apolline artist does not attain beauty by way of following formulae like an alchemist; beauty is a consequence of the metaphysical function of art.

The section concludes by noticing the alignment of German music (this section) with German philosophy (previous section). They point towards a 'new form of existence' – a form of human being dominated by other drives, productive of new cultural forms, no longer individual, and whose systems of affect and response are no longer 'pathological'. We are thus moving, 'in reverse order' from the Greeks, towards a new period of tragedy. This reverse or mirror-image movement has been anticipated several times in the book, for example, in **Section 15**. This is not of course a *repetition* or *imitation* of the pre-Socratic Greek – the Greek experienced the same struggles among the underlying drives of culture, but in their own historical context, so that the Hellenic forms are only instructive 'analogies' for us. History has a cyclical structure in the 'very same' struggles between and 'mixture' of the underlying drives; but each 'repetition' is different as the objectifications of the will manifest into a different phenomenal environment. So, something is emerging that will be a rebirth *specific* to the situation of post-modernity (and, more locally, specific to Germany).[118] The alignment of philosophy and music must have seemed a high point in the book to Nietzsche himself, given his personal creative involvement with both activities, and his programme (outlined here, and further pursued for the next 18 years) to find a new language or strategy for philosophical writing inspired by music. The unity of German philosophy and music is made into a nationalistic shout about the liberation of the German spirit, which has been determined for too long by forms imposed from the outside (specifically 'Latin'; however, compare the metaphor of 'reins' to **Section 15**). Nietzsche, generally averse to the trappings of dialectics, as we have seen, allows himself a (possibly ironic) lapse into Hegelianism at this juncture by claiming that rebirth 'means the return of the German spirit to itself', in parallel to Hegel's world spirit returning to itself in the French Revolution.

SECTION 20

German Education; Revolutionary Epiphany

This section pursues a much more contemporary example of Alexandrian culture: the decline of education, in the form of a 'self-cultivation' [*Bildung*] that is modelled on ancient Greece. (See **Section 18, Note: on 'Bildung'**.) The tone descends to despair, before suddenly and unexpectedly picking up with a tone of joy and an 'exhortation' to arms. In all of Nietzsche's work the idea of a radical momentary turn of history is present. It is powerfully described in *Zarathustra*[119] and *Genealogy of Morality*[120]. This moment – it could almost be called 'messianic', a moment of revolutionary epiphany – is always just about to occur in Nietzsche's works, as if the texts that anticipate it were the final tipping point that trigger it to break loose. He thus anticipates 'that great spectacle in a hundred acts that is reserved for Europe's next two centuries, the most terrible, most questionable, and perhaps also the most hopeful of all spectacles'.[121] In this revolutionary spectacle that follows the epiphanic moment, 'a storm seizes everything that is worn out, rotten, broken, and withered, wraps it in a whirling cloud of red dust and carries it like an eagle into the sky.'[122] This vision of secular salvation is at the heart of Nietzsche's thoughts. In its last paragraph, Section 20 contains one of its most powerful poetic expressions. In passages like these, Nietzsche thinks later (cf. 'Attempt') a dithyrambic Dionysian voice is taking over.

In preparation for the vision of the great revolutionary moment, Nietzsche puts forward the argument that even Goethe, Schiller and Winckelmann, however hard they tried to 'learn from the Greeks', missed something vital about the Hellenic world. The failure of Goethe's *Iphigenia* as a tragedy is proof for the fact. This is a remarkably shrewd, early critical assessment of the weakness – in its avoidance of tragedy – of one of the key texts of German classicism: again Nietzsche demonstrates his extraordinary literary sensitivity here. Of interest is Nietzsche's use of the term 'epigone', meaning 'mediocre imitator of a towering genius'. In many of its most inventive witnesses, for example, Carlyle, Emerson, Heine and Flaubert, the nineteenth century saw itself as the epigonal age, devoid of originality and authenticity. The point is related to Schiller's assessment of modernity in the category of the sentimental. And, again like in the previous section, Nietzsche may agree with the assessment (thus his use of the term epigone), but rejects the implicit pessimistic resignation: the terms 'hope' and 'belief' are used half a dozen times in the section's concluding paragraphs.

Nietzsche argues that whereas the German classicists did manage to set Greek culture as an example for 'self-cultivation' (*Bildung*), this classical educational ideal has been on the wane as the nineteenth century progresses. What follows is a summary of Nietzsche's account of contemporary aesthetics and Greek studies, including the misapplication of concepts of beauty and sublimity, and a scholarly, historiographical approach that must fail to comprehend the 'genius of the Hellenes'. These sentences are directed at many of his soon-to-be-ex-colleagues in Universities. Nietzsche is practically writing his own letter of resignation as a professor of philology. We appear to be now at the lowest cultural ebb, where the task of education has been taken out of the hands of the teachers and professors and handed over to 'the "journalist"'. By the latter, Nietzsche primarily means scholars who see their primary task in writing for regularly appearing academic journals, debating back and forth whatever was the topic of the day, adding incrementally to scholarly knowledge, touching like butterflies lightly on topics and then flying on. In this way the proper task of *Bildung* is comprehensively misunderstood. He lumps such journalists with press journalists in the more usual English sense in **Section 22**. Nietzsche's negative take on modern mass-culture with its new 'democratic' media is clear here (jabs and jokes at journalists of all senses are common in his writings).

In any case, there is no direct causal link between the propagation of the Hellenic ideal of classical character training and the resurgence of tragedy from the spirit of German music. While there may be steps that can be taken to prepare the conditions for a revolutionary moment (rethinking the nature of *Bildung* itself, based upon a more fundamental account of the forces behind cultural history – in other words, writing *The Birth of Tragedy*), it cannot be deliberately caused; even Goethe and Schiller 'were not granted to break open the enchanted gateway leading into the Hellenic magic mountain'. (Note the recurrence of the metaphor of the 'gateway' here [cf. **Section 15**], and the reference of this passage in the title of Thomas Mann's famous novel: *Magic Mountain*.) History cannot be controlled (that illusion is part and parcel of Socratic culture); instead, one can only take advantage of the moment when it arrives and 'accompany the festive procession'.[123]

Nietzsche paints a most colourful picture of 'the growing sterility and exhaustion of present-day culture'. Albrecht Dürer's copper etching of the 'Knight with Death and the Devil' is compared to 'our Schopenhauer; he lacked all hope, but he wanted the truth.' This is praise for Schopenhauer, and there is no one like him now – but also a criticism of his pessimism. So, 'let no one seek to diminish our belief', our 'hope or a renewal . . . through the fire-magic of music' (a reference to the magic fire music in Wagner's *The Valkyrie*). The already mentioned poetic evocation of the revolutionary moment has an interesting feature: Nietzsche's attempt to directly address the reader. 'Yes, my friends, believe as I do in Dionysiac life and in the rebirth of tragedy'. Harking back to classical rhetoric, this new mode of explication foreshadows the speeches of Zarathustra. Nietzsche urges the reader, in playful existentialist variation of the Enlightenment motto *sapere aude* ('dare to think'): 'dare to be tragic human beings'.

SECTION 21

Modern Opera – Wagner's *Tristan and Isolde* as Aesthetic Paradigm

Nietzsche now leaves behind temporarily his analysis of crisis-ridden modernity to focus on the new 'hope' for cultural renewal.

This section is the first complete restatement of the theory of tragedy in the newly emphasized terms of music, myth and modernity. It also demonstrates yet again (in spite of the hero-worship of Schopenhauer and Wagner, and the resonating nationalistic sentiments) that *The Birth of Tragedy* offers a radically modern approach to culture. *The Birth of Tragedy* constructs a theory of aesthetics and of history on the basis of a rejection of pure or absolute states, both in history and in art. Michel Foucault has drawn attention in his essay on 'Nietzsche, Genealogy and History' to the groundbreaking shift in Nietzsche's conception of history: it is not *origins* that Nietzsche is conceptualizing, but notions of *descent*.[124] Thus, in Greek culture *The Birth of Tragedy* focuses on a historically mixed form of culture 'placed between India and Rome', just as in opera it treats an art form that is the product of a fusion of different artistic genres: music and drama. Nietzsche's theory of culture is based on the *interplay* of conflicting elementary forces.

Tragedy is not simply the highest and most profound aesthetic achievement, and therefore also the greatest of cultural productions. It also generates, or perhaps testifies to, health in the 'innermost vital ground of a people'. The Greeks who achieved the most remarkable of military victories over the Persian empire in the first decades of the fifth century BC, were also and at the same time the Greeks of both the Dionysiac 'convulsions' and the tragic Mysteries, and these historical events are all related, with tragedy healing and sustaining the others, albeit briefly. That period exhausted them, and 'who would have expected another' flowering of either the artistic or the political! We are reminded in the **next paragraph** that the favoured of the gods die young, although they also live eternally. Cultural achievement is not measured by endurance (like leather). But there was nothing exceptional about the Greeks in and of themselves (as Nietzsche has repeatedly reminded us, and thus also the 'hope' offered to the German spirit that the same forces can be found in the centre of Europe). Rather, Greece was the more or less accidental site of a remarkable hybrid of cultural forces that created a 'new, third form' in tragedy.

The Dionysiac force, on its own, tends towards the dwindling of the political, and towards nihilistic Buddhism (and we finally have the explanation of the references to Buddhism and India in the previous sections).[125] Of course, it is not 'on its own' even there. Since it exhibits a 'hostility' to politics, a drive to the political must also have been present – again, there are no pure forms. The Apolline, allowed to predominate, tends towards the political, towards worldly greed for power, instantiated in Rome. (Again, the Apolline even here is aware of a threat to its 'survival', and so likewise not on its own.) The term 'politics' derives from the Greek 'polis' meaning city; in the classical period the city was the basic national unit, since the cities were independent states. Nietzsche seems to be using the term 'political' accordingly, to mean whatever brings or forces a group together, giving them a unity of purpose and a 'homeland' and leads them to achievements as a group. In the Apolline, the political is founded upon the 'affirmation of the individual personality'. Nietzsche thus locates key examples of the predominating forms of these forces historically and geographically, seeing in neither anything that modernity would want to emulate as such. Significantly, both represent *metaphorically* the limits of Alexandrian culture – India, because that was the geographical *limit* of Alexander's conquests; Rome, because it was the centre of power in the centuries *after* Alexander.[126] The passage is significant for a different reason: it extends to political forms the domain of those things that can be interpreted through his theory of cultural forces, just as Nietzsche recently did with opera and education. To be sure, here the Socratic/Alexandrian drive is not discussed, but that is because Nietzsche had already pursued the political nature of this now dominant drive in **Section 18** (cf. the discussion of the 'slave class') and will return to it in **Section 23**.

That takes us to **paragraph 3**, and the beginning of one of the most sustained theoretical passages in the book, which extends through **Section 22**. What follows, as we suggested, brings together the key elements of the theory of tragedy from the first half of the book, now recast using the notion of myth, and Schopenhauer's account of music. *The Birth of Tragedy* puts forward a theory of modern music which is decidedly anti-symphonic. The symphony as 'pure' or absolute music is the single-minded Dionysian link to the 'inner nature of things'. As early opera is too far removed from the recognition of the will, the modern symphony is too close to the will to be meaningful.

Its representations cannot be symbolically read; if anything, it indicates *everything*. Moreover, it can have no meaning to an individual listener because its 'meaning' is the destruction of that individual. In tragedy (and, as we shall see, in Wagnerian musical drama) there is a 'division of labour' between music and poetry: the poetic elements of tragic myth and tragic hero take on the task of mediating between the music of tragedy, whose 'universal validity' it channels and concretizes. Nietzsche seems to be demonstrating the structural proximity between classical tragedy and modern opera, based upon an analysis of classical tragedy. In reality it seems to us that Nietzsche worked the other way round, not least since he admitted earlier that our knowledge of music in classical tragedy is more than rudimentary (**Section 17**). It is opera that stands at the cradle of this new theory of music and poetry, and, when he talks about their intimate cooperation in regard to classical tragedy, we can see the idea behind it of Wagner's *Gesamtkunstwerk*, the 'total work of art' forged from a fusing together of ingredient elements across the different artistic disciplines. Nietzsche's musical aesthetic is modelled on Wagner's programme.

By means of tragic myth – word, image, concept and the character of the tragic hero – tragedy provides a 'sublime symbolic likeness' for the listener which concretizes, embeds into form, the incomprehensible musical expressions of the will. Thus in tragedy, the listener is subjected to a benevolent artistic illusion – 'noble deception', Nietzsche says – because it appears as if the music, the supreme medium of expression of the will, was in reality 'merely a supreme presentational device to enliven the plastic world of the myth', *as if* music were subservient to poetry, in other words. 'Myth shields us from music'. Paradoxically, however, the combination of music with myth thus also helps freeing up the full potential of the musical element itself: 'it grants music its supreme freedom for the first time'. In tragedy music may 'indulge' its 'orgiastic feeling of freedom' in a way that would be otherwise (as pure music) impossible. Likewise, myth also benefits from its cooperation with music, because in return for the release of musical potential, music grants myth two things that could not be achieved through words and images (i.e. through poetry) alone. First, it grants great metaphysical significance (see **Section 17**). Also, it is through the music that the spectator achieves a 'foreknowledge' (which Nietzsche also calls Dionysiac wisdom) of the joy (the eternal delight of the will, surging lustfully into existence) reached through destruction (of the individual spectator and the individual tragic hero).

From the vantage point of **Section 21**, the relationship of the Dionysiac and Apolline as it is developed in the first half of the book takes on a new aspect. Derived from concrete critical analysis of Greek tragedy, it is now reformulated to suit modern conditions as the relationship between music and poetic text. Their cooperation does not deprive them of their status as separate artistic forms. On the contrary, their shared task can only work when they remain separate as individual forms. Their hybridity is not a dysfunctional compromise (as in early opera). On the contrary, only through operating within the confines of mutual interplay and cooperation can both fulfil their fullest potential. In fact, classical tragedy serves as a mere case study of secondary importance here, projected for the purpose of introduction to this section, whose main focus is Wagner. From what follows now we become aware that the essence of the theory of symbolic representation is derived from the analysis of modern opera. In fact, a single opera is used as model.

Thus, Nietzsche now 'applies' the categories of his aesthetics of blended forms to Wagner's *Tristan and Isolde*, which Nietzsche regarded as *the* modern opera as such. Or rather: the reader can see quite clearly how he derived these categories *from* the opera. He was moved by *Tristan and Isolde* for all his life. That he had fallen out with Wagner did not change his affection for the piece.[127] Nietzsche's analysis of this opera provides the concepts, the language and, to a certain extent, also the 'compositional' technique of the very text of *The Birth of Tragedy*. (See **Section 16, Note: Nietzsche, Music and Style.**) Nietzsche 'urges' his 'friends' to understand his account through the example of *Tristan and Isolde*. An invocation of 'friends' in this way commenced at the end of Section 20 and will continue. The friends are those who are so disposed or constituted so as to sense the truth of what Nietzsche says, and the specifically (post-) modern profundity and greatness of Wagner's music. The friends are discovered, or perhaps even created, through Nietzsche's writings and Wagner's compositions; there is a parallel here with Euripides 'creating' his proper audience. Nietzsche however comments negatively in the

'Attempt' upon the exclusivity of *The Birth of Tragedy*, its mere preaching to the converted, its failure to create *new* friends.

Nietzsche proposes the thought experiment of listening to the third act of *Tristan and Isolde* merely as a piece of pure music, as a symphony. It is not possible, Nietzsche stresses. Perhaps the music would make no sense *qua* music. Many do after all listen to symphonies, such as those of Beethoven, but it is possible only through the mediation of illegitimate categories of formal beauty. In this case the listener is shielded from the Dionysiac power of the music, not by Apolline myth, however, but rather by Alexandrian misunderstanding and aesthetic insensitivity. Or perhaps the listener would be immediately 'shattered' – Dionysiac wisdom, unmediated, entails the destruction of the wise. So how is it, Nietzsche proposes that his friends ask themselves, that Wagner's opera can be perceived 'as a whole'? It is a *compositum mixtum* that presents us with a vision of the inner nature of things by conceding 'the individual existence' of its listeners. Symbolization means finding representations for musical universalities in the realm of poetic meaning: tragic characters (Tristan), images (the sea), individual actions (yearning), particular affects (the jubilation of Kurwenal). The mode of universality proper to music and the will is symbolized either in the concrete image or the universality of a concept (see **Section 16**).

The symbols function at several levels. We have powerful 'compassion' (*Mitleiden* – like 'compassion' it means literally to feel or be affected along with) for these poetically constructed symbolic concretizations (although of course with our Apolline consciousness we are aware of them as only images on a stage). This compassion saves us from falling into the 'primal suffering' of the world. Moreover, they function cognitively, employing concepts that symbolize and thus offer philosophical insight into, but do not expose us to, the 'idea of the world'. Finally, they function imagistically, as if the 'very realm of sound' becomes visible as *just these* individual figures. All this happens 'just as' in Schopenhauer our everyday thoughts and words save us from – allow us to objectify, conceptualize and thus deal with – the unconscious will. The danger always lurks in the background that our human and cultural protection mechanisms may break down. It is therefore imperative that symbolization succeeds in art.

Note Nietzsche's language here: the images become 'visible' like figures woven in the most delicate of fabrics (*Stoffe*, which means both 'fabric' in the sense of cloth, and, much more generally, 'matter' or 'substance'). This simile continues the leitmotif of veils, and anticipates Nietzsche's use of 'tissue' in paragraphs to come. The idea of symbolic visibility is picked up in later paragraphs with, for example, the 'spiritualized eye'. Also, note the stress we put on 'just these' in the paragraph above. In fact, as Nietzsche will remind us shortly, many images could symbolize the same music – music as the direct expression of the world's will in effect signifies everything. The tragic myth is endowed with highest significance by music; thus the effect that it must be 'just these' images, affects, concepts and characters.

Through its link with the text of myth, music provides the connection between the world of appearances and 'the inner nature of things', not in the sense that one sphere becomes identical with the other or could be confused with it (that would be the 'pathological' confusion of Alexandrian culture). Instead, through its combination with the text of tragic myth, music enables recognition in the spectator of *the difference* between the two spheres. The recognition of this difference takes the form of the 'foreknowledge' of Dionysiac wisdom. **Paragraph 6**, to be sure, expresses the achievement of the Apolline as if it were all deception, but Nietzsche will correct this in the final paragraph of the section. Notice the inclusion of 'ethical doctrine' in the list of component forces in Apolline symbolization; this refers us back to the problem of justice in Aeschylus, so misunderstood by Socrates and Euripides. It also makes a nice contrast to Nietzsche's critique of the merely moral interpretation of tragedy in **Section 22** – the key point here is that morality is a component of the aesthetic, rather than either its origin or a substitute for it.

While **paragraph 5** discussed the various elements of the words and images that make up the tragic myth, **paragraph 7** turns to two key aspects of tragic music which make the former into symbols. Between these two is a 'pre-established harmony' (a reference to Leibniz's solution to the mind/body problem[128] – Nietzsche accordingly discusses just that problem at the end of the paragraph). That is, the drama becomes 'fully realized' only through music; and music becomes fulfilled as well as symbolized through drama. Nietzsche is describing here Wagner's attempt to construct a new psychological relationship between music and dramatic action, so that both shadow one another more intimately than had been attempted and possible in 'early opera' (where the two aspects occurred only alternately). The music predetermines the individuals and objects on stage; specifically, it prefigures their action through melodic line and structures their relations through harmony. Characters on stage are 'simplified' (characters in tragedy are ideal, Nietzsche has already observed, not the lifelike and well-rounded psychological beings of Euripides) because they correspond to melody – that is, as the 'undulating line' of musical notes. And the relationships between characters, in turn, becomes the simultaneous relationships among these note sequences – that is, harmony. The overall emphasis is firmly on harmony. Characters are not originally individuals, but rather their essence is determined and revealed through relationships. Melody begins as the unfolding of harmony (Nietzsche is thinking of the musical structure of *Tristan and Isolde*). This idea of undulating lines, and the 'vertical' harmonic relations between them, leads Nietzsche to the metaphor of a 'delicate tissue' [*zartes Gespinnst*], continuing the leitmotif of veil, net, fabric and so forth. In this way the drama becomes more profound and insightful than any 'poet of the word' could hope for. We *see* the stage 'infinitely enlarged' (because the images on the stage are symbols of insight into the *Ureine*) but also 'illuminated from within' (raised to their highest significance). Again, note the metaphor of an 'enlarged' or 'penetrating' vision, which Nietzsche is employing throughout this section and the next.

Nietzsche adds, fascinatingly, that music can clarify for us 'the genesis of the word'. Here, Nietzsche alludes to the process by which language (words, images, concepts) are formed by a progressive distancing from primal engagement in the world (see **Note on Philosophy of Language in Nietzsche**). Not only can the musically inspired symbol take us towards that primal experience, but it can reveal the process of distancing as such. This is a methodological point. We have been stressing throughout how Nietzsche believes that the account of tragedy, music and so forth, are interesting and important in themselves, but are also and at the same time accounts of a new methodology for philosophy. Here, philosophy by using musical tools can investigate the genesis of language.

We must not think, Nietzsche argues in **paragraph 8**, that the Apolline delusion is something positive or meaningful in itself, relieving us of the Dionysiac understood as a mere 'burden'. Rather, all meaning and significance comes from music. With respect to the insight of music, the Apolline forms are contingent (there could be others, for the same music). The proper metaphysical analysis does not lead us to mind and body, where to the hidden mind only one body corresponds and that body expresses it. Starting from that point we might even think (as the theorists of early opera did) that the word was mind, and music the body. Rather, the proper metaphysical analysis is Kantian or Schopenhauerian: appearance and thing-in-itself. In the latter the idea of any real correspondence makes no sense because the two halves of the 'correspondence' exist in entirely different senses. There is no expression, unless music makes it so.

Still, it appears that the Apolline has won a 'complete victory' over the Dionysiac. But that is only half the story, an effect of the inner illumination of symbols. Such a view ignores the fact that Apolline drama only becomes fully realized and metaphysically significant – only becomes myth – through music. More, it ignores the 'foreknowledge' into Dionysiac joy. (This idea is further pursued in the next section.) To be sure, there is the beautiful Apolline 'tissue'; but 'taken as a whole' tragedy has an effect beyond the possibilities of the Apolline, here described as the Apolline negating itself and its 'visibility'. This is the point to which the argument of *The Birth of Tragedy* was headed right from the outset, the end of its 'undulating line' (Nietzsche has applied Wagner's compositional strategy in the gradual unfolding of this overall position). It is important to note that in musical tragedy or opera both do not speak the same language, but speak *each other's language*; the real victory of art, as Nietzsche's wording here suggests, is Apollo's subordination under the yoke of Dionysus, because 'finally it is Apollo who speaks that [language] of Dionysos'. 'Language' might here be used metaphorically. As Nietzsche has just been saying, the Dionysiac has no language as such, and the previous sentence says 'speak with Dionysiac wisdom' instead. Equally likely, though, is that Nietzsche is referring to a transformative effect on language itself: under the influence of music, language gains the possibility of speaking a truth that, otherwise, is essentially excluded. In tragedy or Wagnerian opera the 'difficult relationship' of the deities 'could be symbolized by a bond of brotherhood'.[129]

SECTION 22

The Aesthetic Listener

This section parallels Sections 7 and 8 – it takes the recast aesthetics of music to the problem of the spectator, or in this case the modern 'listener'. To do this, Nietzsche must also add detail to the idea of the 'negation' of the Apolline, introduced at the end of the previous section. The 'friend' is again evoked as one who has listened, will now understand what has been heard, and thus can testify on Nietzsche's behalf.

The section begins with the omniscient eye which no longer sees surfaces, but penetrates to the heart of things; an eye that sees after vision has been negated (at the end of the previous section); in other words, the eye of a blind prophet like Tiresias. (Note the many instances of 'as if' in these sentences. The language of vision is simply symbolic of the mode of 'insight' granted by musical drama.) What the 'friend' will realize is that the Apolline forces of visibility are 'at their highest pitch', and yet what happens is not the 'static, contented, will-less contemplation' of the true Apolline artist. That is, the aim of this process is not mere form, the pleasure of the beautiful, and the cool disinterest characteristic of the epic – the world justified as a specifically Apolline aesthetic phenomenon. The qualities of the Apolline are not missing, but in the process of their destruction they are seen through, so to speak, and thus valued for what they become expressions of. How can this happen, Nietzsche asks. The question very neatly parallels the 'how can the work be perceived as a whole' question of the previous section. Just as, in the latter, the answer is Apollo, so here the answer is the Dionysiac, which puts the Apolline into its service.

The key word is 'limits'. The Dionysiac 'leads the world of appearances to its limits where it negates itself'. This should sound familiar. It is the same structure as the crisis of Alexandrian man, because of the insights of Kant, Goethe and Schopenhauer. At stake here is not the presumptive universality and optimism of Alexandrianism, which, when crumbling, opens the path to a tragic culture. Rather, here Nietzsche is describing a process *within* the phenomenon of tragedy itself, whereby the Apolline images come to speak the language of Dionysus. The symbolization of Dionysiac wisdom functions in tragedy because the words, images or concepts (the appearances) are made to confront their own limits as appearances, negate themselves and in that negation become Dionysiac symbols for the first time. Tragedy/opera thus hits the spectator with the realization that the world is will through pointing to the limitations of the world of appearance. This gives us another reason why late modernity, in crisis and awaiting the rebirth of tragedy, should be called 'tragic culture' – it enacts this same symbolic negation. Here Nietzsche is clearly working on his account of the origin of language and the possibilities for a recovery of that origin through art (see our discussion in **Section 8**).

Nietzsche now turns to a continuation of his intermittent and often very bitter attack on contemporary aesthetics, which he accuses of never having been able to repeal the original mistakes of Aristotle and Euripides. The tradition of Aristotle is attacked for the account of 'catharsis' in the *Poetics*: the function of tragedy is to purify or purge the emotions of pity and fear in the audience.[130] This, Nietzsche believes, is not aesthetic because it is pathological, that is, it obsesses over passions and affects as the basic phenomena. Euripides is censured (though not by name) for his moralistic vision of tragedy, repeated more recently by Schiller, which again is simply not aesthetic. Thus the central accusation: contemporary critics and philosophers of art (like the anti-Wagnerite rationalist critic Gervinus) would not know art if it bit them on the backside; they simply have no aesthetic feeling. Nietzsche quotes Goethe, who, because he 'never succeeded in treating any tragic situation artistically without some lively pathological interest', avoids the tragic in his work. If we remember, Nietzsche pointed earlier (**Section 18**) to Goethe's *Iphigenia* as an example of its author's limited penchant for the tragic. Goethe asks whether for the Greeks it might have been a matter 'for aesthetic play' even when they treated 'subjects of the most intense pathos'. Provided, of course, we do not think of the aesthetic in opposition to the serious (see **Foreword**). Nietzsche answers emphatically in the affirmative: we moderns can 'raise ourselves above the pathological-moral process' to the level of 'play' in our appreciation of 'musical tragedy'.

This means that the rebirth of tragedy is accompanied by the complementary process of the rebirth of the *aesthetic listener* in contemporary culture. Such an aesthetic listener replaces the partly morally minded, partly scholarly critic, by which Nietzsche really means the whole mass of the public, prepared by their deficient education, by the approach typical in academic writing, and by the press, to be such deaf listeners. What is the artist to do with such listeners? The same thing as the Renaissance composers confronted by laymen: pander to them so successfully as to lose sight of the fact one is merely pandering. Thus, there are dramas or operas that excite everyday, public-sphere kinds of affects – 'current political and social events', nationalism, war, parliamentary factionism, crime, etc. Or, a bit more noble, dramas that stimulate moral or religious energies. None of these dramatic or musical works are actually *art*. This interest of the public is merely a 'substitute for the mighty artistic magic', and can even lead to 'a cult of tendentiousness'. Such criticism creates a form of sociability – a form of human interaction, conversation, mutual stimulation, which *should* be the underlying condition for any *Bildung*. But here the sociability is 'meagre and unoriginal'. Confronted with works by Beethoven and Shakespeare, the critically exhausted public are out of their depth. If we recall the *political* importance that Nietzsche invested in tragedy (the beginning of **Section 21**), this meagre sociability is tantamount to a political critique of a 'people' that is incapable of being a people. (See **Section 18, Note: on 'Bildung'**.)

There are some contemporaries, however, with 'nobler and more delicate faculties' who were touched temporarily by, say, Wagner's *Lohengrin*, but lacked 'a hand to take hold of them' – that is, lacked a Nietzsche to guide them. Without that guide, even so extraordinary an experience would have to fade.[131] One essential pillar of Nietzsche's philosophy as it emerges here is his notion of pedagogy. The Cultural Revolution envisaged cannot succeed without being put into practice by its protagonists in such a way as to assist in the training of future protagonists. Nietzsche has developed a new mode of writing very often directly addressing the reader (the 'friends' in these sections; likewise, Zarathustra communicates through speeches with an audience), and his general concern for the training of the reader is inbuilt as a concern of his new style.

SECTION 23

The Still Untroubled Unity of the German Spirit

This is perhaps the least adventurous and convincing section of the whole of *The Birth of Tragedy*. Nietzsche seems obliged to make concessions to the belligerent German nationalism of the day, even though he has already distanced himself at several points in the book from the war culture of the Bismarck regime. There is no doubt that *The Birth of Tragedy* breathes more of the spirit of Swiss than German culture. The immediate inspiration was found in Basel with its peculiar academic atmosphere and preoccupations (Bachofen, Burckhardt) and patrician traditions (public lectures).[132] Nietzsche entered into intense social contact with Wagner not in Germany, where he first met him at a party in 1868, but from 1869, after he had arrived in Basel, in Tribschen, Lake Lucerne, where Wagner was living at the time. In some of his later letters Nietzsche thought of himself as Swiss[133]: Nietzsche had relinquished his German passport with his call to Basel, but he did not ever apply for Swiss citizenship either, so that technically speaking Nietzsche was stateless for most of his life. With the extolling of the virtues of the German character here Nietzsche therefore runs the risk of inconsistency. He also compromises the validity of his aesthetics of mixed states, of in-betweenness, and of a plurality of basic drives, by invoking the 'pure and vigorous core of the German character' to be uncovered from underneath layers of foreign influences. Reading the passage, the impression arises from the way it is worded that Nietzsche is not totally convinced of what he is saying here.

Paragraph 1 invites readers to participate in an experiment gauging to what extent they are an 'aesthetic listener', and examine their own reaction to the 'miracle' that occurs on the tragic or musical dramatic stage. (Nietzsche could, indeed might as well, be referring here to Hume's famous discussion of miracles.[134]) Do we perhaps fail to see it at all? Or, like Euripides and Socrates, do we simply fail to understand it, seeing only that it contradicts psychological principles (the situation is similar to the nascient aesthetic listener, except that Euripides and Socrates *actively* dismiss it according to their principles, rather than the experience fading). Again, do we recognize the miracle but only as something children believe in (or, more or less equivalently, something that we know through scholarship that the ancients believed but we don't, any more); or something else? The aesthetic listener above all is 'equipped' to apprehend myth, without 'mediating abstractions' (e.g. aesthetic formulae or religious concepts) – this returns us all the way to the 'intuition' in paragraph 1 of **Section 1**. The paragraph then shifts from the experiment to a description of the role of myth, which (1) alone can prevent the aimless meandering of art (even Apolline art); (2) which serves the proper *Bildung* of young people; (3) which provides the first, immediate manner of interpreting life and the world; and (4) which forms the 'powerful, unwritten laws' of culture and state.

A central metaphor in this passage is the contrast between a nomadic existence ('meandering' 'wandering', 'seek', 'chase') and a settled existence ('place of origin', gods of the hearth). Without myth 'all cultures lose their healthy, creative, natural energy' (become 'hungry' and thus futilely gather knowledge and cultural forms from all over the world and from antiquity). Moreover, only the horizon of myth unifies a 'cultural movement' (gives a home). With the latter point, we are back to the political point made in **Section 21**. Socratism is determined to destroy myth, Nietzsche reminds us, and leads us to this modern predicament. The predicament accelerated during the Renaissance with the rediscovery of, and passionate interest in, the ancient world (particularly of course the post-Hellenic world: the period of Alexander and of Rome). In Germany, though, Nietzsche implies, this was rightly resisted until recently. Here he cites Luther, and especially the Lutheran chorale.[135]

Modern Germany is contrasted with 'civilized' France. Nietzsche adapts the old argument of the superiority of German cultural nationhood, not founded on its overflowing wealth of features but on its deficiencies, on what it lacks compared to other nations (in this case, scholarly knowledge of and appreciation for other cultures, and an identity of culture and people). The greatness of the German people lies in its potential for depth, manifest in German language and culture, rather than, as is the case with France, in the high level of 'exterior' civilization. Nietzsche maintains that formerly in France there was an 'identity of people and culture' – the 'depth' in the people matched the manifestations in the exterior culture. Now, that culture has become rootless in its modern manifestations, the people follow suit. German backwardness in this regard avoids this 'horrifying' result, because the core of German identity remains unaffected by the depravities of modern culture. Nietzsche writes, 'this questionable culture of ours still has nothing in common with the noble core of our national character'. This 'ressentiment'-based defence of German backwardness as its potential for future greatness and advantage over the other nations is the clearest indication in this text of Nietzsche's youthful adherence to the clichés of German cultural chauvinism. In his later work he vigorously rejects this stereotypical argument and replaces it with a hard-hitting critique of the provinciality and backwardness of German culture (see for example '**Attempt**').[136]

Paragraph 4, restates, like a rapid series of leitmotifs, the central analysis of tragedy. Three observations should be made. First, Nietzsche maintains that art prolongs the life of myth and prevents it from destruction: 'All Greek art and, particularly, Greek tragedy delayed the destruction of myth'. The collapse of myth, and with it religion and proper national identities, was precipitated by the anti-aesthetic Socratic drive. Secondly, we should ask how can the Greeks be 'our radiant leaders' if the issue at stake is the *purity* of the German character from external influences? Nietzsche's answer is that there is a difference between following the model of the Greeks and imitating their cultural forms (see **Section 3, Note: Nietzsche, German 'Hellenism' and Hölderlin**). As we have stressed, one cannot turn back history and 'become Greek'. Nevertheless, this whole paragraph serves to temper the overt nationalism of much of the rest of this section. Third, Nietzsche here contrasts the value of the 'stamp of the eternal' (by which he means metaphysical, Dionysiac) with the 'historical' (meaning any number of things associated with Socratic/ Alexandrian culture: journalism, a scholarly approach to the ancient world, 'worldliness' and the 'frivolous deification of the present'). This discussion should be compared with **Section 10**.

The Birth of Tragedy constructs an analogy of contemporary German culture with Greek classical culture. Replicating the frontline of the Franco-Prussian war in terms of a cultural frontier, Nietzsche singles out Latin culture as the enemy. However, Nietzsche sounds rather tentative here, the whole passage being riddled with qualifications, as if he was repeating a formula on demand. Invoking the German spirit he ventures that 'some of us will perhaps tend to believe' that a rejection of Latin influence would be a beginning, and that the Franco-Prussian war 'might be some outward preparation'. (The term 'Latin' is carefully chosen, to designate both France and the Catholic church that Luther struggled against, by contrast of course to the Greeks.) That latter claim is immediately qualified: there is no point in fighting unless one is the aesthetic listener tuned to the 'gods of the hearth'. (In Greek mythology, Hestia never leaves the house of the gods; thus it means domestic, rooted myth.) This reads as if Nietzsche was damning the Bismarckian war tendency with faint praise. The rejection of what is foreign must be motivated in recourse to German cultural role models, not in the heat of German entanglement in war.

SECTION 24

Justification of the World as Aesthetic Phenomenon Radicalized – Theory of Musical Dissonance

In this section Nietzsche recasts, one last time, the account of tragedy in order to complete the elaborate metaphor of vision (from **Section 21**), and introduce a new musical category: dissonance. The explicit aim is to finish off the problem of tragic pleasure from **Section 16**, using the new notion of 'aesthetic listener' (or 'spectator'). To do so, Nietzsche dwells at length on the notion of an 'Apolline deception' in 'musical tragedy' as an ideal mix of artistic forms.

Paragraphs 1 and **2** state the argument thus far in terms of Apolline deception. The Dionysiac music 'discharges' itself in an Apolline 'middle world' (see **Section 7**), while Apolline images are intensified and visible to an unprecedented extent. Paragraph 2 rephrases the theorem of symbolization in modern musical tragedy. Through its alliance with music, semblance in tragedy becomes aware of itself. But not in the sense of merely being aware of itself as semblance. The Apolline is always aware of this (unless it is pathological), it is even aware, Nietzsche says, that this semblance floats as beautiful illusion on the turbulent seas of the will (**Section 4**). Such awareness is what makes possible the 'calm delight' of the Apolline forms of art. Rather, 'semblance' becomes aware of its new status as *not even semblance* but symbolic expression of a specifically metaphysical dimension. The aesthetic spectator is no longer satisfied with the image – pleasure in semblance is no longer complete once the semblance has been 'negated'. Now there is a supervening pursuit of a 'yet higher satisfaction'. He or she wants to 'tear the veil' and 'uncover the secrets', but the 'complete visibility' of the symbolic surface prevents this. We are, Nietzsche says, 'compelled to look' and yet also 'filled with desire to go beyond looking'. This enhanced effect can only happen in the mixed, hybrid form of art that is tragedy, or Wagnerian musical drama.

Depth can be experienced, but not in the visibility of what lies behind the images. Instead, depth of meaning can be gleaned only negatively, in the negation and destruction of semblance as semblance, the emergence and destruction of heroic individuality through fate. The forces that lie behind appearances show themselves at work: tragedy reveals them as active in the background, constantly conjuring up appearances in humanly comprehensible forms and destroying them. Destruction functions symbolically in two ways, evidently: as the literal negation of the image in its transformation to symbol, and as an insight into the cyclical creative/destructive forces of nature with respect to which all appearances are transitory. The double sensation of perceiving images and receiving an inkling of their transitoriness enables us to comprehend that 'the world is deep, and deeper than day is aware', as Nietzsche puts it in the 'Midnight' poem in *Zarathustra*.

Paragraph 3 invites us to 'translate' this account of the aesthetic spectator into the tragic artist. This in itself is interesting: the maker of art (or rather the forces that instantiate themselves in the maker) experiences matters in the same way as the spectator. The two processes are mirror images of one another and art bridges them. There are several implications of this. First of all, this helps us to understand how Nietzsche could claim, as in **Section 7**, that the chorus and the audience too function as dramatists. Secondly, this idea helps us to see why Nietzsche rejects the emphasis on technical aspects of writing and production found in Euripides (and in Aristotle's *Poetics*, which is in effect a 'how to' manual for aspiring dramatists). Art should arise from intuition or instinct, not from technical rules and processes (and obviously should be judged in the former manner also). Thirdly, it punctures the romantic idea of the individual creative genius. Rather, the artist as individual is more or less a complete accident, a favourable conjunction of forces which express themselves through him or her and which (as universal forces) are also found in the spectator. Here, it means Nietzsche can quickly change gear from the analysis of spectator to artist (and by **paragraph 6**, back again).

At the heart of Nietzsche's new aesthetic of the tragic lies the paradoxical question of an artistic 'beauty' of the ugly (where 'ugly' stands in for all the pain, struggle, unfulfilment and destruction in tragic drama). This is asked initially from the point of view of the tragic artist; in other words, the question is why does the artist write or compose such terrible things? The theoretical difficulty lies in understanding why the depiction of ugliness is preferred, without this preventing the artist being an artist; that is, without this overstepping the boundaries of the aesthetic sphere "into the territory of pity, fear, or the morally sublime' (cf. **Section 22**). The fact that everyday reality incorporates terrible things is no reply, because the question is not about reality but about art (which always provides a 'higher delight'). Obviously then, tragic art does not imitate nature in any straightforward sense, but provides a 'metaphysical supplement', a way of overcoming it. ('Supplement' is an interesting word, entailing that we consider nature or reality as in some way deficient. It is the Dionysiac wisdom, though, that both shows the deficiency *and* makes possible the supplement.) What, however, does tragic art overcome or 'transfigure'? Not the reality of appearances, because it makes us look at the clearest and most brightly illuminated appearance while telling us 'This is the hour-hand on the clock of your existence!'; myth is the immediate recourse we have to understanding ourselves and our world (**Section 23**).[137]

With this foray into an aesthetic of the ugly, Nietzsche more than compensates for his concessions to contemporary German provincialism, as he made them in **Section 23,** and again in **paragraph 8** of this section where hope is again found for 'the development of the German character'. The formulation of an aesthetic of the ugly places Nietzsche in the company of the European avant-garde of aestheticians and artistic practitioners whose aim it was to accommodate the phenomena of contemporary modern culture in a new and adequate aesthetic theory and practice. Here, Wagner (cf. **Section 16**) finds himself in close proximity with positions of other European artists in this area, Flaubert and Baudelaire, for example, or even Tennyson or Dickens. The parameters of aesthetic theory have to be considerably widened to accommodate for dystopian visions of destruction, suffering and fracturing.

To answer the question of transfiguration (*Verklärung*), Nietzsche returns once more to his initial statement of intent in **Section 5** to work towards a 'metaphysics of art'. He repeats that 'only as an aesthetic phenomenon do existence and the world appear justified'. This initial sentence has now been verified. It means, Nietzsche infers, 'that tragic myth in particular must convince us that even the ugly and disharmonious is an artistic game which the Will, in the eternal fullness of its delight, plays with itself'. The metaphysical reality of the will is not a moral phenomenon; destruction and ugliness are simply other modes of its activity, they cannot be judged with respect to creation and beauty. Or, if you prefer, the activity of the will simply is justice (as Nietzsche implies in speaking of the mode of justice found in Aeschylus, and also in **Section 25)**. The restless activity of the will is best seen as an aesthetic phenomenon, since this activity (like all art, including the Apolline and to some extent even science) strives to console or create delight through transfiguration.

The aesthetic phenomenon that achieves an art of even the ugly occurs when music aligns itself with the fully realized drama of tragic myth. In new modern opera the dark and terrifying world of the will is thus presented musically in the symbolic reality of tragic myth that mediates between the world of appearances and the inner nature of things. As an astonishing coda to the whole book Nietzsche ends this section with an adulation of a specifically musical 'ugliness': 'musical dissonance'. When we encounter musical dissonance, 'we want to listen, but at the same time want to go beyond listening'. Dissonance, 'as indeed music generally', Nietzsche claims, is the only true illustration of the justification of the world. In musical dissonance, any superficial 'classical' notions of beauty as harmony are stripped away and art symbolically represents the fullness of being. Through the phenomenon of musical dissonance Nietzsche hopes to shed some light on the 'difficult problem of the effect of tragedy'. If we remember: Nietzsche maintained that Aristotle's answer of catharsis did not address this problem, because it moved the focus away from aesthetics and sideways into an area of pathology, and that Goethe, though fully aware of the aesthetic dimension of the question, evaded an answer. Only modern opera fully poses the question and answers it radically. In musical tragedy the aesthetic experience consists of going to the limits of sensual perception and reaching some form of symbolic understanding.

With the discussion of the phenomenon of dissonance Nietzsche has arrived at the high point of an aesthetics of new music, the springboard for music theory and practice into the twentieth century. The Modernist music of the Second Viennese School around Arnold Schönberg is founded on the exploration of dissonance (See **Section 16, Note: Nietzsche, Music and Style** for discussion of the phenomenon of dissonance in Wagner and its correlation with the composition of *The Birth of Tragedy*). Art in general is not supposed to be instrumental in opening up the closed mountain of the truth of the world and achieve by indirect means what science and philosophy are incapable of. Instead, *only* tragic music drama can show the true dual nature of the world, because only the connection between tragic myth and music makes it possible to reveal the interdependency of the world of appearances with the inner nature of things.

The last two paragraphs change tone abruptly and awkwardly, moving from the metaphysics and aesthetic of musical tragic drama to the cultural politics of Germany. The section ends with another adulation of the German genius having suffered enough of repression during that 'long period of indignity' when it 'lived in the service of treacherous dwarfs'. Despite this, the German spirit 'has remained whole' (see previous section), the 'Dionysiac capacity' of the people remains in 'magnificent health'. It is like a slumbering knight (the imagery that follows is from Wagner's *Siegfried*). Evidence for this unreduced Dionysiac capacity is not only that German music has embraced the possibilities of tragic drama and dissonance, but also that its capacity for myth remains (presumably, Wagner's extensive use of Northern European mythology is meant). An awakening and homecoming is overdue.

SECTION 25

The Study of Dissonant Man

Nietzsche concludes that he has finally succeeded in bringing together the phenomenon of ancient tragedy and modern musical drama. Metaphysically, they are one and the same phenomenon, under dramatically differing historical and cultural conditions, both capable of a theodicy of even the 'worst of all worlds'. (The reference is to Leibniz and his attempt to show that the existing world is the 'best of all possible worlds'; Leibniz is ruthlessly parodied by Voltaire in *Candide*.[138]) Just as the former testifies to the 'Dionysiac capacity' that the Greek people had, so the latter testifies to the possibilities now opening up for German culture partly because of the dominance of a Socratic culture in crisis. If, however, as Nietzsche has been arguing, nineteenth-century music in Germany, from Beethoven to Wagner, and above all Wagner's musical dramas, are evidence of a reawakening of Dionysiac capacity, then (because the two drives cannot flourish apart) the Apolline must 'already have descended among us'. The image is a joke at the expense of the *deus ex machina* which, literally, referred to stage machinery that allowed actors playing gods to descend from above the stage (perhaps initially hidden by a piece of cloud scenery, and often, like here, right at the end). Here, though, the descent must *already have happened*, part therefore of the fabric of cultural events, rather than being an additional and separable dramatic device at the end of a play. There is an additional joke: the cloud is part of the Euipidean/Socratic stage machinery, which was required (Nietzsche argued) by the dialectical method and all that it entails for the nature of drama. So, the cloud is also the cocoon that the Apolline hid and protected itself within (**Section 14**), and from which it has emerged, metamorphosed into a form specific to conditions of modernity. Future generations, Nietzsche comments, will see its beauty.

The Birth of Tragedy is many things, but its peculiar significance is as an anthropological theory of culture – that is, the study of the nature of human existence from the evidence of cultural phenomena, and also the deeper understanding of the nature and evolution of cultural forms from out of an account of the human. Thus, it is appropriate that, in a striking and memorable phrase, Nietzsche utilizes the musical phenomenon of dissonance as an anthropological metaphor: 'imagine dissonance assuming human form – and what else is man?'. Dissonance is thus associated with the peculiar hybridity of man as a changing *compositum* of biology, spirit and culture, site of competing cultural drives, and of a struggle between instinct and conscious deliberation – this all anticipates what Nietzsche later calls 'man as an incomplete (or "indetermine") animal' (*nicht festgestelltes Tier*).[139]

Here in *The Birth of Tragedy* the task is to understand tragic art; accordingly the anthropological focus is on understanding the relation between the human (understood as a particular objectification of the will where creative, artistic drives come to fruition, and where there can be spiritual awareness of this) and culture (understood as both the product of the human, and as forming the human in *Bildung*). Culture is perceived of here as a kind of externalized material space of internalized human instincts. But the human dimension is already a relation (it is a dissonance). The products of tragic culture are what allow us to represent this fact symbolically to ourselves, raising for the first time the possibility of a fundamental anthropology that would be able to use that symbolism as its object of study. Art, more specifically musical tragedy, is the highest form of cultural activity because it completes man's existence in symbolic form by reminding us (and giving us deep solace and delight in the recognition) of our multidimensioned human nature. Tragedy keeps alive the pain caused by the victory of man over nature, the dismemberment of the whole into individuals, and *also* as a reminder of the primal joy of existence as will. Thus, it is through the detour of culture that we make up for the missing link with nature, and which thus also makes possible authentic social and political relations. Culture is therefore the necessary realization of the human condition in history.

Because of Nietzsche's insights, were we to be 'translated' back to the life of a Greek in a dream, we would have an 'intuition' of the beauty around us not as today's scholars do (as an end in itself). Rather, we would see it as a symbolic evidence of the respect and understanding these people had for the Dionysiac root of their being. But we would also be reminded of the titanic struggle they faced to live, the suffering it took to achieve this beauty.

CHAPTER 4

RECEPTION AND INFLUENCE

CONTEMPORARY RECEPTION OF *THE BIRTH OF TRAGEDY*

The Birth of Tragedy is a manifesto. Its young author goes against the grain of his own time and culture, a rebel also against the boundaries of the academic subject of philology in which he was schooled and employed (he was a professor of philology at Basel). The reading experience can be very moving. Certainly, this is because we are struck by the vigour of some of the new ideas and the originality of symbolic construct used to introduce them. But it is moving also because of our awareness that with this first of Nietzsche's outings as a philosophical writer he cuts himself off from those who had predicted (and aided) his brilliant future as professor of philology. Nietzsche's first book is also his last in terms of contemporary public recognition. The book shocks his 'friends' and makes him many enemies. Upon publication, the philologist Ulrich von Wilamowitz-Moellendorff delivered a searing polemic and tore the book to pieces: in several areas he demonstrates how Nietzsche gets the philological facts wrong or distorts them, and how he belittles the high standards of recent German philological achievement. What follows is a short public outburst of exchanges pro and contra *The Birth of Tragedy*. Nietzsche's friend Erwin Rhode shows how Moellendorff has misquoted Nietzsche. The dedicatee of the book, Richard Wagner[1], intervenes on his behalf with a patronizing newspaper piece, much of it not responding to the detail of Moellendorff's argument. Wagner's intervention probably does Nietzsche more harm than good, because Nietzsche emerges as the grand master's hireling. And on it goes.[2] This heated quarrel is proof of the fact that with *The Birth of Tragedy* a new voice had emerged that wanted to shake things up and was duly misunderstood. With its unexpectedly radical (and for the cultured citizens of the Second Reich uncomfortably 'modern') new theories located on the intersection of culture, history and aesthetics,

The Birth of Tragedy added an avant-garde element into the otherwise dull mix of cultural, academic and mainly military-political ingredients that helped shape the foundational moment of German national unification of 1871. (Nietzsche talks about the link between military campaign and aesthetic theory in the **Foreword**). We need to bear in mind that it is perhaps hasty to make a straight claim for this book as a German contribution to a German historical event: the fact that it was written in Switzerland is of no small importance;[3] the situation of a seemingly comfortable existence in quasi-exile has no doubt encouraged Nietzsche's radicalism and bridge-burning.

THE 'AFTERLIFE' OF *THE BIRTH OF TRAGEDY*: SOME EXAMPLES

We believe that we can safely make the claim that *The Birth of Tragedy* is one of the most important and interesting books to reach us from the second half of the nineteenth century, on a par with, for example, Nietzsche's own *Zarathustra*, Darwin's *Origin of Species* (1859), Marx's *Capital* (1867–94) or, right at the end of the century, Freud's *Interpretation of Dreams*.

Of course, the most infamous influence of Nietzsche was the use his works were put to by twentieth-century fascist politics. His work was used for the wrong reasons by the wrong people and by a movement in desperate need of theoretical legitimization that used anything eclectically and regardless of suitability, including Kant, Goethe and Hölderlin. That Nietzsche's work was politically abused to that extent was only in small part his fault: Nietzsche's strategic use of hyperbole, occasionally stereotypical use of national and racial categories, and general political naïveté all opened his work to that kind of appropriation. The association with the avowedly anti-Semitic Wagner is also telling. More clear, though, is Nietzsche's general distrust of nationalism and militarism, while in later years he became a staunch anti-anti-Semite.[4]

To illustrate the book's significance as initiator of future developments in cultural theory and practice, a brief glance at its reception in three diverse areas of modern culture may suffice: psychology, modernist art and cultural anthropology. Our commentary itself provided much detail to the story of this influence, particularly upon philosophy.

Psychology

A direct link opens up between *The Birth of Tragedy* and twentieth-century psychological theory. 'Nietzsche and Freud are like two discourses set up face to face', Paul-Laurent Assoun concludes in his study on *Freud and Nietzsche*.[5] With Freud's first major publication, *The Interpretation of Dreams* at the turn of the century, the parallel with *The Birth of Tragedy* is immediately discernible: the theme of both books is the reading of dreams; likewise, the conflict between instinct and consciousness; both share the conception of the relationship between ontogenetic (the stages of growth of something) and phylogenetic (the evolutionary stages of something) factors. The main interest of both lies in exploring the mediating power of dreams. Nietzsche's focus is more on a psychology of culture, with an investigation of instinct as the source of cultural development, whereas Freud puts greater emphasis on the structure of the individual psyche and highlights sexual drives as the hidden determinants of personal identity. With Nietzsche, Freud holds that consciousness tends to destroy our dream worlds and cuts us off from the hidden parts of our self. Both work on the assumption that – as Freud puts it – dreams are 'the royal road to a knowledge of the unconscious activities of the mind'.[6] In his 'An Attempt at Self-Criticism' Nietzsche points out that he is discussing culture in terms of mental health. The talk is of 'symptoms', 'degeneration' and 'neuroses'; at one point he refers his findings into the hands of a medical consultant: 'this is a question for psychiatrists' (p. 7), as if he was actively bequeathing these concerns to future practitioner/theorists in this field. In Section 1 of the main text, Nietzsche mentions a psycho-pathological phenomenon of dream semblance confusing itself with the object of semblance. Elsewhere he uses terms such as 'sublimation', 'repression', 'objectification', etc.. All of these reappear in a key capacity as elements of Freud's and other psychologists' theories.

Both Nietzsche's and Freud's theories contain a visionary element of an ideal state of existence which is linked with aspects of mental health and psycho-hygiene: the health of an individual or of cultural systems is dependent on the healthy relationship of consciousness and subconscious forces, with dream energy as the intermediary sphere of imagined being. Thus, it can be argued that much of the foundations are laid in *The Birth of Tragedy* for subsequent individual and collective cultural psychological theory. Immediately after Nietzsche's death, therefore, the book comes to fruition and gains the status that was denied to it during its author's lifetime: that of a foundational, epochal text.

Modernism

The Birth of Tragedy has had the most profound impact on the aesthetic philosophies and the styles of European Modernism during the first half of the twentieth century.[7] The novelist Thomas Mann garners the title *The Magic Mountain* (1924) from it (cf. **Section 20**); and the French composer Florent Schmitt calls one of his compositions 'Dionysiaques' (1911). Within philosophy, in the late 1930s Martin Heidegger gives a long series of lectures on Nietzsche; the first set is entitled 'The Will to Power as Art', and includes a sustained discussion of Nietzsche's first book.[8]

Going back to earlier times before the beginning of 'modernity', from a perspective of the end of the modern period, is a much-practised figure of thought in art, literature and politics of the first half of the twentieth century. The appeal of *The Birth of Tragedy* is as a theoretical reference point for modernist re-evocations of ancient myths. T.S. Eliot makes contact with Nietzsche largely via Frazer's *The Golden Bough. A Study in Magic and Religion* (1890–1915)[9]. Apart from references to Zarathustra's mountain journeying in part V of the poem, *The Waste Land* contains central references to Wagner's *Tristan and Isolde*, alluding to the significance granted to this opera in *The Birth of Tragedy*. Generally, Eliot's theory of culture in *The Waste Land* with its decline in mass culture seems to echo that of *The Birth of Tragedy*. Eliot's play *Murder in the Cathedral* was meant as an illustration of Nietzsche's theory of tragedy. Some of Ezra Pound's poetry is devoted to reviving the preconscious artistic culture of pre-Socratic Greece, in accordance with Nietzsche's propagation of the tragic dithyramb (e.g. in **Section 8**): the first of the *Cantos* of 1917 is a good example.[10] Attempts are also being made far and wide to conceive of new holistic forms of artistic expression based on limiting the censoring, repressing power of consciousness. Thus, it might be daring, but possible to construe a link between modernist techniques of 'stream of consciousness' or 'écriture automatique'[11] with the description of instinctive artistic production in *The Birth of Tragedy*.

The composer Gustav Mahler provides evidence of *The Birth of Tragedy's* direct influence in the creation of a new language of musical Modernism. A strong case could be made particularly for his symphonies numbers 1 to 4, but also especially number 6, to be regarded as direct attempts at applying the musical aesthetic theory developed in *The Birth of Tragedy*. Completely in line with Nietzsche's theorem of musical hybridity, Mahler moves away from the idea of 'absolute music'. The aim is to extend the possibilities of music in Nietzsche's sense[12] by setting poetry at various musical junctures, much of it from the collection of folk-poetry mentioned in *The Birth of Tragedy* (**Section 6**): *Des Knaben Wunderhorn* (*The Boy's Magic Horn*). However, according to Adorno,[13] all of Mahler's symphonies, even those which do not set poetry, can principally be read in this way, because the 'purely musical' ones are also aimed at developing a new musical language of identifiable imagery. A host of other composers could be named to demonstrate Nietzsche's enormous impact on new music, Richard Strauss for instance, or Mahler's pupil Arnold Schönberg. The latter refers directly to the terminology of *The Birth of Tragedy* with the title of one of his key compositions, the Symphonic Poem *Transfigured Night* (Verklärte Nacht), which radicalizes Nietzsche's inheritance beyond Mahler's possibilities. Schönberg experiments with the very material of composition by seeking to extend the boundaries of tonality itself.[14]

In the area of twentieth-century theatre, there are a number of developments that can be directly linked with *The Birth of Tragedy*.[15] Antonin Artaud, especially, needs mentioning. In *Theatre of Cruelty*, Nietzsche's ideas of the devastating effect of the tragic can be identified.[16] However, Artaud is not as interested as Nietzsche in the notion of the tragic as Apollonian transfiguration of Dionysian existential experience. 'Metaphysical solace' is not what Artaud has in mind. In *The Theatre and its Double*, particularly in the essay 'The Theatre and the Plague',[17] we find an unmitigated Dionysian version of Nietzsche's theory of the tragic. His interest is in theatre as vehicle for the breakdown of individuation and civilized standards of social behaviour under the intoxicating spell of a Dionysian rage. An extreme reading of Nietzsche's text perhaps, but one clearly inspired by it. Via Artaud, Nietzsche's legacy is disseminated in a variety of new approaches to theatre, Grotowski, Boal, etc. In the theatre reform of Peter Brook, whose London based Theatre-of-Cruelty-workshop of

1964 opened up ways of renewal for the theatre, the legacy of *The Birth of Tragedy* lives on in the theory and practice of English theatre.

Cultural Anthropology

The Birth of Tragedy puts an end to classicist and romantic historicist visions of Greece as a paradise lost whose nostalgic revocation was meant to counterbalance or alleviate the misery of existence under conditions of modernity. Instead, Nietzsche comes to Greece from the opposite end, as a result of his embrace of modernity. He asks, how do the forces at work in the development of the five phases of Greek history (from the Greek Iron Age to Attic tragedy, cf. **Section 4**) manifest themselves in cultural history in general and, more specifically, where in his own contemporary cultural environment can they be located. The result is a 'scientific' view of Greek culture and myth that foreshadows twentieth-century positions in Cultural and Social Anthropology. The book points forward towards psychological approaches to culture associated with the writings of conservative theorists of cultural decline such as Oswald Spengler, C.G. Jung and Arnold Toynbee. Jungian terms such as 'collective unconscious' (cf. for example, **Section 8**) and 'archetype' (cf. for example, **Section 15**) appear to be directly derived from *The Birth of Tragedy*.[18] In the English-speaking world there is one project in particular that is directly linked with it: Frazer's aforementioned grand-scale work of comparative mythology, *The Golden Bough*, incorporates *The Birth of Tragedy's* impulses.[19] Influential social anthropologists like Bronislav Malinowski[20] and theories of structural anthropology such as those of Claude Levi-Strauss can also be seen against the backdrop of *The Birth of Tragedy's* achievements.[21] But it has also left its mark on Marxist culture-theories, such as Benjamin's, Adorno's[22] and what are broadly called 'post-modern' conceptions of culture such as Foucault's.[23]

The Birth of Tragedy is a transitional, future-oriented text on the threshold between old, even ancient, and modern contemporary culture. Its value lies in that it has contributed greatly to separating one from the other by demonstrating where precisely the new relevance lies of ancient history as an impulse for the modern. The book has aided an epochal re-evaluation of cultural history looked at from a radicalized perspective of late modernity. There is a wealth of evidence for its enormous impact on themes and developments in twentieth-century thought, and its influence is no doubt still ongoing. It is hoped that this commentary might contribute to that in a small way, even though a detailed account of the intellectual events it inaugurated or stimulated cannot be part of its remit; this would by far supersede its tasks as an introduction. But a last question remains: was Nietzsche 'right' in what he said about tragedy? A renowned Swiss classical philologist, Joachim Lutacz, has recently drawn attention to a trend to rehabilitate the book in an area where it was originally thought of as a failure: that of Greek philology. From about the second half of the twentieth century onwards, it was gradually being acknowledged that *The Birth of Tragedy* not only summarized the contemporary state of research regarding the origins of tragedy correctly (Nietzsche did not add anything to the argument as it had been familiar to generations of philologists since the second half of the eighteenth century: all had been following the account in Aristotle's *Poetics*. Astonishingly, Lutacz points out, not even Nietzsche's argument that tragedy springs from music, was new!), but that it also asked new questions about the cultural and philosophical significance and context of tragedy; questions which conventionally established positivist Greek philology of the Wilamowitz-Moellendorff variety failed to posit and was unable to recognize as valid. It is therefore with a fair dose of irony of history, Lutacz thinks, that Nietzsche's true contribution in the actual field of philology was first recognized by a number of pupils of none other than Ulrich von Wilamowitz-Moellendorff's, the original philologist adversary to the book's wider philosophical perspective and sexton of Nietzsche's reputation as philologist and philosopher during his lifetime.[24]

STUDY QUESTIONS

These questions are roughly in the order of presentation of Nietzsche's book. They should be used to help you extend and deepen your understanding of Nietzsche.

1. Is aesthetics a 'science'? What does Nietzsche mean, in the end, by each of these two terms?
2. What reasons might Nietzsche have had for writing about the Greeks, instead of writing directly about late-nineteenth-century Europe?
3. What implications follow from Nietzsche's stress on underlying art-drives, instead of on individuals?
4. Why is it important not to confuse the terms 'semblance' or 'appearance' with 'illusion'?
5. What examples of genealogical method of analysis can you find in the book?
6. Why does an audience enjoy watching a tragedy? What is the philosophical problem here, and how does Nietzsche address it?
7. What does it mean to 'justify' existence – as opposed to such alternatives 'understanding' it, 'dealing with' it, 'accepting' it or 'ignoring' it?
8. How would one's interpretation of Nietzsche's philosophy have to change if one did not stress the mutual necessity of the two art-drives?
9. Have a close look at one or more of the key examples Nietzsche uses in the book: Aeschylus' *Prometheus*; Sophocles' *Oedipus the King* and *Oedipus at Colonus*; Raphael's *Transfiguration*; Shakespeare's *Hamlet*; Beethoven's *9th Symphony*; Goethe's *Faust*; Wagner's *Tristan and Isolde*. How convincing is his interpretation?
10. How are the art-drives related to ethical norms?

11. What are the three types of symbolization Nietzsche envisages, and why is the third type favoured over the other two?
12. In what ways does Nietzsche not just talk about, but *employ*, symbolization in his book?
13. If one must be an aesthetic listener, or even an artist, in order to understand art, what hope is there for the rest of us?
14. What exactly is Nietzsche's largely implicit critique of Christianity as a moral system or as a metaphysical view of the nature of reality?
15. Read Plato's *Symposium*. In what ways is the depiction of Socrates there akin, or not, to the portrait Nietzsche gives?
16. Read one or more of Euripides' plays. Do you find Nietzsche's observations about these plays accurate or insightful?
17. Is Nietzsche, by the end of the book, successful in describing a 'music-making Socrates', or is he describing something that would simply *replace* Socratic culture?
18. In what sense might it be true that science, when it reaches certain points, becomes art?
19. In what ways is *The Birth of Tragedy* composed like a piece of music?
20. In what ways was Nietzsche correct in saying that contemporary culture is in 'crisis'?
21. In writing about the contemporary world, what kinds of things might Nietzsche have had in mind under the heading 'myth'?
22. Consider what Nietzsche, at the time of writing *The Birth of Tragedy*, would have had to say about traditional philosophical topics, such as free will, personal identity or objective knowledge?
23. Do you recognize Nietzsche's descriptions of modern education? What kind of an education system do you think Nietzsche might have encouraged?
24. Is Nietzsche's idea of the aesthetics of the ugly valid, or important? Obviously, dissonance was a key category of the ugly for Nietzsche; are there others that are significant within modern art, and can they be given a Nietzschean analysis?
25. What are the differences, if any, between biology and culture?
26. What does Nietzsche mean in saying that the human is 'dissonance'?

NOTES

INTRODUCTION

1 As our 'baseline' translation, we use *The Birth of Tragedy*, trans. and ed. Raymond Geuss and Ronald Speirs, Cambridge: Cambridge University Press, 2007. It helpfully includes other key early writings of Nietzsche. The standard German text is the first volume of the *Kritische Studienausgabe*, ed. Giorgio Colli and Mazzino Montinari, Berlin: Walter de Gruyter, 1988. (Inexpensively reissued in 1999 by dtv.) For introductory reading, cf. James I. Porter, *The Invention of Dionysus. An Essay on the Birth of Tragedy*, Stanford, CA: Stanford University Press, 2000, also James I. Porter's essay 'Nietzsche and Tragedy', in Rebecca W. Bushnell (ed.), *A Companion to Tragedy*, Oxford: Blackwell, 2005. Less introductory studies include M.S. Silk and J.P. Stern, *Nietzsche on Tragedy*, Cambridge: Cambridge University Press , 1983; Chapters 4–6 of Keith Ansell-Pearson (ed.), *A Companion to Nietzsche*, Oxford: Blackwell, 2006; and David B. Allison, *Reading the New Nietzsche*, Lanham, MD: Rowan & Littlefield, 2001. Also: Dale Wilkerson, *Nietzsche and the Greeks*, London: Continuum, 2006. See also **Further Reading.**

2 Sarah Kofmann, *Nietzsche and Metaphor*, London: Athlone Press, 1993, pp. 2–3.

CHAPTER 1

1 Thus, for example, elements of its metaphysics of art live on in notions of emancipation linked with aesthetic reconciliation in Critical Theory. Cf. for instance, chapter 4 of David R. Ellison, *Ethics and Aesthetics in Modernist Literature*, Cambridge: Cambridge University Press, 2001. Also, Richard Wolin, *Walter Benjamin. An Aesthetic of Redemption*, Berkeley, CA: University of California Press, 1994. Adorno's *Aesthetic Theory*, London: Routledge, 1984, and Herbert Marcuse's as outlined for instance in *Eros and Civilisation*, Boston, MA: Beacon, 1955, (cf. especially chapter 7: 'The Aesthetic Dimension') incorporate Weimar positions of revolutionary aesthetics as amplified in *The Birth of Tragedy*. See also Thomas Jovanovski, *Aesthetic Transformations. Taking Nietzsche at his Word*, New York: Peter Lang Publishing, 2008.

2 See Philippe Lacoue-Labarthe and Jean-Luc Nancy, *The Literary Absolute*, trans. Philip Barnard and Cheryl Lester, Albany, NY: State University of New York Press , 1988.

3 Cf. facsimile of the first edition title page in, Friedrich Nietzsche, *Handschriften, Erstausgaben und Widmungsexemplare. Die Sammlung Rosenthal-Levy im Nietzsche-Haus in Sils Maria*, ed. Julia Rosenthal, Peter André Bloch, David Marc Hoffmann, Basel: Schwabe, 2009.

4 Although it cannot be proven conclusively from Nietzsche's papers or remaining personal reference library (the Herzogin Anna Amalia Bibliothek Weimar, Germany, holds the remainder of Nietzsche's library, approximately 1100 volumes).Thomas H. Brobjer, 'Nietzsche as German Philosopher', in Nicholas Martin (ed.), *Nietzsche and the German Tradition*, Bern: Peter Lang Publishing, 2003, pp. 40–82, does not agree. He holds that Nietzsche never read any Leibniz, Wolff, Fichte and Schelling, and that first-hand acquaintance with Hegel's work is doubtful. Brobjer goes as far as to argue that Nietzsche, therefore, cannot be called a German philosopher at all. However, at certain junctures in *The Birth of Tragedy* it seems, in fact, as if Nietzsche was trying to counter Hegel with recourse to Fichte: Nietzsche's model of identity through non-identity, applied in connection with the interplay of the two drives, has a Fichtean tinge. There are so many instances of Nietzsche *not* revealing his sources that we cannot attach too much significance to Nietzsche not name-checking or referencing any particular influences. Michael Allen Gillespie, *Nihilism Before Nietzsche*, Chicago, IL: University of Chicago Press 1996, from p. 246, investigates 'Nietzsche's Debt to Speculative Idealism', and emphasizes the proximity of his position particularly to those of Fichte's in the area of metaphysics of will. 'His description of Dionysus as an absolute subject in *The Birth of Tragedy* is typical and indicative of his debt to Fichte'. p. 248.

5 See the discussion in Walter Benjamin, *The Origin of German Tragic Drama*, trans. John Osborne, London: Verso, 2009.

6 Cf. in a new translation in 5 vols., Johann Jacob Bachofen (1861), *Mutterrecht (Mother Right): A Study of the Religious and Juridical Aspects of Gyneocracy in the Ancient World*, New York: Edwin Mellen Press, 2009.

7 This link first explored by Alfred Bäumler, later notorious as a glowing Nazi advocate, *Bachofen und Nietzsche*, Zürich: Verlag der Neuen Schweizer Rundschau, 1929. Cf. most recently Frances Nesbitt Oppel, *Nietzsche on Gender, Beyond Man and Woman*, Charlottesville: University of Virginia Press, 2005, where the link is documented between Bachofen and Nietzsche in chapters 2 and 3: 'The "Secret Source": Ancient Greek Woman in Nietzsche's Early Notebooks', and '*The Birth of Tragedy* and the Feminine', pp. 36–88. On Bachofen and Nietzsche particularly pp. 48–49.

8 Nietzsche had in his possession a translation into German, published in 1858, of Emerson's first two series of essays: Ralph Waldo Emerson, *Versuche (Essays)*, Hannover: Carl Meyer, 1858, which is still in his personal reference library in Weimar (shelf mark C701, cf. footnote 4). This is one of Nietzsche's most cherished books, as

the overabundance of reading traces (different styles of handwriting point to different periods of use: first in the early 1860s, inspiring the early essay on 'Fate and History' of 1862, then definitively again in the early 1880s) demonstrate that Nietzsche left in it. He took it everywhere with him, and its ideas and stylistics inspired him throughout his complete writing career. Thus, he adapted Emerson's notions of history, poetry, heroic personality, etc. and the initial idea for the Zarathustra-project (including the early notion of the 'Overman': Emerson calls one of his essays 'Die Höhere Seele', 'The Over Soul' in the original) is most likely to have been inspired by it: on p. 351 Nietzsche comments on a sentence of Emerson's on Zarathustra, the ancient sage, in the margin with: 'that's it!' ('Das ist es!').

9 See the discussion in Walter Benjamin, *The Origin of German Tragic Drama*, trans. John Osborne, London: Verso, 2009.

10 Charles Baudelaire, *The Painter of Modern Life and other Essays*, London: Phaidon, 1970; *Les fleurs du mal* (The Flowers of Evil), Oxford: World's Classics, 1993.

11 Walter Pater, *Studies in the History of The Renaissance*, Oxford: World's Classics, 1998.

CHAPTER 2

1 Though Roger Hollindrake, *Nietzsche, Wagner and the Philosophy of Pessimism*, London: Allen and Unwin, 1982, p. 78, suggests that *The Birth of Tragedy* also inspired Wagner who, when he first received a copy, on 3 January 1872, entered a new creative phase in the composition of *Der Ring* by immediately starting *Götterdämmerung*, Act III scene 1.

2 Schlegel's famous essay of 1800 *On Incomprehensibility* deals with the difficulties and pitfalls of irony, defined as the incomprehensible as such. The style of the essay supports this finding and allows Schlegel to rest his case. In Kathleen Wheeler, *German Aesthetic and Literary Criticism*, Cambridge: Cambridge University Press, 1984, pp. 32–39.

3 Marshall McLuhan, *Understanding Media: The Extensions of Man*, New York: McGraw-Hill, 1964, p. 7.

4 It is also common for the book to be described in three parts: (1) the account of tragedy, (2) the death of tragedy, (3) the conditions of modernity and of the rebirth of tragedy. This only matters insofar as we believe that the two-part description captures something essential about the meaning and compositional strategy of the book.

5 Cf. Barbara von Reibnitz, *Ein Kommentar zu Friedrich Nietzsche, "Die Geburt der Tragödie aus dem Geist der Musik", Kap. 1–12*, Stuttgart: Metzler, 1992, who argues in this way and whose extensive and exhaustive commentary only covers sections 1–12.

CHAPTER 3

1 Concerning Nietzsche's style, see Heinz Schlaffer, *Das entfesselte Wort. Nietzsche's Stil und seine Folgen*, Munich: Hanser, 2007.

2 For a particularly clear example of the later Nietzsche's use of these contrasts, in terms reminiscent of the earlier tragedy book, see *Beyond Good and Evil*, transl. R.J. Hollingdale, London: Penguin, 1990, section 59.

3 The word *Optik* means both the science of optics, and the assemblies of optical elements that might be typical of that science (the human eye, microscopes, etc.); it also carries a metaphorical meaning similar to the English phrase 'point of view'.

4 See for example, Thomas H. Bobjer, 'Nietzsche's Reading and Knowledge of Natural Science: An Overview', in Gregory Moore et al. (eds), *Nietzsche and Science*, Aldershot: Ashgate, 2004, pp. 21–50.

5 Cf. Walter Benjamin, *The Origin of German Tragic Drama*, trans. John Osborne, London: Verso, 2009. Benjamin uses the phrase 'abyss of aestheticism', p. 103. By focusing only on early Nietzsche, Benjamin does not see (or admit to seeing) that Nietzsche himself already viewed matters this way.

6 *Beweisen*, as it is used in this paragraph, means more 'evidence' in an empirical or legal sense than 'proof' in a philosophical sense. Nietzsche is accusing himself of having arrogantly raised himself above the level of mere evidence; this links to the claim, near the end of the section, about philology.

7 This refers to the female followers of Dionysus; the etymology of the Greek word is 'mad' or 'frenzied'.

8 Nowhere in the 'Attempt' does Nietzsche dwell on the Apolline, but his retrospective yearnings for a new original poetic style of writing at least suggest ideas still broadly related to those put forward in the early book under the category of symbolization: Nietzsche is still searching for forms of poetic transfiguration.

9 Note that the German word *Lust* is used in the next section, to describe the underlying Dionysiac condition. 'Disinclination' is a serviceable translation of *Unlustigkeit*, but misses the overtones of 'dour' or 'humourless'.

10 Freud raises a similar point in the conclusion to *Totem and Taboo*. Standard Edition of the Psychological Works, vol. 13, London: Routledge, 1950, pp. 3–200.

11 *Philosophy in the Tragic Age of the Greeks*, trans. Marianne Cowan, Washington, D.C.: Regnery Publishing, 1962, pp. 23–25.

12 This is also how Deleuze reads it in *Nietzsche and Philosophy*, New York: Columbia University Press, 1983.

13 In 'On Those Who are Sublime' in part 2 of *Thus Spoke Zarathustra* is an exemplary moment where this revised Apolline appears.

14 The debates on Nietzsche and Germany are summarized in Stephen E. Aschheim *The Nietzsche Legacy in Germany 1890–1990*, Berkeley, CA: University of California Press, 1994.

15 Cf. Curt Paul Janz, *Zugänge zu Nietzsche. Ein persönlicher Bericht* ('Approaches to Nietzsche. A Personal Report'), Basel: Schriftenreihe der Stiftung Basler Orchester-Gesellschaft (Proceedings of the Foundation Orchestra Society, Basel), 2007; on Nietzsche's musical development from big, hybrid, musical drama to symphonic form (Wagner replaced by Brahms) to musical miniatures. Janz quotes a letter of Nietzsche to Hugo V. Senger of November 1872 concerning the importance of miniature forms. Nietzsche's last composition is a symphonic poem called *Hymn to Friendship*, read as indicative by Janz of his 'Brahmsian' turn.

16 'Metaphysics' means two things here. First, and foremost, it means the many and widely varied attempts to evaluate 'this world' negatively by way of the positing of a world above, beyond or behind it. Throughout his career, Nietzsche is thinking of philosophy in the tradition of Plato. However, Nietzsche's philosophy certainly includes ideas (such as, say, the will-to-power), for which at least a certain strategic, perspectival or heuristic validity is claimed, which resemble metaphysical claims. In this second, limited and problematic sense, one can still talk about Nietzsche's metaphysics: a type of philosophy that has somehow twisted free of Plato, without thereby ceasing to be philosophy. Among many other places, this twisting free is discussed very clearly by Martin Heidegger, *Nietzsche*, 2 volumes, trans. David Farrell Krell, London: HarperCollins, 1991, and by John Sallis, *Crossings: Nietzsche and the Space of Tragedy*, Chicago, IL: University of Chicago Press, 1991.

17 This is borne out by a recent publication, a Buddhist reading of the opera, no less, that strangely confirms Nietzsche's critique. It is argued here that the heathen mythological personnel of the four operas of *The Ring* is reborn in this last of Wagner's operas in Christian reincarnation. Paul Schofield, *The Redeemer Reborn – Parsifal as the Fifth Opera of Wagner's* Ring, New York: Amadeus Press, 2007.

18 Friedrich Nietzsche, *Human, All Too Human*, trans. R.J. Hollingdale, Cambridge: Cambridge University Press, 1996, p. 264.

19 *Unpublished Writings from the Period of 'Unfashionable Observations'*, transl. Richard T. Gray, San Francisco, CA: Stanford University Press, 1999, p. 7.

20 Nietzsche's choice of the mythological god pair is linked with Schiller's system of anthropological drives, outlined in the influential Essay *On the Aesthetic Education of Man in a Series of Letters* (1795), Bristol: Thoemmes Press, 1994.

21 Cf. Weaver Santaniellol (ed.), *Nietzsche and the Gods*, Albany, NY: State University of New York Press, 2001.

22 Cf. John Richardson, *Nietzsche's New Darwinism,* Oxford: Oxford University Press, 2004, who argues (and provides conclusive evidence) that in spite of Nietzsche's overt hostility to Darwin and his critique of one of the cornerstones of Darwin's survival theory: he has fully adopted Darwinism in its fundamental principles and

built upon it as the foundations of his methodology for investigating and critiquing culture. A major point of difference is that Nietzsche seeks to replace the survival instinct with 'the will to power', an important correction with consequences for cultural theory and practice.

23 Cf., for example, Max Nordau, *Entartung* (Degeneracy), Berlin: Duncker, 1892. It is also found in Stevenson's fictionalized form for example in *The Strange Case of Dr. Jekyll and Mr. Hyde* (1886). For a good overview of the development of this offshoot of evolutionary thinking, cf. Elof Axel Carlson, *The Unfit. A History of a Bad Idea*, New York: Cold Spring Harbor Laboratory Press, 2001. Also, see *The Cambridge Companion to Darwin*, Jonathan Hodge, Gregory Radick (eds), Cambridge: Cambridge University Press, 2003.

24 There are many points of contact between a German idealist branch of evolutionary thinking and the later English variety. Cf. for instance Sarah Eigen et al. (eds), *The German Invention of Race*, Albany, NY: State University of New York Press, 2006, which investigates notions of developmental thought in ethnography from Kant onwards; also Stephen Jay Gould, *The Structure of Evolutionary Theory*, Harvard: Harvard University Press; 2002. Darwin in the *Origin of Species* (1859) frequently references the work of the great explorer, geographer, zoologist, botanist, volcanologist and South American freedom fighter Alexander von Humboldt, a close friend of Goethe and contributor to a Schiller journal.

25 Cf. Gregory Moore, *Nietzsche, Biology and Metaphor*, Cambridge: Cambridge University Press, 2002.

26 Similarly, 10 years later Nietzsche will return to the historical figure of Zoroaster in order to dramatize alternative possibilities for the present.

27 The famous whip adage (*Thus Spoke Zarathustra* part 1/18, 'On Old and Young Little Women') has been interpreted in an inoffensive way (see Janz, *Zugänge*, p. 15). Cf. also Frances Nebitt Oppel, *Nietzsche on Gender*, Charlottesville, VA: University of Virginia Press, 2005; Kelly Oliver and Marilyn Pearsall (eds), *Feminist Interpretations of Friedrich Nietzsche*, Philadelphia, PA: Pennsylvania State University Press, 1998.

28 Philipp Blom, *The Vertigo Years, Change and Culture in the West, 1900–1914*, New York: Basic Books, 2008, argues that the course of cultural and political developments before 1914 is substantially influenced by insecurities in gender roles. The argument can be extended backwards to the second half of the nineteenth century.

29 Although there are important differences, we should not miss the relation to the account of sexual love given by Aristophanes in Plato's *Symposium*, trans. Alexander Nehemas and Paul Woodruff, Indianapolis, IN: Hackett, 1989. Aristophanes' presentation is explicitly rejected by Socrates later in the dialogue. However, this occurs only for Socrates to replace it with a treatment of love that

NOTES

likewise depends upon two distinct principles (there it is poverty and resourcefulness) which have an ideal goal (the birth of wisdom), but are forever without unity.

30 The term is used in musical analysis and refers, for instance, to opera that does not follow the alternating recitative/aria pattern. Nietzsche discusses this in section 19. In Wagner's operas there is a continuous presence of both musical and dramatic elements intertwined.

31 Nicholas Martin, *Nietzsche and Schiller. Untimely Aesthetics*, Oxford: Clarendon, 1996.

32 *On the Aesthetic Education of Man in a Series of Letters* (1795), trans. Reginald Snell, Bristol: Thoemmes press, 1994, letter 15, p. 76.

33 In the late 1860s, Nietzsche sketched out a thesis on teleology in Kant, one of the primary concerns of which is the nature of *organism*. See Elaine P. Miller. 'Nietzsche on Individuation and Purposiveness in Nature' in Keith Ansell-Pearson (ed.), *A Companion to Nietzsche*, Oxford: Blackwell, 2006.

34 *Unpublished Writings,* 1999, p. 7.

35 We can see Freud's *Interpretation of Dreams* foreshadowed in these findings, less than three decades in the future (1899/1900), for more detail cf. **Chapter 4, Reception and Influence**.

36 See discussion of allegory in Robert Hollander's 'Introduction' to Dante *The Inferno*, trans. Robert and Jean Hollander, New York: Anchor, 2002.

37 Cf. John Sallis, 'Shining Apollo', in *Nietzsche and the Gods*, pp. 57–73.

38 Schiller uses 'logischer Schein' (cf. 26th letter) as to mean 'wrong semblance'. This chimes with Nietzsche's accusations levelled at the Socratian tendency and science later (cf. from **Section 13** onwards). Is Nietzsche getting his metaphors mixed up, insofar as he seems to link light and luminosity with mere semblance or illusion (the third sense)? That would be to think Platonically. The Dionysiac is the 'darkness' (see **Section 9**). But light and dark are not opposite values they are complementary functions in the healthy organism. See also Jacques Derrida's treatment of a related passage in Aristotle in 'White Mythology' in *Margins of Philosophy*, trans. Alan Bass, New York: Harvester, 1982.

39 For a brief account of Kant on 'appearance' see Douglas Burnham and Harvey Young, *Kant's Critique of Pure Reason*, Edinburgh: Edinburgh University Press, 2007, pp. 36ff.

40 The later Nietzsche abandons this third sense precisely because he abandons the notion of true being. A specifically phenomenological account of Nietzsche's use of *Schein* is to be found in Martin Heidegger, *Nietzsche* and John Sallis, *Crossings: Nietzsche and the Space of Tragedy.*

41 As will be discussed in **Section 21**, the boat imagery and the symbolism it carries for Schopenhauer is also of central importance to Wagner who incorporates a boat scene in *Tristan* as an essential

element of that opera's plot. Nietzsche himself uses the image as a leitmotif (see **Sections 14** and **21).**

42 The text is a running skirmish with Platonic thought, so this is not the last time we will refer to these passages. On art as mere illusory copy, see *The Republic*, trans. Robin Waterfield, Oxford: Oxford University Press, 2008, 595Aff. On the allegory of the cave (and the Platonic metaphors of light, shadow and darkness), 514a–521b. On *The Republic* in general, see Darren Sheppard, *Plato's Republic*, Edinburgh: Edinburgh University Press, 2009.

43 For a discussion of the Kantian basis of this notion in terms of 'exteriority', see Douglas Burnham, *Kant's Philosophies of Judgement*, Edinburgh: Edinburgh University Press, 2002, pp. 65–78.

44 Arthur Schopenhauer, *The World as Will and Representation,* trans. E.F.J. Payne, New York: Dover, 1969, vol. 1, p. 152. Notice also that Nietzsche and Schopenhauer also differ greatly in their use of the term 'Trieb', which for Schopenhauer is the lowest grade of the objectification of the will, blind and uncreative. (See Vol. 1, p. 149.)

45 Thus, Nietzsche in 1871 is rejecting what in 1886 he might call Schopenhauer's pessimism of weakness, and in the positive characterization of the Dionysiac there is a hint of the pessimism of strength. What concerns the later Nietzsche is the role of 'solace' in all this, which either is not a pessimism at all (for it ascribes an intrinsic value to existence), or falls all too easily back into a romantic pessimism of weakness.

46 Not unlike Hölderlin's free verse odes, Ezra Pound's and other modernists' poetic form of free-flowing 'stream of consciousness' techniques (see **Chapter 4, Reception and Influence**).

47 Foucault develops this idea into a philosophical-historical practice. See *The Order of Things, An Archaeology of the Human Sciences*, London: Routledge, 2002, or the essay 'The Subject and Power', in *Essential Works of Foucault* 1954–1984, vol. 3, London: Penguin, 2000, pp. 326–48.

48 A comparison is set up again, as in *The Birth of Tragedy*, in Section 7 of 'Richard Wagner in Bayreuth'. Fourth and last of the *Untimely Meditations*, 1876, ed. Daniel Breazeale, trans. R.J. Hollingdale, Cambridge: Cambridge University Press, 1997, between Aeschylus and Wagner, cf. pp. 222–26, the term 'dithyrambic dramatist', p. 223.

49 Friedrich Nietzsche, *Twilight of the Idols,* trans. R.J. Hollingdale, London: Penguin, 1990, p. 117. See also the distinction between model and example in the penultimate paragraph of this note.

50 Cf. Johann Jacob Winckelmann, *Gedanken über die Nachahmung der griechischen Werke in der Malerei und Bildhauerkunst* (1755) ['Thoughts on the Imitation of Greek Works in Painting and Sculpture'].

51 Indicative for this new outlook attracted to the dark side is the important study of early Greek culture by Nietzsche's friend Erwin Rhode, Nietzsche's original co-combatant defending *The Birth of*

Tragedy against philological attack. Rhode's book: *Psyche. Cult of Souls and Belief in Immortality in the Greeks* of 1894 underpins in many areas *The Birth of Tragedy*'s pioneering investigations of the Ur-history of Greek culture by providing and interpreting a wealth of source material, for example, in 'The Cult of the Chthonic Deities', 'Dionysian Religion in Greece' and 'Its Amalgamation with Apolline Religion'. It appeared first in English translation London: Routledge and Kegan Paul, 1925, reprinted London: Routledge, 2000.

52 Cf. Silke-Maria Weineck, *The Abyss Above. Philosophy and Poetic Madness in Plato, Hölderlin, and Nietzsche*, New York: State University of New York Press, 2002, where these questions are addressed, particularly in pp. 4 and 5

53 Ibid., p. 65.

54 The distinction is based upon Kant's analysis of exemplarity in §§46–9 of *Critique of Judgement*, trans. Werner S. Pluhar, Indianapolis, IN: Hackett, 1987. See chapter four of Douglas Burnham, *An Introduction to Kant's* Critique of Judgement, Edinburgh: Edinburgh University Press, 2000.

55 Françoise Dastur, 'Hölderlin and the Orientalisation of Greece', *Pli, The Warwick Journal of Philosophy*, 10 (2000), pp. 156–73, here p. 167.

56 They also share a predilection for the hymnic, free-form dithyrambic style. Apart from the poetry, Hölderlin's portfolio of work includes a tragedy in verse (*The Death of Empedocles*), an epistolary novel (*Hyperion*) and translations from Greek and Latin. Through a rendering of 'foreign' work, his complete translation of two of the most outstanding Greek tragedies, Sophocles's *Oedipus Tyrannos* and *Antigone*, Hölderlin realizes the full potential of his own poetic powers, a process he identifies as central also for an understanding of Greek culture.

57 Schopenhauer, *World of Will and Representation,* 2 volumes, trans. E.F.J. Payne, New York: Dover, 1969, vol. 1, p. 354.

58 See the slightly different reading in M.S. Silk and J.P. Stern, *Nietzsche on Tragedy*, Cambridge: Cambridge University Press, 1983, p. 198.

59 Nietzsche is thus distinguishing between a naive emotional affect and some other manner in which art can affect us profoundly. This is the meaning of Nietzsche's later attacks on the disinterestedness of Kantian aesthetics. For a discussion of how Nietzsche takes up aesthetic concepts from Kant and Schopenhauer and integrates them with his conception of basic drives, see Jill Marsden, *After Nietzsche*, Basingstoke: Palgrave, 2002.

60 It is thus rather tempting to think of him as Nietzsche's first *Übermensch* (overhuman or superman).

61 Johann Wolfgang von Goethe, *Wilhelm Meisters Lehrjahre*, in Erich Trunz (ed.), *Goethes Werke* Hamburger Ausgabe, vol 7, Munich: Beck, 1965, p. 515. The best translation of this novel

is still by Thomas Carlyle, *Wilhelm Meister's Apprenticeship*, Edinburgh: Oliver and Boyd, 1824.

62 Of the 74 compositions edited by Janz, 14 are songs. Cf. Friedrich Nietzsche, *Der Musikalische Nachlass*, Curt Paul Janz (ed.), Basel: Bärenreiter, 1976. Compositions listed in Janz, *Zugänge*, pp. 19–20.

63 Between 1810 and 1820 Beethoven made more than 200 arrangements of Irish, Scottish, Welsh, English and other folk songs.

64 Nietzsche enthuses over Beethoven's Seventh Symphony partly because Wagner praises it enthusiastically.

65 For example, Friedrich Lange's *Geschichte des Materialismus* (History of Materialism) and Rudolf Virchow's 1858 *Die Cellularpathologie*, explicating organicist theories. Nietzsche's private reference library is held at Herzogin-Anna-Amalia Library, Weimar. (see **Chapter 1, note 4**) Cf. also 'Nietzsche's Library', The Nietzsche Channel.

66 For Schopenhauer, 'extensive magnitudes' (quantities that are distributed in space and time) have reality in appearance only. However, 'intensive magnitudes' – temperature, the intensity of an electric charge, and so forth – lie at the very limits of the explanatory powers of the sciences of appearance, and already refer beyond themselves to the *Ur-Eine*. A similar distinction could be made between 'quantity' and 'quality'. Accordingly, also, Nietzsche prioritizes melody and harmony above rhythm and metre. The former are to be thought of as qualities not quantities; or, if they are thought of as quantities, they are intensive rather than extensive. Thus, they are not confined to the level of appearances, but can carry Dionysiac symbolic weight. The relevant discussion in Schopenhauer occupies §§17ff in *The World As Will and Representation*, with the discussion of 'natural forces' and, shortly thereafter, the notion of 'affections of the will'.

67 There is a scientific, analytical dimension to naturalism that takes it beyond 'realistic' mimesis: Cf. Zola's Introduction (1868) to *Thérèse Raquin*, London: Penguin, 1962, pp. 22–23, 'In Thérèse Raquin . . . I have chosen people completely dominated by their nerves and blood, without free will, drawn into each action of their lives by the inexorable laws of physical nature. I had only one desire: given a highly-sexed man and an unsatisfied woman, to uncover the animal side of them and see that alone, then throw them together in a violent drama and note down with scrupulous care the sensations and actions of these creatures. I simply applied to two living bodies the analytical method that surgeons apply to corpses.'

68 *Unpublished Writings*, 1999, p. 7

69 Aristotle, *Poetics,* trans. Richard Janko, Indianapolis, IN: Hackett, 1987. See also part 1 of Paul Ricoeur, *Time and Narrative*, vol. 1, trans. Kathleen McLaughlin and David Pellauer, Chicago, IL: University of Chicago Press, 1984.

70 Cf. part II of Theodor Wiesengrund-Adorno, 'World Spirit and Natural History, An Excursion to Hegel', *Negative Dialectics*, London: Continuum, 1973, pp. 300–360.

71 This methodological problem is hardly unique to Nietzsche, but it remains the case that few authors left such an expanse of unpublished writings. Given Nietzsche's critique of conventional concepts of an author's conscious intention, a case could be made to accord equal status to the notebooks; similarly, given the frequent games of hide and seek that Nietzsche plays with his readers, it might be that the notebooks are more straightforward and less restrained. Such arguments aside, a good rule of thumb followed by most Nietzsche scholars is to make use of unpublished material only where it constitutes an elaboration of an idea also found (in at least an abbreviated state) in publications. See Daniel Breazeale (ed. and trans.), *Philosophy and Truth: Selections from Nietzsche's Notebooks of the Early 1870's*, Amherst, MA: Humanity Books, 1979.

72 Again, see Derrida's 'White Mythology'.

73 Cf., for example, Antonin Artaud, 'Theatre and the Plague', in *The Theatre and its Double*, London: Calder, 1970, pp. 18–19. Artaud also picks up on the metaphor of illness and plague in this passage.

74 The word more commonly translated as 'representation', for example, in Kant or in the title of Schopenhauer's magnum opus, is *Vorstellung*. Although *Darstellung* is a technical term in Kant, its more common meanings lean to the theatrical and might be better served by 'portrayal'; '*Darsteller*' means actor. Nietzsche is speaking of the birth of the theatrical as such.

75 See Douglas Burnham, *Reading Nietzsche*, Durham: Acumen, 2005, pp. 180–82.

76 *Poetics*, 51a36–51b12.

77 Nietzsche, with his interest in the education of the readers of the future is himself not above such contempt.

78 The reference may be to Comet Swift-Tuttle, discovered in 1862; significantly, only a few decades earlier it had been proved that a comet's tail always points diametrically *away* from the sun.

79 Horkheimer and Adorno use the term equally broadly; cf. Adorno/ Horkheimer's *Dialectic of Enlightenment* (1947), San Francisco, CA: Stanford University Press, 2002.

80 Although in *The Antichrist*, Nietzsche treats Jesus more positively, as a lost and misinterpreted possibility of human health and development. Trans. Judith Norman, Cambridge: Cambridge University Press, 2005.

81 The trial was characterized by an 'irresolvable conflict'; the death of Socrates itself exhibits at least one feature of the tragic. And again, Socrates has a limited insight into the true nature of his fate, in accordance with the convention of tragedy.

82 Cf., for example, *Genealogy of Morality (GM)*, ed. and trans. Maudemarie Clark and Alan J. Swensen, Indianapolis, IN: Hackett, 1998, pp. 19–23.

83 In Plato's early dialogues, it is likely that we get a more or less accurate image of method, style and ideas of Socrates. Later, Plato develops his own distinctive position, and 'Socrates' is more a fiction. On Nietzsche's analysis, however, the 'new' ideas remain within the Socratic domain.

84 Frederic Jameson, *The Political Unconscious. Narrative as a Socially Symbolic Act*, London: Routledge, 1983. Cf. also the standard monograph of Ian Watt, *The Rise of the Novel. Studies in Defoe, Richardson and Fielding*, Berkeley and Los Angeles, CA: University of California Press, 1957. Georg Lukàcs in *The Theory of the Novel* (1916) speaks of 'the "half-art"' of the novel. See Michael McKeon, *Theory of the Novel. A Critical Anthology*, Baltimore, MD: Johns Hopkins University, 2000, section 11, pp. 185–218.

85 Indeed, the writing structure reproduces this concept: except in those cases where Nietzsche is clearly reminding us of the results of the first half of the book, the notion of Apolline more or less disappears from sections 13 to 20. It only makes its reappearance when the 'hope' for cultural renewal arises.

86 See, for example, section 296 in *Beyond Good and Evil*; the poem 'At Midnight' in *Zarathustra*.

87 For example, just prior to Socrates' death in *Phaedo*, trans. G.M.A. Grube. Indianapolis, IN: Hackett, 1977.

88 See especially *Symposium*.

89 This analysis of the relation between science and the world it studies appear again often in twentieth-century thought, for example in Heidegger's 'The Question Concerning Technology' in David Farrell Krell (ed.), *Basic Writings*, San Francisco, CA: Harper, 1993.

90 As a symbol, the *ouroboros* (tail eating snake) means either self-reflexivity (thus, for example, it is used on a famous 1812 image of Kant), infinity, or cyclical return (as in the later's Nietzsche eternal return, see *Thus Spoke Zarathustra,* Part III, 2, 'On the Vision and Riddle' 2, p. 137).

91 For example, the gateway into the cycle of Eternal Return 'On the Vision and Riddle' 2, p. 136. The idea of revolutionary transformation through the concatenation of the three time fields (past, present and future) is one of Nietzsche's most fascinating concepts. The present is the turning point, the zero-hour or the moment of noon (or perhaps midnight) in this construction where past is transformed into future.

92 See also the discussion of the position of artist and philosophy in the commentary to the **Foreword**.

93 The increase in the significance of myth corresponds to a dramatic lessening in the frequency of the term 'symbol'. Among other things, this plasticity of language creates a strategic impression of anachromism: while 'symbolization' feels like a contemporary theoretical concept to be used with respect to ancient Greece, myth feels decidedly archaic in the modern world.

94 The verb 'express' is here '*darstellen*', with its theatrical connotations, and elsewhere 'expressions' is '*Ausdrücke*'; definitely not to be translated as 'represents' or 'representations' for reasons obvious enough.

95 See Georges Liébert, *Nietzsche and Music*, Chicago, IL: University of Chicago Press, 2004; Brian McGee, *The Tristan Chord: Wagner and Philosophy*, Holt, 2002; and the 1996 special issue of *New Nietzsche Studies*, ed. Babich and Allison, New York: Fordham University Press, 1996. Thomas Mann, *Doctor Faustus: The Life of the German Composer Adrian Leverkuhn, as Told by a Friend*, New York: Modern Library, 1966. The novel gathers its music theory content from Adorno's *Philosophy of Modern Music*, and contains long passages on dissonance. See James Schmidt, 'Mephistopheles in Hollywood', in Cambridge Companion *to Adorno*, Cambridge: Cambridge University Press, 2004.

96 Charles Rosen, *The Classical Style. Haydn, Mozart, Beethoven*, London: Faber and Faber, 1997, p. 348.

97 Theodor Wiesengrund Adorno, *Mahler: A Musical Physiognomy*, Chicago, IL: Chicago University Press, 1996, p. 7.

98 See the discussion of 'sequences of words' in the last section of 'The Dionysiac World View'.

99 Cf. *Zeit- und Lebenstafel*, Nietzsche Werke, ed. Karl Schlechta, Munich: Hanser, 1956, vol III, pp. 1361–64. Our translation

100 A very useful overview of the role of myth in German cultural theory down to Nietzsche in George S. Williamson, *The Longing for Myth in Germany: Religion and Aesthetic Culture from Romanticism to Nietzsche*, Chicago, IL: Chicago University Press, 2004. It is important to realize that Nietzsche was by no means the first to contemplate the intellectual problem nor the cultural possibilities of myth. In addition to the many anthropologists, Nietzsche was influenced by two examples: the 'Oldest Program towards a System in German Idealism', a fragment from the 1790s most often attributed to Hegel, which speaks of a reinvigoration of mythology, albeit in alignment with reason (see translation and commentary in David Farrell Krell, *The Tragic Absolute. German Idealism and the Languishing of God*, Bloomington, IN: Indiana University Press, 2005); likewise Schelling's 1842 *Historical-Critical Introduction to the Philosophy of Mythology*, trans. Mason Richey and Marcus Zisselsberger, Albany, NY: State University of New York Press, 2008.

101 *Poetics*, 49b25–27.

102 In these remarks Nietzsche's philological conscience comes to the fore. He refrains from speculation where historical source material is scant. He was very well informed in the area of ancient music theory and practice. Evidence for this is the copy of an extremely detailed, scholarly, and still largely topical monograph in Nietzsche's private reference library, Rudolph Westphal, *Geschichte der alten und mittelalterlichen Musik* (History of Ancient and Medieval

Music), Breslau: Leuckart, 1865, heavily annotated by Nietzsche with marginalia and underlining. Shelf mark C216, Nietzsche Estate, Herzogin-Anna-Amalia Library, Weimar.

103 Examples might be the storm sequences in Beethoven's Sixth, or Rossini's *The Barber of Seville*. Presumably, though, Nietzsche would have distinguished between 'tone painting' and 'tone or symphonic poem', the latter a form widely disseminated in nineteenth- and early-twentieth-century European music, in the wake of Berlioz's experiments with symphonic form; Liszt, in many ways musical teacher to Wagner, excelled in the genre with works such as *A Faust Symphony*, *Orpheus* and *Tasso*; Strauss, for instance with *Thus Spoke Zarathustra*, Schoenberg and Bartok continue the tradition. On the register of Nietzsche's musical compositions are three symphonic poems. Cf. Janz, *Zugänge*, p. 19.

104 See Aristotle, *Poetics*, 54a16ff.

105 Jacob Burckhardt, *Civilisation of Renaissance in Italy*, trans. S.G.C. Middlemore, London: Penguin Classics, 1990.

106 This concept is a constituent element of philosophical 'hermeneutics' since Wilhelm Dilthey. See Hans-Georg Gadamer, *Truth and Method*, London: Continuum, 2006.

107 It might be advantageous to draw a parallel here between this third element of what Nietzsche identifies as 'modern' with twentieth-century notions of the 'post-modern' (see **Chapter 4, Reception and Influence**).

108 Houston Stewart Chamberlain, *The Foundations of the 19th Century*, trans. John Lees, New York: Adamant Media Corporation, 2003.

109 Oswald Spengler, *The Decline of the West*, trans. Charles Francis Atkinson, abridged, Oxford: Oxford University Press, 1991.

110 See the notion of the 'antiquarian' in *Untimely Meditations*, p. 67.

111 For a brief account, see Burnham and Young, *Kant's* Critique of Pure Reason, Edinburgh: Edinburgh University Press, 2007, pp. 138–42.

112 Again, the concept of a post-Socratic mode of human existence will develop in Nietzsche's later work to the idea of the 'free spirit' and also the 'overman'.

113 For a discussion of the tendency of post-Enlightenment thought to think its own condition in terms of the tragic, see David Farrell Krell, *The Tragic Absolute*.

114 The question of to what extent Nietzsche's ideas here constitute a true advance beyond Platonic metaphysics, conceived broadly, is a fascinating one; likewise the question of whether the new tragic culture envisaged will be able to avoid the death experienced by Greek tragedy. Nietzsche, in the 'Attempt', obviously feels he has failed. Heidegger and especially Sallis (Martin Heidegger, *Nietzsche* and John Sallis, *Crossings: Nietzsche and the Space of Tragedy*) provide a full discussion.

115 Cf. John Wenham (ed.), *Claudio Monteverdi, 'Orfeo'*, Cambridge Opera Handbooks, Cambridge: Cambridge University Press, 1986,

here particularly Nigel Fortune 'The Rediscovery of Orfeo', pp. 78–118.
116 For a much more full discussion, see Nicholas Martin, *Nietzsche and Schiller. Untimely Aesthetics*, Oxford: Clarendon Press, 1996.
117 See §§7–9 of *Critique of Judgement*. For a discussion, see chapters one and two of Douglas Burnham, *An Introduction to Kant's Critique of Judgement*.
118 See discussion in **Section 3, Note: Nietzsche, German 'Hellenism' and Hölderlin.**
119 Cf. Part III, section 2: 'On the Vision and Riddle', pp. 134–38.
120 Cf. Third Treatise, the end of section 27: 'All great things perish through themselves, through an act of self-cancellation', etc. p. 117.
121 *Genealogy*, p. 117.
122 There is a dialogue between this passage and Walter Benjamin's 'Ninth Thesis on the Philosophy of History'. Compare Nietzsche's jubilant vision of revolutionary transfiguration with Benjamin's depressed view of historical progress (in the light of the Hitler-Stalin Pact of 1939) that renders revolutionary intervention progressively impossible :'. . . this is how one pictures the angel of history . . .' 'Theses on the Philosophy of History' (1940), in *Illuminations*, Hannah Arendt (ed.), London: Fontana, 1972, pp. 245–55, here p. 249.
123 The concept has considerable affinities with Alain Badiou's notion of 'fidelity': see Part V of *Being and Event*, trans. Oliver Feltman, London: Continuum, 2006.
124 Michel Foucault, 'Nietzsche, Genealogy, History', in Paul Rabinow (ed.), *The Foucault Reader*, London: Penguin 1991, pp. 76–100, cf. especially pp. 76–90.
125 Robert G. Morrison, *Nietzsche and Buddhism, A Study in Nihilism and Ironic Affinities*, Oxford: Oxford University Press, 1999. Freny Mistry, *Nietzsche and Buddhism, Prolegomenon to a Comparative Study*, Berlin: deGruyter, 1981. Also Part III, *Nietzsche and the Gods*, pp. 87–136.Interest in Eastern thought was widespread in the nineteenth century in Europe, and Schopenhauer and Nietzsche were not exceptions. However, hampered by the available translations and commentaries, misunderstanding was no less widespread. Here, Buddhism is oversimplified as nihilism.
126 Those interpreters of Nietzsche who see Socratic culture as an excessive, one-sided victory of the Apolline can point to this section, with Rome following on from Greece's decline. However, not only does Nietzsche never actually suggest this, but he is also merely naming examples and specifically *political* (rather than artistic) examples at that. These examples also happen to have the irresistible advantage of providing a neat geographical and historical metaphor (Greece 'between' India and Rome). Finally, given the essentially cyclical nature of history for Nietzsche, chronology of itself is rarely useful evidence.
127 See Janz, *Zugänge*: 'On 27 December 1888, ten days before his mental breakdown, Nietzsche writes to Carl Fuchs, who is working on a

book on Wagner, "On no account leave out *Tristan*: it is the capital work and fascinating beyond all comparison in all the arts."' P. 28, (our translation).

128 See, for example, 'A New System of Nature', in G.W. Leibniz, *Philosophical Essays*, Roger Ariew and Daniel Garber (ed. and trans.), Indianapolis, IN: Hackett, 1989.

129 One contradiction of the text may be pointed to here on the level of metaphorical symbolization: the two deities are here symbolically linked as brothers, whereas earlier they appear gendered in opposite ways.

130 Aristotle, *Poetics*, trans. Richard Janko, Indianapolis, IN: Hackett, 1987.

131 The star that shone briefly is probably a reference to *Eta Carinae*, a wildly variable star that had a flare-up in 1870.

132 Cf. David Marc Hoffmann (ed.), *Nietzsche und die Schweiz*, Zürich: Strauhof, 1994; also, Andrea Bollinger and Franziska Trenkle, *Nietzsche in Basel*, Basel: Schwabe, 2000.

133 *Nietzsche in Basel*, p. 20.

134 *Enquiries Concerning Human Understanding*, ed. P.H. Nidditch, 3rd edn., Oxford: Oxford University Press, 1975.

135 Nietzsche's views on Luther are complex. In *Beyond Good and Evil*, he is celebrated as chief architect of modern German language (section 248). However, see *Gay Science 358,* and again *Genealogy*, p. 106: 'Luther, the peasant . . .'

136 For example, 'the desolation of the German spirit . . .', *Genealogy*, p. 115.

137 'Transfiguration' is the standard translation of *Verklärung*; however, we should not miss that the root of the latter is not figure or form, but *clarity*. In accordance with Nietzsche's optical metaphor, the term is about making visible or even rendering transparent.

138 See G.W. Leibniz, *Theodicy*, trans. E.M. Huggard, Chicago, IL: Open Court, 1998. Francois Voltaire, *Candide: Or, Optimism*, trans. Theo Cuffe, London: Penguin, 2005.

139 *Beyond Good and Evil*, section 62.

CHAPTER 4

1 Indeed, a draft of a part of the book was given to Wagner's wife, Cosima as a birthday present.

2 The contributions are collected in a slim volume Karlfried Gründer (ed.), *The Quarrel about the Birth of Tragedy*. (Der Streit um Nietzsches *Geburt der Tragödie*, [contributors are Erwin Rhode, Ulrich von Wilamowitz-Moellendorff and Richard Wagner]), Hildesheim: Olms, 1989.

3 Cf. our brief discussion of Nietzsche's political loyalties and status in the **Foreword** and **Section 22.**

4 Most of the damage was caused by his sister and the Weimar Nietzsche Gesellschaft under her chairmanship who exploited Nietzsche's

use of hyperbole, etc., manipulated the vast fragmentary output of the ideas he bequeathed, and even occasionally falsified the work.
5 Cf. Paul-Laurent Assoun, *Freud and Nietzsche*, London: Continuum, 2006, where the link is investigated in fullest detail, here p. 189.
6 Sigmund Freud, *The Interpretation of Dreams*, Standard Edition of the Psychological Works, vols. 4 and 5, London: Hogarth, 1975, here vol. 5, p. 608.
7 Cf. Leon Surette, *The Birth of Modernism. Pound, Eliot, Yeats, and the Occult*, Montreal: McGill-Queens University Press, 1994, discusses Nietzsche's trail in the works of some of the leading modernists writing in English. For further discussion of Nietzsche's relation to contemporary literary production and criticism, see Douglas Burnham and Melanie Ebdon, 'Philosophy and Literature', in *The Continuum Companion to Continental Philosophy*, ed. John Mullarkey and Beth Lord, London: Continuum, 2009.
8 The four volumes are collected into two in Martin Heidegger, *Nietzsche*, trans. David Farrell Krell, San Francisco, CA: Harper & Row, 1991. See Paul Gordon, *Tragedy after Nietzsche, Rapturous Superabundance*, Chicago, IL: University of Illinois Press, 2000. The Heideggerian tradition, and dealing with Nietzsche's account of art generally and tragedy particularly, can be found in Denis Schmidt, *On Germans and Other Greeks: Tragedy and Ethical Life*, Bloomington, IN: Indiana University Press, 2001; David Farrell Krell, *The Tragic Absolute. German Idealism and the Languishing of God*, Bloomington, IN: Indiana University Press, 2005; and John Sallis, *Crossings: Nietzsche and the Space of Tragedy*, Chicago, IL: University of Chicago Press, 1991.
9 Originally published in 2 volumes in 1890, the project grew to 12 volumes for the third edition of 1915. This edition was reprinted in 15 volumes (Basingstoke: Palgrave MacMillan, 2005). Frazer himself edited an abridged one-volume version in 1922; this edition is currently available as a paperback edition, London: Penguin, 1996. To Modernists like Eliot and W.B. Yeats, *The Birth of Tragedy* and *The Golden Bough* formed part of a package of influences.
10 Cf. Kathryn Lindberg, *Reading Pound, Reading Nietzsche. Modernism after Nietzsche*, Oxford: Oxford University Press, 1987.
11 There is a whole French line of Nietzsche reception including, of course, in Modernism. Cf. Jacques Rider, *Nietzsche en France*, Paris: Presses Universitaires de France, 1999.
12 Alma Mahler, in *Gustav Mahler, Memories and Letters*, London: Cardinal, 1990, reports Mahler's overall rejection of Nietzsche's atheistic philosophical position and his unhappiness with Nietzsche's later anti-Wagnerian stance. This view has recently been corrected as oversimplified. There is a rich seam of evidence, both on a personal and musical level, for the growth of Mahler's artistic identity in close proximity with Nietzsche's early positions. Cf. particularly the Mahler section in William J. McGrath, *Dionysian Art and*

Populist Politics in Austria, New Haven, CT: Yale University Press, 1974, where Mahler's early contacts with Nietzsche are explored.

13 Theodor Wiesengrund-Adorno, *Mahler. A Musical Physiognomy*, Chicago, IL: University of Chicago Press, 1996. Cf. particularly chapters 1, 3 and 6.

14 For a comprehensive account, see Georges Liébert, *Nietzsche and Music*, trans. David Pellauer and Graham Parkes, Chicago, IL: University of Chicago Press, 2004.

15 Cf. T. John L. Styan, *Modern Drama in Theory and Practice*, particularly vol 2: *Symbolism, Surrealism and the Absurd*, Cambridge: Cambridge University press, 1983.

16 Cf. 'The Own and the Foreign Orient. Schlegel, Nietzsche, Artaud, Brecht. Notes on the Process of a Reception' in Erika Fischer-Lichte et al. (eds), *The Dramatic Touch of Difference*, Tübingen: Narr, 1990.

17 Antonin Artaud, *The Theatre and its Double*, London: Calder, 1970.

18 Cf. Paul Bishop, 'Jung and Nietzsche', in *Jung in Contexts. A Reader*, London: Routledge, 1999.

19 Cf., for example, the section XLIII, 'Dionysus', Penguin edition, pp. 464–71.

20 Malinowski clarifies his indebtedness to *The Birth of Tragedy* as a foundational text inspiring his own innovative approach in an early essay, 'Observations on Nietzsche's "The Birth of Tragedy"' 1904/05, in Robert J. Thornton, Peter Skalnik, (eds), *The Early Writings of Bronislaw Malinowski*, Cambridge: Cambridge University Press, 1993.

21 Tracy B. Strong, *Nietzsche and the Politics of Transfiguration*, Chicago, IL: University of Illinois Press, 2000, deals with Nietzsche's conception of anthropology, outlining similarities and differences in the approaches to anthropology in Rousseau, Nietzsche and Levi-Strauss.

22 Particularly, Adorno/Horkheimer's *Dialectic of Enlightenment* (1947), San Francisco, CA: Stanford University Press, 2002, shows strong echoes of Nietzsche's psychology of culture in its juxtaposition of 'primeval' Greek and Enlightenment culture.

23 For a comprehensive discussion of Nietzsche's impact on post-modern theory, see Clayton Koelb (ed.), *Nietzsche as Postmodernist. Essays Pro and Contra*, New York: State University Press, 1990. Of more recent philosophers who have taken *The Birth of Tragedy* seriously, see especially the first chapter of Giles Deleuze, *Nietzsche and Philosophy*, trans. Hugh Tomlinson, London: Continuum, 2006.

24 'Fruchtbares Ärgernis': Nietzsche's 'Geburt der Tragödie und die gräzistische Tragödienforschung', in *Nietzsche und die Schweiz*, Zürich: Strauhof, 1994, pp. 30–46, cf. particularly pp. 41–44.

FURTHER READING

THE TEXT

Nietzsche makes extensive use of metaphors, wordplay, puns and so forth. This is why his work is notoriously difficult to translate. As our 'baseline' translation, we use *The Birth of Tragedy*, trans. and ed. Raymond Geuss and Ronald Speirs, Cambridge: Cambridge University Press, 2007. It helpfully includes other key early writings of Nietzsche, for example, the seminal essay (though unpublished by Nietzsche) 'On Truth and Lying'. There are other good recent English translations, for example, Douglas Smith's *The Birth of Tragedy*, Oxford: World's Classics, 2000, or Shaun Whiteside's *The Birth of Tragedy*, London: Penguin, 1994. The first translation of *The Birth of Tragedy* into English (1909) is also still in print and one of the best, partly owing to the historical proximity of styles of German and English: William A. Haussmann, ed. Oscar Levy, vol. 1 of *The Complete Works of Friedrich Nietzsche: The First Complete and Authorised English Translation*, in 18 vols, London: Foulis, 1909–13.

Some of Nietzsche's word artistry simply cannot (fully) be rendered, and any reader of *The Birth of Tragedy* in translation will have to make do with an approximation. For linguistically adventurous readers, it might be advisable to compare with the English versions and/or check key terms or passages against the German original, if need be with the help of a dictionary. The standard German text is the first volume of the *Kritische Studienausgabe*, ed. Giorgio Colli and Mazzino Montinari, Berlin: Walter de Gruyter, 1988. (Inexpensively reissued in 1999 by dtv.)

Facsimile of the first edition title page with the title vignette of Prometheus Unbound, drafted by Nietzsche, in Friedrich Nietzsche, *Handschriften, Erstausgaben und Widmungsexemplare. Die Sammlung Rosenthal-Levy im Nietzsche-Haus in Sils Maria*, ed. Julia Rosenthal, Peter André Bloch, David Marc Hoffmann, Basel: Schwabe, 2009.

Publication History and Bibliography

William H. Schaberg, *The Nietzsche Canon. A Publication History and Bibliography*, Chicago, IL: University of Chicago Press, 1995.

Biography

Curt Paul Janz, *Nietzsche Biographie*, 3 vols, Munich: Hanser, 1978.
Rüdiger Safranski, *Nietzsche. A Philosophical Biography*, London: Granta, 2003.

Introductions

For introductory reading cf. James I. Porter's essay 'Nietzsche and Tragedy', in Rebecca W. Bushnell (ed.), *A Companion to Tragedy*, Oxford: Blackwell, 2005, pp. 86–104 or James I. Porter, *The Invention of Dionysus, An Essay on the Birth of Tragedy*, Stanford, CA: Stanford University Press, 2000. Less introductory studies include M.S. Silk and J.P. Stern, *Nietzsche on Tragedy*, Cambridge: Cambridge University Press, 1983; Chapters 4–6 of Keith Ansell-Pearson (ed.), *A Companion to Nietzsche*, Oxford: Blackwell, 2006; and David B. Allison, *Reading the New Nietzsche*, Lanham, MD: Rowan & Littlefield, 2001. Any monograph on Nietzsche and his work contains a section on this first book, for example, Gianni Vattimo, *Nietzsche: An Introduction*, trans. Nicholas Martin, London: Continuum, 2002; Michael Tanner, *Nietzsche*, Oxford: Oxford University Press, 1994; or R.J Hollingdale, *Nietzsche. The Man and his Philosophy*, Cambridge: Cambridge University Press, 1999; Walter A. Kaufmann, *Nietzsche: Philosopher, Psychologist, Antichrist*, Princeton, NJ: Princeton University Press, 1974, and also Arthur C. Danto, *Nietzsche as Philosopher*, Chichester: Macmillan, 1965. A collection of critical material on Nietzsche, Peter R. Sedgwick, *Nietzsche: A Critical Reader*, Oxford: Blackwell, 1995.

Commentary

The most detailed and comprehensive commentary, albeit in German and only of sections 1–12 (which the author deems to be the only ones worthy of commentary): the doctoral thesis of Barbara von Reibnitz, *Ein Kommentar zu Friedrich Nietzsche, "Die Geburt der Tragödie aus dem Geist der Musik", Kap. 1–12*, Stuttgart: Metzler, 1992. No longer in print, David Lenson, *The Birth of Tragedy, A Commentary*, Boston, MA: Twayne, 1987.

Relevant Notebooks

Daniel Breazeale (ed. and trans.), *Philosophy and Truth: Selections from Nietzsche's Notebooks of the Early 1870's*, Amherst, MA: Humanity Books, 1979.

Richard T. Gray (transl.) *Unpublished Writings from the Period of 'Unfashionable Observations'*, San Francisco, CA: Stanford University press, 1999.

THE BIRTH OF TRAGEDY AND NIETZSCHE'S NEW STYLE OF PHILOSOPHY

The best analysis of Nietzsche's idea of style in connection with Nietzsche's programme of philosophical reform in his early work: Sarah Kofmann, *Nietzsche and Metaphor*, London: Athlone Press, 1993: also, in overall perspective, Heinz Schlaffer, *Das entfesselte Wort. Nietzsche's Stil und seine Folgen*, Munich: Hanser, 2007. Gilles

Deleuze, *Nietzsche and Philosophy*, New York: Columbia University Press, 1983. Gregory Moore, *Nietzsche, Biology and Metaphor*, Cambridge: Cambridge University Press, 2002. Silke-Maria Weineck, *The Abyss Above. Philosophy and Poetic Madness in Plato, Hölderlin, and Nietzsche*, New York: State University of New York Press, 2002.

THE BIRTH OF TRAGEDY AND THE GERMAN TRADITION

Schopenhauer, *World of Will and Representation*, 2 vols, trans. E.F.J. Payne, New York: Dover, 1969. Richard Wagner, *Prose Works*, ed. and trans. W.A. Ellis, London: Kegan Paul, Trench, Trübner, 1899. Keith Ansell-Pearson, *Nietzsche and Modern German Thought*, London: Routledge, 1991. Nicholas Martin (ed.), *Nietzsche and the German Tradition*, Bern: Peter Lang Publishing, 2003, here particularly pp. 40–82, Thomas H. Brobjer, 'Nietzsche as German Philosopher'. Nicholas Martin, *Nietzsche and Schiller. Untimely Aesthetics*, Oxford: Clarendon Press, 1996. See the discussion of Creuzer's Romantic theory of symbolization, so central to Nietzsche, in Walter Benjamin, *The Origin of German Tragic Drama*, trans. John Osborne, London: Verso, 2009. Nietzsche incorporating Romantic theory of irony, particularly Friedrich Schlegel's as outlined in his essay *On Incomprehensibility* (1800), in Kathleen Wheeler, *German Aesthetic and Literary Criticism*, Cambridge: Cambridge University Press, 1984, pp. 32–39. Two of Friedrich Schiller's essays of particular relevance for *The Birth of Tragedy*: *On Naive and Sentimental Poetry*, London: Ungar, 1966; *On the Aesthetic Education of Man in a Series of Letters* (1795), Bristol: Thoemmes Press, 1994. A discussion led in *The Birth of Tragedy* of notions of Greek 'serenity' as introduced in Johann Jacob Winckelmann, *Gedanken über die Nachahmung der griechischen Werke in der Malerei und Bildhauerkunst* (1755) ['Thoughts on the Imitation of Greek Works in Painting and Sculpture']. Of Goethe, at least two works need mentioning (apart from the poetry) that had a profound impact on Nietzsche: Johann Wolfgang von Goethe, *Wilhelm Meisters Lehrjahre*, in Erich Trunz (ed.), *Goethes Werke* Hamburger Ausgabe, vol. 7, Munich: Beck, 1965, p. 515. The best translation of this novel is still by Thomas Carlyle: *Wilhelm Meister's Apprenticeship*, 1824. And *Faust*, Parts 1 and 2, *Goethes Werke* Hamburger Ausgabe in 14 vols, ed. Erich Trunz, Munich: Beck, 1981, vol. 3. The best recent translation is by David Luke, *Faust Part 1*, Oxford: Oxford World's Classics, 1998; *Faust Part 2*, Oxford: Oxford World's Classics, 2008.

NIETZSCHE, TRAGEDY AND PHILOSOPHY

Schopenhauer, *World of Will and Representation*, 2 vols, trans. E.F.J. Payne, New York: Dover, 1969. Richard Wagner, *Prose Works*, ed. and trans. W.A. Ellis, London: Kegan Paul, Trench, Trübner, 1899. For a discussion on art and tragedy in Nietzsche, cf. Julian Young, *Nietzsche's Philosophy of Art*, Cambridge: Cambridge University Press, 1992; Arthur Nehamas, *Nietzsche: Life as Literature*, Cambridge, MA:

Harvard University Press, 1985. Denis Schmidt, *On Germans and Other Greeks: Tragedy and Ethical Life*, Bloomington, IN: Indiana University Press, 2001. John Sallis, *Crossings: Nietzsche and the Space of Tragedy*, Chicago, IL: University of Chicago Press, 1991. Martin Heidegger, *Nietzsche*, trans. David Farrell Krell, San Francisco, CA: Harper & Row, 1991. Gilles Deleuze, *Nietzsche and Philosophy*, trans. Hugh Tomlinson, London: Continuum, 2006. For an understanding of some of the motives in Nietzsche's treatment of Socrates, cf. Plato's *Symposium*, trans. Alexander Nehemas and Paul Woodruff, Indianapolis, IN: Hackett, 1989. On art as mere illusory copy, see *The Republic*, trans. Robin Waterfield, Oxford: Oxford University Press, 2008, 595Aff. On the allegory of the cave (and the Platonic metaphors of light, shadow and darkness), 514a–521b. On *The Republic* in general, see Darren Sheppard, *Plato's Republic*, Edinburgh: Edinburgh University Press, 2009. Silke-Maria Weineck, *The Abyss Above. Philosophy and Poetic Madness in Plato, Hölderlin, and Nietzsche*, New York: State University of New York Press, 2002. For a discussion of Nietzsche's indebtedness to Kant and Schopemhauer, see Jill Marsden, *After Nietzsche*, Basingstoke: Palgrave, 2002. Nietzsche's theory of tragedy developed not only in accordance with but also in critical distance ('catharsis') from Aristotle's *Poetics*, trans. Richard Janko, Indianapolis, IN: Hackett, 1987. For a discussion of the tendency of post-Enlightenment thought to think of its own condition in terms of the tragic, see David Farrell Krell, *The Tragic Absolute. German Idealism and the Languishing of God*, Bloomington, IN: Indiana University Press, 2005. Robert G. Morrison, *Nietzsche and Buddhism, A Study in Nihilism and Ironic Affinities*, Oxford: Oxford University Press, 1999. Freny Mistry, *Nietzsche and Buddhism, Prolegomenon to a Comparative Study*, Berlin: deGruyter, 1981. Also Part III, Weaver Santaniellol (ed.), *Nietzsche and the Gods*, Albany, NY: State University of New York Press, 2001, pp. 87–136. Interest in Eastern thought was wide-spread in the nineteenth century in Europe, and Schopenhauer and Nietzsche were not exceptions. However, hampered by the available translations and commentaries, misunderstanding was no less wide-spread. Here, Buddhism is oversimplified as nihilism. For verifying Kant's central role for Nietzsche, cf. Douglas Burnham, *Kant's Critique of Pure Reason*, Bloomington, IN: Indiana University Press, 2008, and Burnham, *Kant's Philosophies of Judgement*, Edinburgh: Edinburgh University Press, 2004.

NIETZSCHE AND MYTHOLOGY

George S. Williamson, *The Longing for Myth in Germany. Religion and Aesthetic Culture from Romanticism to Nietzsche*, Chicago, IL: Chicago University Press, 2004. Dale Wilkerson, *Nietzsche and the Greeks*, London: Continuum, 2006; Weaver Santaniellol (ed.), *Nietzsche and the Gods*, Albany, NY: State University of New York

Press, 2001. Jacques Derrida, 'White Mythology' in *Margins of Philosophy*, trans. Alan Bass, New York: Harvester, 1982. It is important to realize that Nietzsche was by no means the first to contemplate the intellectual problem or the cultural possibilities of myth. In addition to the many anthropologists, Nietzsche was influenced by two examples: the 'Oldest Program towards a System in German Idealism', a fragment from the 1790s most often attributed to Hegel, speaks of a reinvigoration of mythology, albeit in alignment with reason (see translation and commentary in Krell, *The Tragic Absolute*); likewise, Schelling's 1842 *Historical-Critical Introduction to the Philosophy of Mythology*, trans. Mason Richey and Marcus Zisselsberger, Albany, NY: State University of New York Press, 2008.

NIETZSCHE, MUSIC AND WAGNER

Richard Wagner, *Prose Works*, ed. and trans. W.A. Ellis, London: Kegan Paul, Trench, Trübner, 1899. Roger Hollindrake, *Nietzsche, Wagner and the Philosophy of Pessimism*, London: Allen and Unwin, 1982. For a comprehensive account on Nietzsche and music see Georges Liébert, *Nietzsche and Music*, trans. David Pellauer and Graham Parkes, Chicago, IL: University of Chicago Press, 2004. Brian McGee, *The Tristan Chord: Wagner and Philosophy*, Basingstoke: Holt, 2002; Friedrich Nietzsche, *Der Musikalische Nachlass*, ed. Curt Paul Janz, Basel: Bärenreiter, 1976. Paul Schofield, *The Redeemer Reborn – Parsifal as the Fifth Opera of Wagner's Ring*, New York: Amadeus Press, 2007. On classical harmony and dissonance, see Charles Rosen, *The Classical Style. Haydn, Mozart, Beethoven*, London: Faber and Faber, 1997, p. 348. Babette E. Babich, *Words in Blood, Like Flowers. Philosophy and Poetry, Music and Eros, in Hölderlin, Nietzsche and Heidegger*, Albany, NY: State University of New York Press, 2006. Theodor Wiesengrund-Adorno, *Mahler. A Musical Physiognomy*, Chicago, IL: University of Chicago Press, 1996, might be a good example for musical analysis of a post-Wagnerian, post-Nietzschean musical phenomenon.

NIETZSCHE AND THE NOVEL

Thomas Mann, *The Magic Mountain* (1913–24), London: Everyman, 2005, illustrates Nietzschean notions of decadence. *Doctor Faustus: The Life of the German Composer Adrian Leverkuhn, as Told by a Friend* (1943–47), New York: Modern Library, 1966. Exploring political and cultural aspects of Nietzsche's 'artiste's metaphysics', the novel features a composer and gathers its music theory content from Adorno's *Philosophy of Modern Music*; it contains long passages on dissonance. See James Schmidt, 'Mephistopheles in Hollywood', in *Cambridge Companion to Adorno*, Cambridge: Cambridge University Press, 2004, pp. 148–80.

'THE SWISS NIETZSCHE'

David Marc Hoffmann (ed.), *Nietzsche und die Schweiz*, Zürich: Strauhof, 1994. Friedrich Nietzsche, *Handschriften, Erstausgaben und Widmungsexemplare. Die Sammlung Rosenthal-Levy im Nietzsche-Haus in Sils Maria*, ed. Julia Rosenthal, Peter André Bloch, David Marc Hoffmann, Basel: Schwabe, 2009. Andrea Bollinger and Franziska Trenkle, *Nietzsche in Basel*, Basel: Schwabe, 2000. Of great influence on Nietzsche: Johann Jacob Bachofen (1861), *Mutterrecht (Mother Right): A Study of the Religious and Juridical Aspects of Gyneocracy in the Ancient World*, new translation in 5 vols, New York: Edwin Mellen Press, 2009. Alfred Bäumler, *Bachofen und Nietzsche*, Zürich: Verlag der Neuen Schweizer Rundschau, 1929. Cf. most recently Frances Nesbitt Oppel, *Nietzsche on Gender, Beyond Man and Woman*, Charlottesville, VA: University of Virginia Press, 2005, where the link is documented between Bachofen and Nietzsche in chapters 2 and 3: 'the "Secret Source": Ancient Greek Woman in Nietzsche's Early Notebooks', and '*The Birth of Tragedy* and the Feminine', pp. 36–88. On Bachofen and Nietzsche particularly pp. 48–49. Also regarding modern history, Jacob Burckhardt (1860), *The Civilisation of Renaissance in Italy*, trans. S.G.C. Middlemore, London: Penguin Classics, 1990.

NIETZSCHE AND HISTORY

Dale Wilkerson, *Nietzsche and the Greeks*, London: Continuum, 2006. Françoise Dastur, 'Hölderlin and the Orientalisation of Greece', *Pli, The Warwick Journal of Philosophy* 10 (2000), pp. 156–73. Nietzsche was greatly influenced by Jacob Burckhardt (1860), *The Civilisation of Renaissance in Italy*. trans. S.G.C. Middlemore, London: Penguin Classics, 1990. For post-modern adaptation of Nietzsche genealogical theory of history, see, Michel Foucault, 'Nietzsche, Genealogy, History', in Paul Rabinow (ed.), *The Foucault Reader*, London: Penguin, 1991, pp. 76–100.

NIETZSCHE AND SCIENCES

Babette E. Babich, *Nietzsche's Philosophy of Science. Reflecting Science on the Ground of Art and Life*, Albany, NY: State University of New York Press, 1994. Babette E. Babich, Robert S. Cohen (eds), *Nietzsche, Epistemology, and Philosophy of Science. Nietzsche and the Sciences*, 2 vols, Boston, MA: Kluwer, 1999. Gregory Moore and Thomas H. Brobjer (eds), *Nietzsche and Science*, Aldershot: Ashgate, 2004, here particularly Thomas H. Bobjer, 'Nietzsche's Reading and Knowledge of Natural Science: An Overview', pp. 21–50. John Richardson, *Nietzsche's New Darwinism,* Oxford: Oxford University Press, 2004. Gregory Moore, *Nietzsche, Biology and Metaphor*, Cambridge: Cambridge University Press, 2002.

AFTERLIFE OF *THE BIRTH OF TRAGEDY*

Immediate Reactions

Karlfried Gründer (ed.), *The Quarrel about the Birth of Tragedy*. (Der Streit um Nietzsches *Geburt der Tragödie*, [contributors are Erwin Rhode, Ulrich von Wilamowitz-Moellendorff and Richard Wagner]), Hildesheim: Olms, 1989.

Nietzsche and Aesthetic Modernity

Julian Young, *Nietzsche's Philosophy of Art*, Cambridge: Cambridge University Press, 1992. Elements of *The Birth of Tragedy*'s metaphysics of art live on in notions of emancipation and aesthetic reconciliation in Critical Theory. See for instance chapter 4 of David R. Ellison, *Ethics and Aesthetics in Modernist Literature*, Cambridge: Cambridge University Press, 2001. Also, Walter Richard Wolin, *Benjamin. An Aesthetic of Redemption*, Berkeley, CA: University of California Press, 1994. Theodor Wiesengrund-Adorno, *Aesthetic Theory*, London: Routledge, 1984, and Marcuse, *Eros and Civilisation*, Boston, MA: Beacon,1955, (cf. especially chapter 7: 'The Aesthetic Dimension'). See also Philippe Lacoue-Labarthe and Jean-Luc Nancy, *The Literary Absolute*, trans. Philip Barnard and Cheryl Lester, Albany, NY: State University of New York Press, 1988, and Jovanovski Thomas, *Aesthetic Transformations. Taking Nietzsche at his Word*, New York: Peter Lang Publishing, 2008. For a discussion of Nietzsche's 'aestheticism', see Walter Benjamin, *The Origin of German Tragic Drama*, trans. John Osborne, London: Verso, 2009. On the proximity of Nietzsche's 'aesthetic symbolism' with positions taken up by Charles Baudelaire, see Baudelaire, *The Painter of Modern Life and other Essays*, London: Phaidon, 1970; *Les fleurs du mal* (The Flowers of Evil), Oxford: World's Classics, 1993, and Walter Pater, *Studies in the History of The Renaissance*, Oxford: World's Classics, 1998, cf. particularly the 'Conclusion'.

Nietzsche and his Impact on German Culture and Politics

Stephen E. Aschheim, *The Nietzsche Legacy in Germany 1890–1990*, Berkeley, CA: University of California Press, 1994. For Nietzsche's conservative to proto-fascist legacy: Houston Stewart Chamberlain, *The Foundations of the 19th Century*, trans. John Lees, New York: Adamant Media Corporation, 2003. Oswald Spengler, *The Decline of the West*, trans. Charles Francis Atkinson, abridged, Oxford: Oxford University Press, 1991.

Twentieth-Century Psychology

Sigmund Freud, *The Interpretation of Dreams*, Standard Edition of the Psychological Works, vols 4 and 5, London: Hogarth, 1975. Paul-Laurent Assoun, *Freud and Nietzsche*, London: Continuum, 2006.

Aesthetics of Modernism

There are strong affinities between Nietzsche's evocations of tragic rapture and those that can be found in Antonin Artaud's *The Theatre and its Double*, London: Calder, 1970, particularly in his comparison between theatre and the plague. Cf. T. John L. Styan, *Modern Drama in Theory and Practice*, particularly vol. 2: *Symbolism, Surrealism and the Absurd*, Cambridge: Cambridge University press, 1983. There is a whole French line of Nietzsche reception including, of course, in Modernism. Cf. Jacques Rider, *Nietzsche en France*, Paris: Presses Universitaires de France, 1999. For further historical investigations of influences, cf. Paul Gordon, *Tragedy after Nietzsche, Rapturous Superabundance*, Chicago, IL: University of Illinois Press, 2000. Leon Surette, *The Birth of Modernism. Pound, Eliot, Yeats, and the Occult*, Montreal: McGill-Queens University Press, 1994, discusses Nietzsche's trail in the works of some of the leading modernists writing in English. James Frazer, *The Golden Bough*, Basingstoke: Palgrave MacMillan, 2005. Originally published in 2 volumes in 1890, the project grew to 12 volumes for the third edition of 1915; the 2005 edition was later reprinted in 15 volumes. Frazer himself edited an abridged 1 volume version in 1922; this edition is currently available as a paperback edition, London: Penguin, 1996. To Modernists like Eliot and W.B. Yeats, *The Birth of Tragedy* and *The Golden Bough* formed part of a package of influences. 'The Own and the Foreign Orient. Schlegel, Nietzsche, Artaud, Brecht. Notes on the Process of a Reception', in Erika Fischer-Lichte et al. (eds), *The Dramatic Touch of Difference*, Tubingen: Narr, 1990. For further discussion of Nietzsche's relation to contemporary literary production and criticism, see Douglas Burnham and Melanie Ebdon, 'Philosophy and Literature', in *The Continuum Companion to Continental Philosophy*, ed. John Mullarkey and Beth Lord, London: Continuum, 2009. Also on Modernism, cf. Kathryn Lindberg, *Reading Pound, Reading Nietzsche. Modernism after Nietzsche*, Oxford: Oxford University Press, 1987. Theodor Wiesengrund-Adorno, *Mahler. A Musical Physiognomy*, Chicago, IL: University of Chicago Press, 1996 might be a good example for musical analysis of a post-Wagnerian, post-Nietzschean musical phenomenon. William J. McGrath, *Dionysian Art and Populist Politics in Austria*, New Haven, CT: Yale University Press, 1974, where Mahler's early contacts with Nietzsche are explored.

Cultural Anthropology

Early repercussions of Nietzsche's text: Erwin Rhode (1894), *Psyche. Cult of Souls and Belief in Immortality in the Greeks*, London: Routledge and Kegan Paul, 1925, reprinted London: Routledge, 2000. Paul Bishop (ed.), 'Jung and Nietzsche', in *Jung in Contexts. A Reader*, London: Routledge, 1999, pp. 205–41. Bronislav Malinowski clarifies his indebtedness to *The Birth of Tragedy* as a foundational text inspiring his own innovative approach in an early essay, 'Observations on Nietzsche's *"The Birth of Tragedy"* 1904/05, in Robert J. Thornton, Peter Skalnik (eds), *The Early Writings of Bronislaw Malinowski*, Cambridge: Cambridge University Press, 1993. Tracy B. Strong, *Nietzsche and the Politics of Transfiguration*, Chicago, IL: University of Illinois Press, 2000, deals with Nietzsche's conception of anthropology, outlining similarities and differences in the approaches to anthropology in Rousseau, Nietzsche and Levi-Strauss. Adorno's and Horkheimer's *Dialectic of Enlightenment* (1947), San Francisco, CA: Stanford University Press, 2002, shows strong echoes of Nietzsche's psychology of culture in its juxtaposition of 'primeval' Greek and post-Homeric Enlightenment culture.

Nietzsche and Post-modern Theory

For a theory of modern epistemology akin to Nietzsche's, see Michel Foucault, *The Order of Things, An Archaeology of the Human Sciences*, London: Routledge, 2002; also, for a post-modern theory of power derived from Nietzsche's, see Foucault's essay 'The Subject and Power', in Paul Rabinov (ed.), *Essential Works of Foucault 1954–84*, vol. 3, London: Penguin, 2000, pp. 326–48, and Michel Foucault, 'Nietzsche, Genealogy, History', in Paul Rabinow (ed.), *The Foucault Reader*, London: Penguin 1991, pp. 76–100. For a comprehensive discussion of Nietzsche's impact on post-modern theory, see Clayton Koelb (ed.), *Nietzsche as Postmodernist. Essays Pro and Contra*, New York: State University Press, 1990. Of more recent philosophers who have taken *The Birth of Tragedy* seriously, see especially the first chapter of Gilles Deleuze, *Nietzsche and Philosophy*, trans. Hugh Tomlinson, London: Continuum, 2006. Also, Paul de Man, *Allegories of Reading*, New Haven, CT: Yale University Press, 1979.

INDEX

Apolline, Dionysiac and tragedy are all passim.

Adorno, Theodor Wiesengrund 20, 72, 110, 113, 119, 125, 158–9, 173, 175, 180

Aeschylus 5–6, 9, 37, 61, 80–5, 90, 94, 100–1, 115, 138, 150, 170

aesthetics, aestheticism 2, 6, 8, 10, 13, 16, 18, 21–5, 27–30, 36–9, 47–9, 53–5, 62–5, 72, 75, 91–2, 95–7, 107–14, 118–19, 124, 131–3, 135–8, 141–51, 171

affect, affection 41, 91–2, 100, 105, 127–9, 137–8, 142–3

Alexandria/Alexandrian 117, 119–25, 127–30, 134, 137–8, 141, 146

anthropology 6, 10–13, 29–30, 33, 36–7, 48, 66, 80, 96, 106, 114, 153, 155, 159, 175

Antigone 61

antiquity 54, 57, 83, 93, 125, 127, 145

archaic 6, 107

archetype 159

Archilochus 39, 61–5, 113

Aristophanes 93–4, 168

Aristotle 46, 60, 70–1, 83, 87, 95, 98, 100, 114, 116, 142, 148, 150, 169

Artaud, Antonin 78, 158, 173

Attic 58, 60–1, 72–3, 88, 116, 159

Bachofen, Johann Jacob 6, 144, 164

balance, balanced 39, 110

barbarism 49, 101, 106, 121

Baudelaire, Charles 8, 150

beauty 19, 28, 37, 42, 44, 51–3, 63, 83, 116, 129, 131, 137, 149–53

Beethoven, Ludwig van 44, 59, 66, 67, 109, 117, 129, 137, 143, 152, 172, 176

Benjamin, Walter 18, 113, 119, 163–6, 176

Berg, Alban 24, 109

Bildung 116, 122–3, 130–2, 143, 145, 153

Bismarck, Friedrich von 25, 144, 147

Brahms, Johannes 167

Buddhism 133, 167, 177

Burckhardt, Jacob 6, 117, 120, 126, 144

Burnham, Douglas 169–70

Carlyle, Thomas 120, 131

Cassandra 60

character (in drama) 68–70, 82, 88, 92, 96, 104, 116, 135, 137–9

cheerfulness 16, 89, 105, 117, 129 *see* serenity

chorus 8, 27, 68–75, 77–79, 86, 90, 94, 100, 106, 115, 148

Christ, Christianity, Christian 4, 7, 9, 16–17, 20–1, 24, 44, 53, 59, 81, 83–5, 89, 96–7, 115–17, 120, 125, 167, 173

chthonic 19, 55

classical, classicist, classicism 5, 10, 23, 34, 36, 52, 54–6, 64, 67, 72, 81–2, 88–9, 93, 106, 109–10, 117, 119, 125, 127, 131–2, 134–6, 146, 150, 159–60

cocoon 99, 152

Coleridge, Samuel Taylor 36

collective 20, 37, 80, 94, 96, 156

Collective Unconscious 6, 159

comedy 39, 88, 93, 116

comfort, *see* consolation

compassion 136

compose, composed, composer 9, 28, 36, 64, 66, 108, 112–13, 124, 126, 129, 143, 157–8

INDEX